# Ranching Women of

# Colorado

## ⇒ 17 Legendary Ladies ⇐

## Linda Wommack

Caxton Press

First Edition
ISBN # 978-087004-629-2
LCCN# 2019954788
CIP Information available at Loc.gov

Cover and book design by Jocelyn Robertson

Printed in the United States of America
CAXTON PRESS
Caldwell, Idaho
206824

# TABLE OF CONTENTS

# ⋟ ACKNOWLEDGMENTS ⋞

◇◇◇◇◇◇◇◇◇◇◇◇

I have long held an interest in women ranchers. From my fascination and years of research of the life of Ann Bassett, which became the first biography of her, to the stories of Rattlesnake Kate, which I heard during my childhood, their pioneer spirit has stayed with me.

Over the years I have had the privilege of meeting or conversing with a few of the people who knew some of the women whose stories are recounted in this book. I first learned of Josie Bassett from Daun DeJournette in the spring of 1997. Freda Walker Bishop shared a few stories of her grandmother, Evelyn Mantle, in 2017 and early 2018. Meg Anderson, John Lake, and Donna Smith graciously shared their experiences of Tweet Kimball with me, and Deborah Mueller Hruza led me on tours of Tweet's Cherokee Castle and patiently answered all my questions. I am now honored to be a member of the Cherokee Ranch Heritage Leadership Committee.

Newspaper articles regarding many of the ranching women were quite helpful in understanding their place in their respective communities. Historical societies and museums were an invaluable source of information as well as of access to photographs. Once again, the majority of photographs came from the Denver Public Library Western History Department. I am indebted to my friend and colleague, Coi Drummond-Gehrig, for her immense knowledge of historic photographs.

Special thanks go to those who believed in this project and gave freely of their time and advice. First on that list is my husband Frank, who tolerated the many late nights of research and writing, and helped to work out the research obstacles. To

Connie Clayton, who diligently edited the manuscript with wit and humor, and became my support line on many levels, my sincere thanks. A heartfelt thank you to Scott Gipson of Caxton Press who has believed in me and my work for over twenty years. My sincere appreciation for their encouragement and professionalism.

And finally to the pioneer women ranchers who were a strong, spirited group of ladies who set the fence posts, as it were, for those who followed.

~ Linda Wommack, February, 2019

# ⮞ INTRODUCTION ⮜

◇◇◇◇◇◇◇◇◇

The American West has always been known for strong women, and the state of Colorado is no exception. From the earliest days of settlement, Colorado women had a love for the land and built their homesteads and ranches.

The Homestead Act of 1862 brought thousands west for free land, new beginnings, and a new way of life.

For many, it was the dawn of a new dream, and no more so than for the female homesteader. At a time when most women's futures were tied to a husband's prosperity, it was a bold, courageous step for women to step out of the conventional norm. In fact, only about twelve percent of women did so. After the Transcontinental Railroad was completed in 1869, railroad companies advertised free land for coming west by railroad, and even targeted their sales pitches to women:

## Mary Had A Little Farm
*Mary had a little farm - as level as the floor*
*She placed on it a fancy price, and struggled to get more.*
*She kept the land until one day the country settled up*
*And where the wilderness had been there grew a bumper crop.*
*Then Mary rented out her land - she would not sell you know*
*And waited patiently for the prices still to grow.*
*They grew as population came, and Mary raised the rent*
*With common food and raiment now she could not become content.*
*She built her up a mansion fine, had bric-a-brac galore - and every time*
*The prices rose, she raised the rent some more.*
*"What makes the land keep Mary so?" the starving people cry.*
*"Why Mary keeps the land you know" the wealthy would reply.*

*And so each one of you might be "Wealthy, refined and wise,"*
*If you bought some land and held it for the rise.*

What were the reasons these women struck out on their own?

Theirs were not that different from their male counterpart; independence, financial security, adventure, or an escape from the past may have been some of the reasons for such an undertaking. Their reasons were their own.

This anthology includes the stories of very remarkable women ranchers of Colorado. Rumalda Luna Jaramillo Bent Boggs inherited land from her wealthy Mexican family, which she and her husband used wisely and enlarged over time. They created Boggsville, which became a thriving ranching community in southern Colorado. Likewise, Amache Prowers, a Cheyenne Indian, received a parcel of land in southern Colorado that was the beginning of the largest cattle ranch in southern Colorado.

There were women such as Ann and Josie Bassett, who were raised on their family ranch in Brown's Park in the extreme northwest corner of Colorado. Each sister went on to own and operate their own separate ranch. Conversely, Annie and Kitty Harbison were sisters who worked their ranch together. They homesteaded land in what would become part of Rocky Mountain National Park. Kate Slaughterback had a small ranch on the plains of Weld County and happened upon a den of rattlesnakes. For over three hours Kate battled the snakes. When there were no more and all were dead, Kate gathered over one hundred fifty snakes. She made a dress out of the skins and sold the rattles and fangs to the curious. Kate became known as "Rattlesnake Kate," and is a legend in Weld County. Florence McIntire was first known for being the First Lady of Colorado. Following his term as governor, Albert W. McIntire divorced his wife. Florence sued for and won title to their ranch in the San Luis Valley, where she spent the rest of her life as a female rancher.

These are among the many stories of amazing ranching women, and are enhanced by the women's own words and views of ranching life. Excerpts from the diary of Emily French, a homesteader in Elbert County, speak to the loneliness of life on the windblown prairie. From the writings and interviews of Julia Kawcak we learn of the isolation of mountain ranching in Moffat County.

Several of these legendary ladies' ranches still exist and many can be visited by the public. Adeline Hornbek's ranch is managed by the folks at the Florrisant Fossil Beds National Monument. Florence McIntire's ranch property is managed by the Bureau of Land Management, and archaeological studies are conducted on a regular basis. Elizabeth Hutchinson's ranch is owned by the City of Steamboat Springs and tours are available. Rattlesnake Kate's ranch house was moved to the Greeley Museum where it can be seen today. Tweet Kimball's magnificent Cherokee Castle is open to the public during special events. And the ranch homes of Amache Prowers and Rumalda Boggs can be toured at Boogsville. A portion of Evelyn Mantle's ranch is now part of Dinosaur National Monument.

Today, there are more women ranchers in Colorado than ever before. It is a tribute to the struggles and hardships these pioneering women endured that set the way for those who women who work the land today.

# Ranching Women of

# Colorado

≫ 17 Legendary Ladies ≪

# THE UNSETTLED PLAINS

## *Rumalda Luna Jaramillo Bent Boggs*
**Hispanic Heiress**

## *Amache Ochinee Prowers*
**Cheyenne Princess of the Plains**

Homesteading on the eastern plains of Colorado. *Heath Gay*

# Rumalda Luna Jaramillo Bent Boggs
## Hispanic Heiress

Rumalda Luna Jaramillo Bent Boggs received her inheritance of more than two thousand acres of land in today's southeastern Colorado, where the first permanent settlement in the Arkansas River Valley would later be established. This historic settlement, located where the Arkansas River meets the Purgatoire River, would attract several multicultural families. Through their pioneer spirit, these settlers would build a community and frame an economic structure based on agriculture and ranching. Since the 1819 Adams-Onis Treaty, the Arkansas River had been the established boundary between the United States and the Spanish landholdings. This river continued to serve as the international boundary between the United States and Mexico after Mexico won its independence from Spain in 1821. The Arkansas River Valley soon became the major travel route for trade between the United States and the trading centers of Santa Fe and Taos, then in Mexico. William Becknell is credited for making his historic trip from Missouri to Santa Fe, which established the Santa Fe Trail. Known as the "Mountain Branch" of the Santa Fe Trail, which ran directly through the Arkansas River Valley, it was soon congested with trappers, traders and travelers journeying to and fro. The increase in travel became an economic boom for Charles and William Bent and Ceran St. Vrain, who would build the finest trading post along the historic Santa Fe Trail.

Charles Bent, the eldest of the Bent brothers, who would all become instrumental in the frontier trading enterprise, left his home in Westport, Missouri, to venture West with the Missouri Fur Company. Bent spent considerable time on the upper Missouri

River as a trapper, and learned the ways of Indian trading. Bent's quick wit and learning ability brought the attention of another trader among the Plains Indians; Ceran St. Vrain. In 1825, Charles Bent and Ceran St. Vrain formed the Bent, St. Vrain & Company. It was the foundation of a trading empire that covered much of the West, including hundreds of square miles of today's states of Colorado, New Mexico, Arizona, Kansas, and Utah.

Capitalizing on the rich trading opportunities along the mountain branch of the Santa Fe Trail, Bent and St. Vrain chose an area along the south bank of the Arkansas River to build their trading post. The two were able to secure the site in large part due to the help of Lilburn Boggs, an influential member of the Mexican government. Boggs was a brother-in-law to the Bents, having married their sister, Julianna, in 1817. During this time, Boggs was in mourning, as Julianna had recently died following childbirth. Bent and St. Vrain picked a spot along the river, near the mouth of Huerfano Creek, to begin the construction of the trading fort. It would first be known as Fort William, after Charles' younger brother, who by this time had joined his brother on the Colorado plains.

William Bent, the second of the Bent brothers, was born in Westport, Missouri, on May 23, 1809. Deeply influenced by his older brother Charles, William came west to join his brother's business, where he supervised the building of the large adobe fort. William would eventually become the primary manager of the business activities, and bring successful trading operations among the many Indian tribes of the southern plains. Within a year of its opening, the name of the trading fort was changed to Bent's Fort.

This large, square adobe fortress sat on a rise above the river and could be seen for miles in all directions on the open prairie. The fort was not only the first trading post in the area, it also served as the first stockade. Bent's Fort was the center of trade with the local Indians, particularly the Arapaho and Cheyenne. Charles and William Bent maintained friendly relations with the Indians. In 1837, William Bent married Owl Woman, the daughter of White Thunder, the keeper of the Cheyenne Sacred Medicine

Arrows. Through this intermarriage, the first of several in the Arkansas Valley, a relative peace was maintained between the two cultures for several years. While William Bent operated the fort along the Arkansas River, his older brother, Charles, along with Ceran St. Vrain, traveled the Santa Fe Trail between the fort and Santa Fe, handling the trade negotiations. As the southwestern trade increased through their efforts, both men established a permanent home in Taos, the small settlement in the northern area of Mexico. There, Bent

Rumalda Boggs inherited her land from a Mexican land grant. *DPL*

and St. Vrain opened a trading post and soon became heavily involved in the town's civic affairs. Charles Bent soon established himself as one of its most prominent, well-respected residents.

In 1835, Charles Bent met the beautiful widow, Maria Ignacia Jaramillo Luna. Maria's husband, Juan Rafael Luna, had died the previous year. Maria's family were well established in the fabric that was the politics of Mexico. Maria's father, José Raphael Sena de Luna, Sr., was the head of the customs house in Taos, and her mother, Maria Apolonia Jaramillo, was the daughter of Francisco Jaramillo, a successful merchant on the Santa Fe Trail. The Jaramillo family were also related to the Vigil family, who were prominent landowners in northern Mexico, and influential in Mexican politics, with Cornelio Vigil being the mayor of Taos. Ceran St. Vrain, friend and business partner of Bent's, also happened to be a family friend and godfather to Maria's daughter, Rumalda Jaramillo Luna.

Following a year of courtship, Charles Bent and Maria Ignacia Jaramillo Luna were married. Maria brought her four-year-old daughter, Rumalda Jaramillo Luna, into the marriage, whom Bent would later adopt as his own.

In 1843, Maria's brother Cornelio Vigil, together with Ceran St. Vrain, applied for a land grant through the Mexican government. These land grants along the Mexican border with the United States were being offered to Mexican citizens in an effort to fortify the area with landowners who were loyal to the Mexican government in the event of war. The tract of land the two men applied for encompassed more than two million acres, bounded on the north by the Arkansas River, and on the south near today's Colorado-New Mexico border. The land stretched east from the Sangre de Cristo mountain range to the present-day border with Kansas. Perhaps due to the efforts of Vigil's cousin, Donaciano Vigil, who served as secretary to Governor Manuel Armijo in Taos, initial approval for Vigil and St. Vrain's request was granted. In December 1843, Governor Manuel Armijo traveled north from Taos to personally survey the land and approve the grant, known as the Vigil-St. Vrain Land Grant. On January 2, 1844, Governor Armijo wrote to his superiors, including Mexican president Santa Ana, informing them that he had, "closed here the boundaries of this grant and having recorded the same, I took them by the hand and walked with them and caused them to throw earth and pull up weeds, and make other demonstrations of possession."[1]

A year later, Vigil and St. Vrain "quietly" conveyed one-sixth of the land to Vigil's cousin, Donaciano Vigil, another one-sixth to Governor Armijo and a one-sixth portion to Charles Bent. However, by this time the winds of war between the two countries were strong. In May 1846, Mexican troops crossed the border and fired on United States soldiers protecting the southern border. On

May 13, 1846, President James Knox Polk went before the United States Congress, asking for a declaration of war against Mexico.

Charles Bent maintained his prominent position among businessmen of Taos. Bent was so influential, when General Stephen Watts Kearny and the Army of the West arrived in Santa Fe, claiming New Mexico for the United States, he appointed Charles Bent to the office of civilian governor for the new territory. For a time after this appointment, it seemed as if the town of Taos would remain peaceful as the war with Mexico continued; so much so that Kearny and his army troops left the region.

However, the civilian population of northern New Mexico became extremely unruly. Antagonism over the American military takeover of the area caused both the Indians and the Mexicans to cast their alliance with the previous Mexican government rather than supporting the new American authorities. Within a few short months, revolt was in the air in the new United States territory of New Mexico. Mexican sympathizers repeatedly tore down the American flag that flew over Taos Plaza. Several enraged citizens retrieved the flag and nailed it to a tall cottonwood pole, raising it over the plaza, guarding it night and day. The United States Congress later granted permission to fly the flag at Taos Plaza twenty-four hours a day, one of the few places in the country to do so. Yet in the midst of rumblings of revolt and war, two young people from different cultures would find love and form a life together.

Thomas Oliver Boggs, a longtime employee with the Bent brothers, had made several trips along the Santa Fe Trail hauling trade goods by wagon between Bent's Fort and Sante Fe. On one particular trip to the Bent and St. Vrain trading post in Taos, Boggs elected to remain in Taos, working as an employee of the Bent-St. Vrain enterprise. Here, he would meet and fall in love with Rumalda Luna Jaramillo Bent.

Thomas Boggs, born on August 22, 1824, was the eldest of ten children born to Lilburn Boggs and his second wife, Panthea Grant Boone Boggs. Lilburn Boggs' first wife, Julianna Bent, sister of Charles and William Bent, tragically died after giving birth to the couple's second son, William, in 1822. The Boggs and Bent families remained close throughout their years in the West. At the time of Thomas' birth, the Boggs family resided in the small hamlet of Harmony Mission on the Marais des Cygnes River near Papinville, Missouri. There, Lilburn Boggs was a prominent Indian trader at Fort Osage. His mother, Panthea Boone, the granddaughter of the famous frontiersman Daniel Boone, made a home for her family and raised her children. Lilburn Boggs would go on to become governor of Missouri, serving from 1836 to 1840. During his term as governor, Lilburn Boggs issued an executive order in 1838, ordering the Mormons to leave the state of Missouri.

When young Thomas Boggs reached his teen years, he began spending time with his mother's brother, Albert Gallitan Boone, a trader at Fort Osage along the Missouri River. Albert G. Boone noticed the ambition and drive in his nephew. Boone also became keenly aware of the lad's quick learning abilities, as Boggs was able learn several Indian languages. When Boone made the decision to move west and open his own trading post, he took young Thomas O. Boggs with him. Boone opened his trading post near present-day Fort Scott, Kansas. It was here that Boggs gained his experience in the trading business.

At the age of seventeen, Boggs struck out on his own, heading further west. He secured a position as a travel boss with James and Samuel Magoffin's trade wagons. When the group reached Bent's Fort, young Thomas Boggs met his father's friends, the brothers of his father's first wife, for the first time. William Bent offered Boggs employment at the fort, and Boggs readily accepted. It was the beginning of sixteen years that Boggs would work for the Bent brothers in various capacities.

It was during one of the many trips Boggs made along the Santa Fe Trail, hauling trade goods from Bent's Fort to Sante Fe and Taos, that Boggs chose to remain in Taos, working at the trading post owned by Charles Bent.

Boggs spent many evenings socializing at the home of

Charles and Maria Ignacia Bent. The Bent residence, located just off the town plaza area, was a happy home, for by this time Charles and Maria Ignacia had three young children of their own: Alfred, Teresina, and Estafina.

It was here, at the busy Bent home, Boggs became acquainted with Maria Josefa Jaramillo Carson. Josefa, as she known, was the younger sister of Maria Ignacia Jaramillo Luna Bent, and recently married to Christopher Houston "Kit" Carson. During this time, Carson was with John C. Fremont on his second western expedition to California.

When Boggs was introduced to Bent's stepdaughter, fourteen-year-old Rumalda Luna Jaramillo Bent, he was smitten. With Rumalda's affluent family lineage, the beautiful young señorita was considered to be one of the premier young ladies among the elite society of Taos. According to Albert W. Thompson, "Rumalda and Josefa, only three years older, were the belles of Taos when they were young. [They] were intimate associates, noted for their dancing, beauty, and vivaciousness." [2]

None of this mattered to Thomas Boggs, for he had found his true love. With his uncle, Charles Bent's, permission, Boggs began to court fourteen-year-old Rumalda. Although Boggs was fluent in many Native American languages, he possessed only a rudimentary knowledge of the Spanish language, and Rumalda spoke very little English. Despite the language barrier, the two fell in love and were married in May of 1846. It was a marriage that would last more than fifty years.

The happiness of the newlywed couple was soon shattered by the increase of violence in Taos. Mexican resentment against the American invasion during the war escalated. In July 1846, Charles Bent and Thomas Boggs, fearful of the escalation of rioting and violence, left with their wives and family members, including Josefa Carson, for the safety of Bent's Fort, north of where the war was raging.

In late July 1846, General Stephen Watts Kearny and his troops overtook Bent's Fort, claiming it as the headquarters for

Kearny's final onslaught into Mexico. Kearny and his soldiers were treated to a fine reception and welcome.

Samuel and Susan Magoffin were also at Bent's Fort during this time. Samuel and his brother James, operating a trade business along the Santa Fe Trail, had hired Thomas Boggs, bringing them to the fort a few days previous.

While staying at the fort, on July 31, 1846, a pregnant nineteen-year-old Susan Magoffin suffered a miscarriage. William Bent helped the grieving Samuel Magoffin bury the child in a spot outside of the fort. Devastated over the loss of her child, Susan Magoffin later wrote in her journal:

"While [I] was miscarrying a child, an Indian woman easily gave birth to a healthy baby. Within a half hour the Indian woman walked to the river to bathe herself and the child."[3]

For the next few weeks Charles and Maria Ignacia Bent, their three young children, stepdaughter Rumalda, and her new husband, Thomas, as well as Josefa Carson, stayed within the confines of the fort for their safety. General Stephen Watts Kearny and his army entered Santa Fe on August 18, 1846, where they raised the American flag without firing a shot. When news of Mexico's surrender of the northeastern portion of the country reached Bent's Fort, the Bent and Boggs families prepared to return to Taos. As the two families made their way south along the Santa Fe Trail, relieved that the violence of war was over, they were planning for better days ahead, particularly the newlyweds, Thomas and Rumalda Boggs.

Arriving in Taos in early September, Charles Bent found himself in the middle of the formation of a new territorial government under the auspices of the United States. Following negotiations between Mexico and the United States, the boundary between the two countries was moved to the Rio Grande River in Texas.

Charles Bent retained his appointment as governor, now the first governor of New Mexico Territory, approved by the United States Congress. Donaciano Vigil, a second cousin to Maria Bent, was appointed lieutenant governor.

Governor Charles Bent and the members of the new government, along with their families, traveled to Santa Fe for a celebration of the new American territory. On the evening of September 24, 1846, a grand ball was held at the historic Santa Fe structure known as the Palace of Governors, the seat of power for the newly created New Mexico Territory. General Stephen Watts Kearny, acting as proxy for President James K. Polk, conveyed the governmental powers to Charles Bent and the other officials of the new territory. Among the many dignitaries in attendance were several noted Taos businessmen and women. Attending the festivities were Samuel and Susan Magoffin, who had resumed their trading business along the Santa Fe Trail following the loss of their child. Gertrude Barcelo, the owner of a bordello located near the Palace of Governors, was also in attendance. Barcelo was known to be the former mistress of the last Mexican governor, Manuel Armijo.[4] Susan Magoffin, apparently aware of Gertrude Barcelo's business affiliation, was appalled at her appearance at such a grand occasion. Describing Barcelo, Magoffin later wrote: "…decked out in scarlet Canton crepe shawl to be in trim with the Natives, an old woman with false hair and teeth, flaunting that shrewd and fascinating manner necessary to allure the wayward, inexperienced youth to the hall of final ruin." [5]

Just a month after taking office, in early October, Governor Bent began receiving reports of violence and unrest among the people against the new American government. On October 20, 1846, Governor Bent wrote to General Kearny, informing him, "I have my eye on them and shall certainly give them a high berth if the fact can be proven worthy." [6]

Although Governor Bent held out hope for peace in the new territory, the violence continued. During the Christmas season, several arrests were made of those leading the plot to overthrow the new government. The Bent family, relieved that such threats had been thwarted, enjoyed a peaceful Christmas celebration with family.

Following the New Year celebrations of 1847, Governor Bent and his family traveled north to Taos on January 14, for a short, quiet reprieve from governmental duties. Their family time at their beloved Taos home, while blissful, was short-lived.

Several native Mexicans, as well as many of the local Taos Indians, resented the American take-over of their land. Rioting in the streets of Taos rose to revolt, violence and murder. Before dawn on the cold morning of Friday, January 16, bedlam broke out on the streets of Taos when a group of Taos Indians, led by Tomasito Romero, stormed into the local jail and broke out two of their tribal members, held on petty charges.[7]

By the time Sheriff Stephen Louis Lee arrived at the jail, a large group of angry and quite inebriated men had formed a mob. As the group grew larger by the hour, Sheriff Lee was powerless to stop them. Cornelio Vigil, Governor Bent's brother-in-law and a member of the government, tried to reason with the unruly men. Suddenly a few of the men grabbed Vigil and began beating him. Others brought out weapons, including knives. When the men stabbed Vigil repeatedly, others began cutting off body parts: ears, fingers, legs and arms. Terrified, Sheriff Lee attempted to flee the horrific scene but was caught and killed.

Feeling victorious, Romero led the murderous rioters through Taos to the home of Governor Bent. The family members were still asleep in that early morning hour. However, the family cook, preparing the morning meal in the kitchen, heard the approaching mob and alerted the governor. At approximately seven o'clock, as the sun was rising, Bent quickly dressed and came downstairs. Bent was the only man in residence, as Boggs had accepted the job of courier for the military and Carson was in California with General Kearny. Residing in the Bent home with Maria Ignacia and their children, Alfred, Teresina, and Estafina, were Rumalda Bent Boggs and Josefa Jaramillo Carson.

With the women and children safely hidden in an adjoining room, the angry mob shouted and pounded on the front door of the Bent home. As Bent opened the door, hoping to reason with the men, he was shot several times. As Bent fell back inside the home, Maria rushed toward him. A few of the Taos Indians shot arrows inside the house and one hit Maria Ignacia. Still, Maria Ignacia managed to get to the door, close it and bolt it.[8]

In the adjoining room, Josefa and Rumalda used iron spoons and pokers to open a hole through the brick wall of the house. Incredibly, the two young women were eventually able to break through and make an opening large enough for them to get through. Rumalda and Josefa then helped Alfred, Teresina, and Estafina through the opening. By this time the women could hear the sounds of the frenzied mob and knew they had broken into the house. Just as Maria Ignacia managed to get through the hole in the wall, the maniacal mob stormed into the room.

Rumalda Luna Bent Boggs, who was holding her mortally wounded stepfather, looked up in fear when the mob entered the room. Rumalda watched in horror as Tomasito Romero jerked Bent from Rumalda's clutches and threw him to the floor. What happened next is best related by Rumalda Luna Bent Boggs: "He [Romero] proceeded to scalp [Bent] with a bowstring while he was still yet alive, cutting as cleanly with the tight cord, as it could have been done with a knife."[9]

As Romero and his cohorts began mutilating the lifeless body of Charles Bent, Buenaventura Lobato, one of the instigators of the mob violence, rushed into the Bent home. Horrified by the bloody remains of Governor Charles Bent, Lobato admonished Romero and the others for killing the governor. Lobato then ordered the men to leave the Bent residence. They did so, but not before Romero grabbed the scalp of Charles Bent.

Horrified by the death of Charles Bent and the intimidation by the murderous mob, the Bent family members remained in the home in a state of shock. Sometime in the early morning of the following day, a few neighbors managed to sneak to the Bent house under the cloak of darkness and deliver food to the women and children.

Famed mountain man James Beckwourth, a longtime friend of the Bent brothers, had witnessed the murder and rode through the night and half the next day to Bent's Fort with the grim news. Word of mouth traveled faster, as Bent family friend and frontiersman, Charles Autobees, had already broken the devastating news to the Bent brothers. William and younger brother George executed a secret retrieval of Charles' body, necessary given the violent climate of the area. Charles Bent was secretly buried near a wall at Bent's Fort, next to the grave of youngest brother Robert, who was also murdered, on October 20, 1841, scalped by Comanche Indians along the Santa Fe Trail. Several years later the body of Charles Bent was returned to Santa Fe and given an honorable burial.[10]

Romero and his violent mob continued their rampage through the streets of Taos and the surrounding area. Perhaps on instructions from Lobato, the rioters seemed to target members of Governor Bent's family and those associated with him in political office. As the marauders moved through the town, they carried a large wooden board with the scalp of Governor Charles Bent pinned to it, for all to see.

In a stable at the edge of town, the mob cornered two men: Narciso Beaubien, and Pablo Jaramillo, the brother of Maria Ignacia Bent and Josefa Carson. The two men had no chance to defend themselves as the murderous mob lanced them to death. Next they found James W. Leal, an attorney in the governor's office. After the mob tortured the young attorney, they scalped him while still alive and left him to die on the streets of Taos.[11] Jose Raphael Sena de Luna, Sr., Maria Bent's father, was accosted at his home and much of his property was destroyed. Romero and his thugs also ransacked the home of Christopher "Kit" and Josefa Carson, which was near the Charles Bent home.

After two days of the murderous rampage, the violence was finally over. A wounded Maria Ignacia Bent, her three children, and Rumalda and Josefa, finally felt safe enough to leave their home. The women and children joined several other terrified Taos citizens who were offered sanctuary at the fortified home of Padre Antonio José Martinez.

On February 3, 1847, a company of United States volunteer troops, led by Ceran St. Vrain, arrived in Taos. When news of the troop's arrival reached the bloodthirsty mob members, they moved to an old mission church, the San Geronimo de Taos, which their Taos Indian allies had taken over. Within days of their arrival, the United States Army volunteers attacked the mission compound with heavy artillery. The attack lasted the entire day, with casualties on both sides. During the battle, one of the leaders of the mob faction, Pablo Chavez, was spotted by the soldiers. Chavez was wearing the blood-stained coat of Governor Charles Bent. Ceran St. Vrain, a close friend of the now-deceased Charles Bent, was incensed at the outrageous sight and put a bullet in the head of Chavez.

Meanwhile, Boggs had been relieved of his duties and set out with a group of men from Fort Leavenworth to return to Taos and his young bride. Along the way, the group met a man, Lewis Garrard, who was on his way to Bent's Fort. Garrard joined Boggs' group as they followed the Arkansas River to Bent's Fort. When the men finally reached the fort in late March, Boggs was informed of what became known as the Taos Rebellion, and of the murder of his uncle, employer and friend, Charles Bent. Boggs was told that his wife and the other Bent family members were safe. Nevertheless, Boggs left the fort immediately, heading for Taos.

Boggs arrived in Taos in early April, relieved to find his wife unharmed. It must have been a bittersweet reunion, as Rumalda related the horrible experience she and her family went through and that she had no choice but to watch, as her stepfather was brutally scalped alive.

With Carson still in California, Boggs was the only male in his wife's family. Therefore, Boggs felt honor-bound to take over the role of his deceased father-in-law and great friend. Boggs made accommodations for his wife's family and became a guardian to Rumalda's siblings. Boggs also resumed his previous position at Charles Bent's trading post, as well as overseeing the financial interests of the Bent brothers' business until William Bent could make other arrangements.

A few months later, as Taos began to rebuild and order was restored, a series of murder trials were held. The prosecution team was led by Frank Blair, who had served under Governor Bent. Judges during the various trials included Carlos Beaubien, the father of Narciso Beaubien, who had been murdered in the stable, and Joab Houghton, a close friend of the deceased Governor Bent. Lucien Bonaparte Maxwell, brother-in-law of the slain Narciso Beaubien, sat on one of the juries. Throughout the trial proceedings, Ceran St.Vrain, friend and partner of Governor Bent's, served as interpreter.[12]

With Boggs' support and encouragement, Maria Bent, her daughter Rumalda Bent Boggs, and Josefa Carson, all eyewitnesses to the murder of Governor Bent, testified. The women sat on benches along the oblong-shaped courtroom. Lewis H. Garrard, whom Boggs had met on his journey back to Taos, also attended the trials. Of the appearance of the Bent women at the trials, Garrard wrote: "The dress and manner of the three ladies bespoke a greater degree of refinement than usual."[13]

Garrard was particularly impressed with the powerful testimony of the widow, Maria Ignacia Bent. He wrote: "The eyes of the culprits were fixed sternly upon her and on pointing out the Indian who killed the Governor, he [Romero] was aware of her evidence [which] sealed his death warrant."[14]

When the trials were concluded, fourteen men were convicted of murder and sentenced to hang. The gallows for the public hangings were erected and the first of the hangings occurred on April 9, 1847. By all accounts the series of hangings were well attended.

The estate of Charles Bent was eventually settled. Ceran St. Vrain, as the sole landowner of the Vigil-St. Vrain Land Grant, gave the majority of Cornelius Vigil's portion to Vigil's sister, Maria Ignacia Bent, as well as a sizable tract to Vigil's other sister, Josefa Jaramillo Carson. The land that had been deeded to Bent was divided between the four surviving Bent children. Rumalda Luna Bent Boggs received 2,040 acres of land along the Arkansas River where it meets with the Purgatoire River.

In the meantime, United States Colonel Sterling Price, commanding officer for the District of Santa Fe, requested the services of Thomas Boggs. Boggs was again asked to deliver military dispatches between New Mexico Territory and Fort

Leavenworth, Kansas. Later that year, Boggs accepted a position with John C. Fremont's group on yet another trip to California. While in California, Boggs managed to visit with his brother William, and his family, who were living in the northern area near Bodega Bay in the Napa Valley. Impressed with the rich soil and climate of the area, Boggs stayed in California for seven months, leaving in August of 1848.

His trip back to New Mexico Territory was a long journey, traveling south to Sonora and Chihuahua, Mexico, and then north into the United States.[15]

Reunited in Taos with his wife, Rumalda, Boggs sold his home, and he and Rumalda, along with Rumalda's six-year-old sister, Teresina Bent, moved to Santa Fe. There, he opened a mercantile store on the town's main street. Boggs placed a series of ads in the *Santa Fe New Mexican* newspaper, advertising his new business enterprise, located at 78 Main Street.

Boggs' mercantile store did well and he and Rumalda were happy there. In Santa Fe, the first of two children was born to the couple, Carlos Adolfo. A few years later, Boggs sold his business, packed up his young family, and headed west for California. In California's Napa Valley, Boggs joined his brother in farming the fertile soil of the area.

In 1855, after five years of farming and little results, the Boggs family returned to New Mexico Territory and the town of Taos. Not long after his arrival, Boggs entered into a business partnership with his old friend and family member, Christopher "Kit" Carson, and Lucien Maxwell. Maxwell had received a large parcel of land through the Mexican land grants known as the Maxwell Land Grant. Maxwell and Carson had a contract with the United States government to supply provisions and clothing to the Taos Indians, as well as beef to Fort Union.

Boggs moved his family to the Maxwell ranch near the small settlement of Rayado. Indians often roamed the area around Rayado and the Maxwell ranch. Boggs, with his experience as a trader and his fluency in several dialects of the language, seemed to get along with them fairly well. However, during one particular incident, when Maxwell and Carson were away from the ranch, a group of unruly local Cheyenne arrived at the ranch. Boggs sensed something was amiss. In an attempt to placate the Indians, Boggs invited them to join him in a feast later in the day. Boggs then put a plan into motion.

Boggs managed to get a couple of the ranch hands safely off the ranch with instructions to ride the thirty-five miles to Fort Union and bring troops back to the ranch. Next, he alerted the women and asked them to prepare a very large meal. Rumalda Bent Boggs, Josefa Jarimillo Carson, and Maria de la Luz Beaubien Maxwell immediately began cooking. Within a few hours, the meal had been prepared and the women, including twelve-year-old Teresina Bent, began laying out the food for their Cheyenne "guests."

Nearly fifty years after the incident, Teresina Bent Scheurich related her frightening encounter with the Indians:

"I was twelve years old and the chief of the war party saw me and wanted to buy me to make me his wife. He kept offering horses. My, I was so frightened! And while I carried platters of food from the kitchen, the tears were running down my cheeks. That made the chief laugh. He was bound to buy me." [16]

Boggs did his best at Indian diplomacy, gently rebuffing the chief's offer, but the man was insistent. He and his fellow warriors moved to a place directly in front of the ranch house, where the chief told Boggs they would remain until sundown. The chief further instructed Boggs that if the young Teresina Bent was not brought forth, she would be taken by force. [17]

Boggs secured the women inside the ranch house and prepared what defense he could. And then, just as the sun was going down, troops on horseback from Fort Union, including Carson, who had been at the fort delivering goods, galloped toward the Maxwell ranch.

Teresina Bent Scheurich related the relief she felt that day: "The Indians saw them and went away. Then I cried some more, I

The Boggs ranch house located at Boggsville. *DPL*

was so glad."[18]

     Following this unsettling encounter with the Indians, both Boggs and Maxwell began to think about relocating their cattle business. It may also have been due to the increased violence and lack of sufficient military protection, owing to the ongoing Civil War in the east. In any case, both Boggs and Maxwell were keenly aware of the increase in settlers moving west, following President Abraham Lincoln's signing of the Homestead Act in 1862. With the creation of the Colorado Territory in 1861, Boggs and Maxwell began planning a move to the Arkansas River.

     The Arkansas River had been a legendary section along the Mountain Route of the Santa Fe Trail for nearly forty years, when the fur trade was a strong enterprise in the West. With the new emergence of traffic along the trail, Boggs and Maxwell felt the time was right to relocate to the Colorado Territory.

     In the summer of 1862, Boggs and Maxwell moved their cattle to the fertile area where the Purgatoire River joins the Arkansas River. This was the tract of land Rumalda Luna Jaramillo Bent Boggs had inherited following the death of her stepfather, Charles Bent. Thomas Oliver and Rumalda Luna Jaramillo Bent Boggs and Rumalda's half-sister, Teresina Bent, moved to the area later that summer. Accompanying them were Rumalda's mother, Maria Ignacia Jaramillo Luna Bent Ritc, her new husband, Charles, and their infant daughter. Maria Ignacia had remarried two years after the murder of her husband, Charles Bent. A year later, Maria and her new husband, Charles Ritc, had their first child together, a daughter, also named Rumalda.[19]

Rumalda Jaramillo Luna Bent Boggs' land inheritance covered more than two thousand acres, located approximately two miles south of the Arkansas River, and southeast of her uncle's fort. The lush green land was the result of the Purgatoire River running nearly through the center of the acreage. It was here that Thomas O. and Rumalda Bent Boggs envisioned a new ranching community. Rumalda was a strong-willed woman with an independent mind. Born into the influential Jaramillo family of Taos, New Mexico, she also gained a respect for strong community efforts from her paternal family heritage, the Virgil family. With this deeply held belief, Rumalda encouraged her husband.

Thomas and Rumalda Boggs began planning a small settlement. First Boggs built a large nine-room home for his family, as well as Rumalda's family. Boggs picked a perfect spot just a few yards from the west bank of the Purgatoire River. The Boggs home, the first permanent structure in the region, was an adobe structure, in the traditional Spanish Colonial style. The exterior of the home was rather plain, with a series of small windows paned with sheets of mica. Nevertheless, it was a sturdy structure with walls nearly two feet thick.

Inside, the floors were made of hard-packed dirt and then seasoned with pinon ash and ox blood, in the Spanish custom. The walls were whitewashed with a clay substance made of pounded wheat which created a milky, chalky liquid. Rumalda and her mother decorated the interior of the home in the Spanish style, with a variety of wall hangings and traditional furniture.

Next, barns and stables were built. Along with the cattle Boggs and Maxwell were raising, Boggs had also been bringing his sheep from New Mexico to pasture on the fertile land during the summer months. Now, Boggs kept his growing sheep herd at what became "Boggs Ranch," year-round. Thomas Oliver Boggs is credited with being the first to introduce sheep into the Arkansas River Valley and would become known as the "father" of the sheep business in the valley.

When the Civil War ended, most of the soldiers stationed at the Fort Lyon Military Post were mustered out and the fort remained idle for a time. In 1866, a massive spring storm caused the Arkansas River to flood, destroying the fort. Within a year, the new Fort Lyon was constructed a few miles upstream at the point where the Purgatoire River joins the Arkansas River. From this new military post, soldiers were able to protect the ever-increasing groups of travelers on the Santa Fe Trail.

Boggs entered into a contract with Fort Lyon, providing them with meat from his cattle and sheep herds. The fort soon became a marketplace for Boggs' provisions. Rumalda, along with her mother and sisters, planted a large garden, which in time yielded fruits and vegetables that were also sold at the fort.

Thomas Oliver and Rumalda Luna Jaramillo Bent Boggs were quite popular at Fort Lyon. The Boggs couple often invited the soldiers to their home for a meal and conversation. Soon Thomas and Rumalda became known for their kind hospitality and Rumalda's exceptional cooking skills. Off-duty soldiers routinely spent time at the Boggs Ranch.

William Bent, Rumalda's step-uncle and Thomas' uncle, lived a few miles north of the Boggs Ranch, at the mouth of the Purgatoire River, on a small ranch of his own. His son, Robert Bent, also lived nearby, as did Bent's oldest daughter, Mary, and her family. The Bent families were frequent visitors to the Boggs Ranch. In 1867, John Wesley Prowers moved his family and large cattle holdings to the Boggs Ranch. Prowers and Boggs had been friends ever since they worked together shortly after the opening of Bent's Fort. In 1846, Prowers had married Amache Ochinee, the daughter of One-Eye, a Cheyenne sub-chief, medicine man, and friend of William Bent. Amache's father, One-Eye, was one of the many Cheyenne and Arapaho killed at Sand Creek on November 29, 1864. After several military investigations, the United States government, through the Treaty of the Little Arkansas, promised many things to the various Indian tribes, including a 160-acre parcel of land to each of the survivors of the Sand Creek Massacre. Amache Ochinee Prowers received her government appropriation of the 160-acre land grant which was located next to Rumalda Luna Jaramillo Bent Boggs' inherited land through the Vigil-St. Vrain Land Grant.

Just a few yards north and east of the Boggs home, John Prowers built a large, two-story territorial style home for his own growing family. Amache Ochinee Prowers was delighted to learn that her childhood friend Mary Bent, and her husband, lived nearby.

Not long after the Prowers family had settled into their new home, Prowers' sister Mary, Mary's husband, John S. Hough, and their children arrived at the growing settlement. Boggs generously allowed them to move into an older outbuilding with three rooms of living space on one side, and three additional rooms on the other side. John Hough later wrote:

> The families of Boggs, Carson and Ritc were one half Spanish as the wives of these men were Spanish women. The writer's wife being the only woman of Anglo-Saxon blood. The wife of Prowers being a full-blood Cheyenne Indian. Quite a mixture but we all got along very pleasantly.[20]

With the addition of the Prowers and Hough families, as well as the routine social visits of the Fort Lyon soldiers, the Boggs settlement was named "Boggsville," located on the south bank of the Arkansas River. As it was near the Santa Fe Trail, Boggs and Prowers saw the opportunity to expand the settlement as well as their agricultural interests.

Prowers built a trading post and stage stop on the east side of Boggsville which his brother-in-law John Hough operated. Among the many items offered were guns and ammunition, bowie knives, clothing, shoes, boots, Mexican saddles, and canned fruits. They also sold prime beef supplied by John and Amache Prowers'

Hereford cattle, at ten cents a pound. Boggs even opened a post office in one of the front rooms of his home, as a convenience to the travelers as well as the settlers. With the success of the new trading post and stage stop, Boggsville, the first non-military settlement in the Arkansas River Valley, became an important stop on the Santa Fe Trail via the "Boggsville Branch."

With the influx of travelers stopping at Boggsville, Rumalda Boggs and Amache Prowers enlarged their courtyard with features of the hacienda-style New Mexican architecture. The women opened the courtyard for entertainment, providing food, picnics, dancing, and socializing. As more settlers came to the area, a community center was firmly established.

In the winter of 1866-1867, Thomas Boggs, John Prowers, Charles Ritc, and Robert Bent, the son of William Bent, along with the Tarbox brothers, began construction of a seven-mile canal. It was a monumental effort to draw water from the Purgatoire River. When it was completed, the canal served as the anchor of a system of irrigation ditches, known as the Tarbox ditches, that watered more than one thousand acres, including the area of Boggsville. The construction of the canal and the Tarbox ditches became the impetus of the subsequent development of irrigated agriculture around Boggsville that continues to this day.

With the new irrigation system allowing the settlement of Boggsville the needed water for farming, Thomas and Rumalda Boggs planted more than six hundred acres of various crops. Wheat, grains and fodder were grown for feed for the livestock. Fruits and vegetables were raised for the settlement, as well as to sell to the neighbors and travelers, and to market at Fort Lyon. The couple even experimented with new crops such as alfalfa.

Now more and more farmers and ranchers moved to the area. Within a decade, their ranches would encompass much of the area west to the Hardscrabble area near Pueblo, and east to the Kansas border.

Thomas O. Boggs grazed his growing sheep herd on the southern side of the Arkansas River, and John Prowers raised cattle on the northern side. At Boggsville, both men were able to increase their agricultural interests. Within two years, Boggs had a sheep herd of nearly eight thousand, and Prowers' cattle herd numbered nearly the same.

During the Christmas season of 1867, Christopher "Kit" and Maria Josefa Jaramillo Carson moved to Boggsville. Carson had just been relieved of his command at Fort Garland, as the United States army was trimming its forces. Now, awaiting new orders, he needed a place for his pregnant wife and their six children to live. Boggs immediately offered his in-laws the adjoining three vacant rooms of the six-room adobe outbuilding, in which the Hough family occupied the other half. John Carson, a direct descendant of Carson, later remarked, "Back then you had to work together with people in order to survive. Boggsville gave permanency to the area. People knew they would be treated well there. It was a haven where they wouldn't be cheated."[21]

Josefa was relieved to once again be with her sister, Maria Ignacia, as well as her niece, Rumalda Boggs. Rumalda, only three years younger than her aunt, must have been pleased to have her entire family with her once again.

However, upon Carson's arrival at Boggsville, it was obvious to all that his health was declining. Carson must have realized it as well. Not long after his family had settled into their new home, which Carson hoped was temporary, he traveled the few miles to the home of his old friend, William Bent. It was during this visit that Carson met Doctor Henry R. Tilton, the army surgeon at Fort Lyon. After casual conversation, Carson told the doctor of his ailments. Dr. Tilton later wrote, "He was then complaining of a pain in his chest, the origin of which he attributed to a fall received in 1860. It happened while he was descending a mountain."[22]

Dr. Tilton offered to take Carson in his carriage to Fort Lyon for a detailed consultation. After a rigorous exam, Carson was diagnosed with an aneurysm of the carotid artery. Josefa, who was present when the doctor gave the couple the devastating news, struggled amid her pregnancy to keep both her husband and children in optimistic spirits. Doctor Tilton later described the sad event: "The General, as Carson was popularly and officially known, now was a sick man, without long-assured income, [and] was the sole support of a goodly family, and was facing evil days."[23]

Of his first meeting with Mrs. Josefa Carson, the doctor described her as "evidently having been a very handsome woman, at age 39, she had lost much of her beauty."[24]

With the devastating news, Carson's hopes and dreams for his family's future were dashed. Carson had planned to build a home and ranch on the two parcels of land that his wife, Josefa, had inherited from her uncle Cornelio Vigil, through the Vigil-St. Vrain land grant. The land was just north of Boggsville, along the Purgatoire River. Now, Carson realized he would never be able to provide for his family as he had hoped. Back at Boggsville, Josefa did her best to tend to her husband's needs, while also tending to the children. Her niece, Rumalda Boggs, helped with the children and the cooking and cleaning, which provided time for Josefa to rest and take care of herself and her unborn baby.

Then, shortly after ringing in the New Year, Carson was among many Colorado dignitaries called to Washington D. C. by the War Department for a conference on how best to prevent Indian uprisings. In late January 1868, despite his declining heath, Carson agreed to accompany Colorado Governor Alexander C. Hunt, who was also the acting Superintendent of Indian Affairs, on the trip to Washington D. C. There, Carson headed the Ute delegation of chiefs and dignitaries, a delegation that included his friend Chief Ouray, for a peace council with President Andrew Johnson and members of both the U. S. Senate and House of Representatives.

Carson returned to his family at Boggsville after a two-month absence. Carson enjoyed the next two days being reunited with his children and his wife Josefa, who was now in her eighth month of pregnancy. On April 13, 1868, Josefa went into premature labor. After giving birth to a healthy baby girl, a weak Josefa remained in bed for days. Carson named his baby girl Josefita, in honor of her mother and his beloved wife.

As Carson sat by his wife's side, confident Josefa would be

fine, he wrote a letter to a friend, relaying such optimism: "I arrived home on the 11th inst. and found my family well. I was very sick but since my arrival home, I have improved some & hope it will continue."[25]

Josefa was not getting better; in fact, she was growing weaker. On the evening of April 27, 1868, forty-year-old Josefa Jaramillo Carson died.[25] Overcome with grief, there was little Carson could do.[26]

Rumalda Boggs took the Carson children, including two-week-old Josefita, into their home. Thomas Boggs did his best to console his old friend, while John and Amache Prowers tended to the burial of Josefa and comforted a distraught Carson. The following morning, Boggs, Hough, and Prowers dug a grave at the edge of Rumalda's beautiful flower gardens at Boggsville, where the body of Maria Josefa Jaramillo Carson was laid to rest.[27]

After a brief solemn service, a silent Christopher Houston Carson, now a widower with seven children to care for, simply walked away. Years later, the youngest son of Christopher and Josefa Carson, Charles Carson, named for Charles Bent, recalled the time of his mother's death: "That was a terrible time. Father was sick and we children didn't know what would become of us. He just seemed to pine away after mother died."

Doctor Henry R. Tilton later wrote, "Her sudden death had a very depressing effect upon him."[28] In spite of his profound grief, a week after the burial of his beloved wife, Carson, deeply concerned for his children's welfare, sent a letter to Aloya Scheurich. Scheurich was the husband of Teresina Bent, who had lived with her stepsister, Rumalda Boggs, since the death of her father. Not long after her marriage, Teresina's mother, Maria Ignacia Jaramillo Luna, joined her daughter in their new home back in Taos, New Mexico. Carson's letter to Scheurich, dated May 5, 1868, read in part:

> I would be comparatively healthy if the misfortune [of] losing my wife hadn't happened. Those were trying days for me. I have given the necessary orders to have my own body, if I

should die, and that of my wife's, sent together to Taos, to be buried as soon as the weather is cool enough to do so. Please tell the old lady [Josefa's older sister, Maria Ignacia] that there is nobody in the world who can take care of my children but her, and she must know that it would be the greatest of favors to me, if she would come and stay until I am healthier.[29]

Receiving the letter, Maria Ignacia Bent Ritc and daughter Teresina Bent Scheurich, as well as her husband, Aloya, immediately left Taos for Boggsville. It was a long, two-hundred-mile trip, and during that time Carson's health declined. When they arrived on May 15, Boggs informed them that Carson had been taken Fort Lyon the previous day. Boggs hitched his wagon and drove them to Fort Lyon. However, Carson wasn't able to have visitors. Doctor Henry R. Tilton later described the situation: "His [Carson] disease, aneurysm of the aorta, had progressed rapidly; and the tumor pressing on the pneumo-gastric nerves and trachea caused frequent spasms of the bronchial tubes which were exceedingly distressing."[30]

Fearing Carson would not live much longer, Dr. Tilton encouraged the dying man to make out his will. Carson did so, which Tilton wrote out and Carson signed. For the next week, Dr. Tilton did what he could to ease Carson's pain. At 4:25 in the afternoon of May 23, 1868, Carson began coughing and blood spurted from his mouth. "I supported his forehead on my hand while death speedily closed the scene," wrote Dr. Tilton.[31] Carson's last words in Spanish were, "Adios compadre."

The American flag flying high over Fort Lyon was lowered to half-mast in honor of the general. A soldier rode to Boggsville with the news of Carson's death. Thomas Boggs, ready to travel to the fort to bring back the body of his friend, was told there would be no need. The following day, after a brief ceremony which included rifle volleys and the bugling of taps, soldiers led a procession to Boggsville, carrying the casket of brevet General Christopher Carson. When the casket arrived at Boggsville that solemn day, Thomas Boggs and John Prowers had the grave ready.

Christopher Houston "Kit" Carson was buried at the edge of Rumalda Boggs' flower garden, next to his beloved wife, Josefa.

In his will, filed in the Pueblo County courthouse, Carson named Thomas Oliver Boggs as executor.[32] As executor of the meager Carson estate, Boggs and his wife Rumalda also became the guardians of the five under-aged Carson children.[33] The obvious trust that Carson had placed in his old friend, Thomas Boggs, is a testament to their friendship and the high regard Carson had for the Boggs family.

For Thomas and Rumalda Boggs, the added responsibility of raising five additional children must have been difficult. Yet Rumalda, now pregnant with her second child, welcomed the children of her beloved aunt into her home and loved them as her own, particularly baby Josefita. Before the winter had set in, Boggs, along with his son, Carlos Adolfo, managed to complete an addition to their adobe home. Located on the west side, the house now took on a U shape.

On December 9, 1868, thirty-six-year-old Rumalda gave birth to her own daughter, Minnie Boone Boggs, named for Thomas' grandmother, Phoebe Boone. It must have been a bittersweet Christmas that year, the Boggs family celebrating a new addition; and the Carson children missing their parents. Rumalda prepared a very special dinner and extra sweet treats for all the children.

With the spring of 1869, new life, new optimism, and prosperity flourished at Boggsville. There were more than thirty farms and ranches along the Purgatoire River nearby. The community of Boggsville also grew. That year, there were ninety-seven residents living at the settlement. More than twenty buildings were erected to serve the community.

One of those buildings was a schoolhouse. Rumalda insisted on a school for the area's children. The school building, built on the north edge of the property, was completed by the end of the year. John W. Prowers brought in a friend, P. G. Scott, as the area's first teacher. When the school opened in the spring of 1871, children from the local farm and ranches, as well as the children residing at Boggsville, were provided the opportunity for education.[34]

With the new addition of the school, Boggsville became the educational and social center of the community. In the center of the area, Rumalda constructed a courtyard, built in the New Mexican hacienda style, to host parties and community events. Rumalda Luna and Amache Prowers hosted many parties for the locals, educational events for the children, and dinners for the politicians. Presiding over such events, the women were busy with their children and tending to their households. Their husbands were busy as well.

The Boggsville settlement was located south of the Arkansas River. Boggs, Prowers, and Hough constructed a bridge, possibly a toll bridge, across the river.[35] This provided a direct connection to the historic Santa Fe Trail, which followed the north bank of the river. With the construction of the bridge, a shift in traffic along the mountain branch of the trail brought an influx of travelers to the area. As the crossing to Boggsville became more prominent, Boggs hired men to operate the ferries that ran across the river. By 1870, Boggsville also served as a stage stop along the trail. It was a place where travelers could rest, water their horses, and obtain fresh provisions. From there, they would continue their journey along the trail either north to Bent's Fort, east to Fort Lyon, or west to Pueblo. During this time, as many as two hundred individuals resided at Boggsville, primarily employees or tenants who worked in the agricultural operations of Boggs and Prowers.

Boggs raised his sheep on the south side of the Arkansas River and Prowers raised his cattle on the north side of the river. Both men had contracts with Fort Lyon to provide meat for the soldiers. By the early 1870s, Boggs had grown his sheep herd to an impressive seventeen thousand head.

Each year Boggs would invite his neighbors to bring their sheep to Boggsville where he and Rumalda hosted one of their many community events. Boggs would hold the annual sheep shearing contest for all the ranchers. In the center of Rumalda's social garden, she and the other rancher's wives laid out food, including fruit and pies. The children played games on the lush grassland around the area before being called for the picnic. As the sun set, the music started, and dancing in Rumalda's courtyard went on for hours.

In February 1870, the Colorado territorial legislature established Bent County. The new county, named for William Bent, encompassed more than five thousand square miles, from approximately two miles west of Fowler to the Kansas border. In 1871, Boggsville was named as the first county seat. Thomas Oliver Boggs was elected county sheriff, and John Prowers was elected county commissioner. The two men each set up offices in their homes where they conducted the county's business. Within that first year of the community being named as the county seat, Boggs and Prowers were awarded a government contract to operate a post office from Boggsville.

Rumalda Boggs and Amache Prowers continued to host their social events for the citizens, and now the politicians in the area of Bent County also attended. Evidently the socializing paid off for Boggs, as that fall he was elected to represent the citizens of Bent County in the Colorado state legislature.

For the next two years, Boggsville flourished. However, by 1873, the first non-military settlement in the Arkansas Valley began a steady decline.

In 1873, the Kansas & Pacific Railroad had extended their line from the town of Kit Carson, reaching the Arkansas Valley, where a railroad town known as West Las Animas City was established. This new settlement was located upstream along the Arkansas River, approximately two miles north of Boggsville. Eager to capitalize on the new transportation opportunities, one of the first things the new town builders did was to promote a redirection of the travelers to Boggsville, back to the original Santa Fe Trail.

This had a serious impact on the community of Boggsville, as most of the Santa Fe Trail traffic shifted northward and bypassed Boggsville, which remained the agricultural center of Bent County for the next few years.

In 1875, the Atchison, Topeka & Santa Fe Railroad reached

the railroad town. With two railroads serving the area, businesses grew and the population soared. It was during this period that the prosperous town became known simply as Las Animas.

Despite the economic set back, Thomas and Rumalda Boggs remained at Boggsville for the next two years, dependent on the success of Boggs' enormous sheep herd. In 1877, officials at the United States Land Grant offices in Washington D.C., began an investigation into various aspects of the 1843 Vigil-St. Vrain Land Grant. Ultimately, Thomas and Rumalda Luna Jaramillo Bent Boggs received a letter requesting proof of title to Rumalda's inherited two thousand acres of land following the murder of her stepfather in 1846. Boggs dutifully sent what paperwork he had. After receiving another letter asking for further documentation, Boggs sent off a letter of his own. With his many years of service to the government, both as an Indian agent and as a scout for Fremont's expeditions, Boggs asked President Ulysses S. Grant to intervene in the matter. President Grant did so and before the year was out, the government dropped the investigation.[36]

By the end of 1877, Boggs had made the decision to leave the new state of Colorado. Many factors played into his decision; the settlement of Boggsville was losing residents, the economy was growing weaker, and perhaps he was discouraged after the ordeal with the federal government. In any case, Thomas Boggs sold his property and the inherited land of Rumalda Luna Jaramillo Bent Boggs in late 1877. It was the end of a pioneering enterprise in Colorado. With his wife's inheritance, Thomas Oliver and Rumalda Luna Jaramillo Bent Boggs had established the first non-military settlement in Colorado Territory. It was at Boggsville that the rich agricultural empire of the Arkansas Valley had its beginning. Due to Thomas Boggs' vision, the first irrigation system was devised; his friend John Prowers became the cattle baron of southeastern Colorado; and Thomas O. Boggs became known as the first successful sheep rancher in the Arkansas Valley.

Nevertheless, not long after Thomas Boggs left his namesake of Boggsville, there were very few sheep ranchers in the area. Boggs eventually sold the property for thirteen thousand dollars to the John Lee family, who operated the San Patricio Ranch, a cattle ranch running large herds of Hereford and Galloway cattle. The cattle ranchers controlled the range land and harbored a deep antagonism against sheep. The powerful Bent Prowers Cattle and Horse Growers Association requested that the Atchison, Topeka & Sante Fe Railroad arrange shipments of all sheep from Lamar, and refuse shipment of sheep to the Las Animas stockyards.

The Boggs family, including the children of the deceased Carsons, left Colorado and relocated at Willow Springs, later renamed Raton. Here, the couple operated a boarding house at the foot of Raton Mountain. However, not long after the opening of their new establishment, the Boggs found themselves in yet another land claim dispute. Officials of the Maxwell Land Grant Company, which owned a considerable amount of New Mexico land, managed to prove that Boggs had no legal claim to land where his boarding house was located. In due course, the company was able to legally evict the Boggs family from their property.

Discouraged but undaunted, Boggs moved his family to Springer, New Mexico, southeast of Rayado, the area where Boggs had begun his agricultural enterprise over twenty-five years previously. Boggs relocated his massive sheep herd to an area along the Pinavetitos River, approximately thirty-five miles south of Clayton, New Mexico. Boggs spent the summer months tending his flock, living in a small adobe home he had built for himself. Within a few years, Boggs sold off his sheep herd and the land for ten thousand dollars and moved permanently back to Springer, with his wife and young daughter.

Back in Springer, with a portion of the money Boggs had received from his land sale, Thomas and Rumalda agreed to send their fourteen-year-old daughter, Minnie Boone, to St. Louis, Missouri, to complete her formal education. It was a tradition begun by Boggs' uncles, William and Charles Bent (Rumalda's stepfather), repeated by the Carson family, and now carried on by the Boggs family. With Minnie Boone Boggs away at school, Thomas and Rumalda settled into their life together. Ironically,

*40*

Boggs found employment as an agent for the Maxwell Land Grant Company, the same company that had forced him to abandon his business at Willow Springs. Boggs' duties included traveling to the company's properties, visiting with the Mexicans living on company grant land for years, and negotiate the removal of unauthorized settlers from the company's land. Rumalda had raised both Carlos and Minnie as devout Catholics; however, she did worry about her young daughter so far away without a proper chaperone.[37]

Boggs detested his job. He was getting older and perhaps due to his own experience with government intrusion regarding land grants, he no longer had the tolerance for government or corporate suppression. And he was unhappy with his time away from Rumalda. After two years with the Maxwell Land Grant Company, Boggs quit.

Not long after Boggs returned to Springer and his beloved Rumalda, another ironic happenstance befell the Boggs couple. During one of her several visits home from school, Minnie Boone Boggs informed her parents that she was in love with a local man. He was George Alexander Bushnell, an Englishmen who was employed as an auditor for the Maxwell Land Grant Company, the same company that Boggs had recently worked for.

Rumalda was very pleased with the prospect for her beloved daughter, but Thomas Boggs had reservations. After much discussion, Thomas and Rumalda allowed the young couple to become betrothed. However, Rumalda insisted that her daughter finish her schooling.

On December 9, 1884, Minnie Boone Boggs and George Alexander Bushnell were married in Springer, New Mexico. The groom had purposefully chosen the date of the wedding, as it was Minnie Boone Boggs' birth date. The wedding was the social event in Springer, covered in detail in the local newspaper, the *Las Vegas Optic*.

In April 1887, Minnie Boone Boggs Bushnell gave birth to Thomas and Rumalda's first grandchild, Charles Lilburn Bushnell. Thomas and Rumalda were overcome with joy. Rumalda doted on the child and Thomas "spoiled him shamelessly."

Their joy turned to sadness two months later when tragedy struck the Boggs family. The Boggs' son, Carlos Adolfo (known as Charlie), and his wife, Eva, lived on small ranch between Springer and Raton, not far from his sister Minnie Boone Boggs Bushnell's home. In mid-June 1887, Charlie had just returned home from Raton with a wagon load of supplies. Sometime that evening,Charlie Boggs was murdered in his home. The murder was never solved, although the authorities suspected the victim's wife, Eva Matheny Boggs.

Thomas and Rumalda Boggs held the funeral for their son in their home in Springer, New Mexico. Following the solemn service, thirty-eight-year-old Carlos Adolfo "Charlie" Boggs was buried in the local cemetery in Springer. Not long after the burial, Eva Matheny Boggs left the area and was never heard from again.

Shortly after the birth of Minnie's second child, Thomas George, born in 1891, Thomas and Rumalda left Springer and moved in with their daughter Minnie and her growing family. George Bushnell, by this time a very successful businessman in Raton, had built a large home for his family in Clayton, some eighty miles southeast of Raton. Thomas O. Boggs, now sixty-seven years old, was in failing health. Living with Minnie and the grandchildren was a delight for Rumalda. She doted on her grandchildren and took care of her ailing husband. Rumalda insisted on cleaning her own quarters in the large house, despite the services of the Bushnell's hired help. Even with his poor health, Thomas enjoyed his grandchildren as well.

Shortly before the birth of Thomas and Rumalda's third grandchild, Rose May, born in 1893, Thomas O. Boggs suffered a stroke which left him paralyzed. In September 1894, Boggs contracted pneumonia and his lungs filled with fluid. On September 29, 1894, Thomas Oliver Boggs, founder of Boggsville, died in the home of his beloved daughter, Minnie. The funeral services for the patriarch of the Boggs family was held in the Bushnell home, with burial in the nearby Boot Prairie Cemetery.[38] Rumalda Luna Jaramillo Bent Boggs, now a widow, remained in the home of her daughter and son-in-law. Rumalda rebounded from her grief when her fourth grandchild, George, was welcomed into her world in 1896. Rumalda was at her daughter's side when tragedy once again struck her family. At the age of thirty-three, Minnie's husband, George Bushnell, died from complications after contracting pneumonia. Now mother and daughter, both widows, depended on each other. Albert W. Thompson, then a citizen of Clayton, who knew Rumalda Luna Jaramillo Bent Boggs, later described the woman as "a dark-eyed beauty with a daintiness of face and figure she kept into her old age."[39]

For the next few years, Rumalda helped her daughter, Minnie, as she raised her children. Rumalda thoroughly enjoyed her grandchildren. They were happy times in the twilight years of this pioneering woman.

At the age of seventy-five, Rumalda Luna Jaramillo Bent Boggs died on January 13th, 1906. Her obituary, printed in the local paper, *The Clayton Citizen*, on June 16, 1906, referred to Rumalda Luna Jaramillo Bent Boggs as "One of New Mexico's most respected women and the last oldtimer."

Rumalda's daughter, Minnie Boone Boggs Bushnell, held the funeral for her beloved mother in her home.[40] Following the service, Rumalda Luna Jaramillo Bent Boggs was buried next to her husband of fifty years, Thomas Oliver Boggs, in the Boot Prairie Cemetery near Clayton, New Mexico.[41]

Rumalda Luna Jaramillo Bent Boggs, the strong independent woman of Spanish descent, created a multi-culture community with her Anglo husband. Through her pioneering spirit, she laid the foundation for the many women ranchers of Colorado.

# Notes

1. Lavender, *Bent's Fort*, pg. 245.
2. Thompson, "The Death and Last Will of Kit Carson," *The Colorado Magazine*, 1928.
3. Drumm, *Down the Santa Fe Trail and Into New Mexico: The Diary of Susan Shelby Magoffin*, pg. 61.
4. Lavender, *Bent's Fort*, pg. 286.
5. Drumm, *Down the Santa Fe Trail and Into New Mexico: The Diary of Susan Shelby Magoffin*.
6. Lavender, *Bent's Fort*, pg. 293.
7. Simmons, *Kit Carson & His Three Wives*, pg. 72.
8. ibid.
9. *New Mexico Magazine*, "Insurrection in Taos," April 1942.
10. The body of Robert Bent was later reinterred in St. Louis, Missouri.
11. Simmons, *Kit Carson & His Three Wives*, pg. 73.
12. Lavender, *Bent's Fort*, pg. 316.
13. Gardner, "Tragedy in Taos," *The New Mexico Magazine*, October 2000.
14. ibid.
15. Boggs, William, "Narrative," *The Colorado Magazine*, March 1930.
16. Sabin, *Kit Carson Days*, Vol 2., pg. 633.
17. Simmons, *Kit Carson & His Three Wives*, pg. 87.
18. ibid.
19. For whatever reason, writers have spelled this fourth daughter of Maria as "Romalda." Even more confusing, writers have also confused the two sisters' names, thereby interchanging the two women in their history.
20. Hough, John S., Early Day Colorado Election. Manuscript Collection, MSS232, FF16. Colorado History Center.
21. ibid.
22. Sabin, *Kit Carson Days*, Volume 2, pg. 792.
23. ibid.
24. Carson letter dated April 16, 1868. *Simmons, Carson & His Three*

*Wives*, pg.175.

25. The adobe outbuilding which served as the last home of Carson and where Josefa died washed away when the Purgatoire River flooded in 1921.

26. Josefa's marker in the Taos Cemetery incorrectly gives her death date as April 23.

27. Christopher "Kit" Carson and his wife, Josefa, were later reinterred in Taos, New Mexico. Simmons, *Carson & His Three Wives*, pg.175.

28. ibid, pg. 142.

29. Shikes, *Rocky Mountain Medicine*, pg. 236.

30. Sides, *Blood and Thunder*, pg. 395.

31. Thompson, The Death and the Last Will of Kit Carson, Colorado Magazine, 1928.

32. Carson's oldest son, William, received his education at the University of Notre Dame, courtesy of General William T. Sherman.

33. The schoolhouse at Boggsville, was the first schoolhouse in what would become Bent County.

34. Francis W. Cragin Collection, Colorado History Center.

35. William Boggs Collection, Colorado History Center.

36. Thompson, The Death and Last Will of Kit Carson, The Colorado Magazine, 1928.

37. Clayton Memorial Cemetery records. Clayton, New Mexico.

38. Thompson, Albert W., Thomas O. Boggs, Early Scout and Plainsmen," The Colorado Magazine, 1930, pg. 152-160.

39. "Recollections of Minnie Boone Boggs Bushnell Burch," Albert W. Thompson Collection. MSS 79BC, Center for Southwest Research, University of New Mexico.

40. Ibid.

41. Clayton Memorial Cemetery records. Clayton, New Mexico. Sadly, both grave sites of Thomas and Rumalda Boggs have been lost in the cemetery records.

# Amache Ochinee Prowers

**Cheyenne Princess of the Plains**

In the spring of 1828, brothers Charles and William Bent of
Missouri were scouting the lush Arkansas River Valley, home to
the "Mountain Branch" of the Santa Fe Trail. At the time, the
Arkansas River served as the international boundary between the
United States and Mexico. The Santa Fe Trail was the major trade
corridor for travelers between the Mexican settlements and St.
Louis, Missouri, the "Gateway to the West."

The Bent brothers, while searching for the perfect location
for a frontier trading fort, were met by a group of Cheyenne
Indians. Through sign language and an interpreter, Cheyenne sub-
chiefs Yellow Wolf and Lone Bear expressed interest in a trading
post and directed the Bent brothers to the perfect location: the
north side of the Arkansas River, along the Santa Fe Trail.

Two years later, in 1830, the Bent brothers, in partnership
with Ceran St. Vrain, another Missouri trader among the Plains
Indians, established the Bent, St. Vrain & Company, which became
the foundation of a trading empire that covered much of the West,
encompassing hundreds of square miles of what would become
Colorado, New Mexico, Arizona, Kansas, and Utah. The men
built a large adobe fort, located along the Arkansas River near the
mouth of Huerfano Creek, in today's southeast Colorado. First
known as Fort William, the stockade was later renamed "Bent's
Fort."

The Cheyenne and Arapaho tribes were encouraged by
Lone Bear and Yellow Wolf to trade at Bent's Fort. The two sub-
chiefs became good friends with the Bent brothers and came to the
new fort often. In fact, William Bent married a Cheyenne woman,
Owl Woman, in 1837. It was an exceptional union of two cultures,

as Owl Woman was the daughter of White Thunder, the keeper of the Cheyenne Sacred Medicine Arrows.

Not long after his marriage into the Cheyenne tribe, William Bent was involved in a confrontation with a Kiowa warrior. When the warrior pulled a knife, Lone Bear intervened, and the Kiowa warrior thrust his knife into the eye of Lone Bear. Lone Bear survived the attack and was forever known as One-Eye, or Och-I-Nee. Some time later, Bent became extremely ill, suffering from a severe throat infection which prevented him from swallowing. His wife, Owl Woman, did what she could. Owl Woman became fearful after her husband declined for several weeks, losing weight and only growing weaker. Finally, Owl Woman resorted to her Cheyenne ways. She sent for the Cheyenne medicine man One-Eye.

After One-Eye examined his friend's throat, he returned to William's bedside with a handful of tiny, prickly sandburs, about the size of a pea.[1] One-Eye used an awl to make a hole through each of the sandburs, being careful not to prick himself with the sharp barbs. Then he strung a long strand of sinew through each of the sandburs and dipped the entire strand into warm marrow fat. Owl Woman watched in horror as One-Eye placed the prickly sandbur strand in the back of Bent's throat. Holding on to the strand, One-Eye used a small tree branch to push the lubricated sandburs down Bent's throat. After a brief time, perhaps only seconds, One-Eye slowly pulled the sinew string. A mass of putrid puss clung to the prickly sandburs. One-Eye continued the procedure for a few days until Bent could finally swallow a sip of water and then broth. In time, Bent made a full recovery. From then on, Bent would allow no one other than his friend One-Eye to treat his family.[2]

One-Eye felt the same kinship for his friend William Bent. In 1846, One-Eye brought his wife to the comfort of Bent's fort where she gave birth to a daughter they named Amache Ochinee, which means "Walking Woman." Susan Magoffin was staying at the fort following a miscarriage during her westward journey. The unhappy entry in her journal mentioning the Indian woman with

Amache was the daughter of Cheyenne chief One-Eye. She married John Wesley Prowers. Together, on land she received through Indian reparations, the couple operated the largest cattle ranch in southern Colorado. *DPL*

the new baby at the river referred to One-Eye's wife bathing his new daughter, Amache Ochinee.[3]

Life for young Amache was centered in a West of changing and merging cultures. While living the traditional Cheyenne life, her father One-Eye, a peaceful Cheyenne chief of the Council of Fourty-Four, was also a great friend to William Bent, and camped often near the fort. Thus, at a very young age Amache lived within two cultures. Amache spoke fluent Cheyenne and Spanish and understood English, although she seldom spoke it.

Growing up near the fort, Amache had a best friend in Mary Bent, the daughter of William Bent and Owl Woman. In the summer months, the Cheyenne hunters would often allow the girls to lasso colts from their herd of horses, and occasionally the two young girls were allowed to follow the buffalo hunters. It was at Bent's Fort, in 1857, that the beautiful teen-aged Amache met John Prowers, a young trader in the employ of Bent's Fort.

Like the Bent brothers, John Wesley Prowers was also born in Missouri, near Westport, in 1839. Prowers had a difficult childhood and spent very little time attending school. In 1856, at the age of eighteen, Prowers left Missouri in the company of Robert Miller, then Indian agent for the tribes of the Upper Arkansas region. The two arrived at Bent's Fort in the early summer with wagons loaded with annuity goods for the local Indian tribes. Prowers spent the next two months at Bent's Fort, where he passed out bacon, beans, cornmeal, coffee, oatmeal, salt, sugar, clothing and blankets to the Arapaho, Cheyenne, Kiowa and Apache tribes.

Prowers stayed on at Bent's Fort, first working as a clerk and later leading supply wagons along the Santa Fe Trail for William Bent.

Prowers, who was fluent in Spanish and several Indian dialects, found the young Cheyenne maiden Amache Ochinee very pleasant to be around. Years later, her daughter Ida recalled in an interview that her mother, while understanding English, cleverly spoke it only when she chose to. In any case, romance ensued, and with council from William Bent, One-Eye allowed the marriage of his daughter to the enterprising Prowers.

The wedding of twenty-two-year-old John Wesley Prowers and fifteen-year-old Amache Ochinee took place at Fort Supply in Indian Territory, in 1861. The newlyweds moved into a private section of Bent's Fort. Amache was accustomed to life at the fort and felt quite comfortable there. However, being married to a white man brought about some new adjustments for the young Cheyenne woman. Amache never really learned to prepare meals to her husband's liking, despite hours of instruction. Amache and John Prowers eventually struck a balance whereby they split the cooking duties. On the other hand, Amache very much enjoyed wearing the clothing of the Anglo-Victorian world. Although she never wore a corset, as she grew older she dressed in a very dignified style. In the summer of 1861, Prowers returned to his home state of Missouri on a freighting trip for William Bent. He took his new bride with him so that she could experience the sights of a place she had never known. While there, Prowers met with an old friend, John Ferril, to purchase a herd of cattle. With every bit of his savings, Prowers purchased one hundred head of Hereford cattle. John and Amache Prowers returned to the Upper Arkansas Valley and Bent's Fort with the cattle by the fall of that year. William Bent was happy to allow Prowers' cattle to graze at the fort, the cattle eventually providing food for the army.

The following year, after a freighting trip for Bent, Prowers returned to the fort where he was greeted by Amache with the news that they were going to have a baby. Now with a baby on the way and a family to think of, after seven years of freighting for Bent on the Santa Fe Trail, Prowers struck out on his own.

Prowers moved his herd of cattle to an abandoned Indian reservation on Caddoa Creek in the fall of 1862. The site had been established earlier that year for a reservation for the Wichita Caddoa Indians. Three large stone buildings had been erected by the time the Indians were to be brought to the reservation in the fall of 1862. However, the Civil War had broken out in the nation, and the site was abandoned. Prowers was able to purchase the reservation land and stone buildings from the United States government in 1863. It was here that Prowers could graze his cattle, the first to do so year-round, and sell to the military for troops stationed at Fort Lyon.

On July 18, 1863, at Bent's Fort, Amache gave birth to Mary, the first of their nine children. Later that summer Prowers moved his young family to the new area which would eventually become the center of his cattle empire.

Amache quickly adapted to life on the ranch. In time, two more children were born at the ranch, Katharine and Susan. When Amache was able, she enjoyed helping her husband with the cattle. The couple worked well together, and Prowers began to trust her views and opinions regarding their cattle enterprise.

In 1863, Prowers purchased the first of several prized Kentucky bulls. With this first bull, at a cost of nearly two hundred and fifty dollars, Prowers began crossbreeding his Missouri Hereford cows. He was the first in Colorado to bring Hereford cattle to his land and the first to crossbreed the stock. Prowers eventually was able to furnish beef, considered the best in Colorado, for the army troops at Fort Lyon and elsewhere. However, this was a long and costly venture for John and Amache Prowers. To make ends meet, Prowers continued his employment with William Bent.

By this time, with the country in the midst of the Civil War, Bent had relinquished his fort to the United States government, with the understanding it was only for the duration of the war. Prowers stayed at the fort where he operated the supply store for the army. With his ability to speak fluent Spanish as well as converse in several Indian dialects, Prowers also acted as interpreter between the Arapaho and Cheyenne tribes living in the area and the military officers. With Amache's help, Prowers was able to make a small profit by supplying the fort with his beef. It seemed to be an amicable arrangement for all, until the horrible night of November 28, 1864.

A severe snowstorm had hampered a military troop advancement toward the Arkansas River. Nevertheless, Colonel John M. Chivington, leading his newly created "100 Day

Volunteers," guided his horse briskly along the Bijou Creek Trail which would lead to the Arkansas River Valley. The one-time Methodist elder and Civil War hero of Glorieta Pass, itching for another glorious battle, now had the coveted orders from his district commander, General Samuel Curtis: "The Indians are to be fully subdued or exterminated. There will be no peace until the Indians suffer more."[4]

Chivington led the Colorado Third Regiment and three companies of the Colorado First Regiment south toward the Arkansas River. Major Hal Sayr and his troops, guided by Jim Beckwourth, arrived at Camp Fillmore, where they were greeted by members of Company E of the First Regiment.

Early the next morning, Monday, November 28, Chivington ordered a group of soldiers from the Colorado Third, under Lieutenant Joseph Graham, to head across the river toward William Bent's ranch at the mouth of the Purgatoire River. Captain Cook was ordered to take Company E of the First Colorado Cavalry, to the John W. Prowers ranch along the Arkansas River, at the mouth of Caddoa Creek. Both Cook and Graham received additional orders to "put the place under guard, allowing no one to leave."[5] Irving Howbert, who was under Graham's command, recalled, "In order that the news of our approach should not reach the Indians, every man whom we met on the road was taken in charge, and guards were placed at all ranches for the same purpose."[6]

The siege of the Prowers and Bent ranches was significant to Chivington's secrecy on several levels. William Bent was the father of half-breed sons, believed to consort with the enemy. John W. Prowers was married to Amache Ochinee, the daughter of One-Eye, who had previously bravely walked into Fort Lyon with the peace letter from Black Kettle, pledging peace with the white man that led to the council at Camp Weld earlier that year, something Chivington strongly opposed.

That cold winter night of November 28, 1864, changed Amache and John Prowers' life forever. In the dead of night, Captain Cook and his soldiers with Company E of the First

Colorado Cavalry stormed into the Prowers residence, placing the home and John Prowers in particular under armed guards. When the nightmare was over, Colorado Territory was changed as well.

It was later revealed that this action was taken to prevent Prowers from warning his Cheyenne friends and family of the impending attack at their camp along Sand Creek. It must have been an agonizing two nights for Amache. Her father One-Eye, her mother, and Cheyenne family members were camped at Sand Creek. The troops, led by Colonel John Chivington, attacked the peaceful Indian camp the following morning, Thursday, November 29, 1864. When it was over, hundreds lay dead, including Amache's father. Eyewitness accounts from both soldiers and Indians estimated the number of casualties at approximately one hundred and fifty, with two-thirds of the dead being women and children, lying on the blood-soaked ground.

On the morning of Friday, November 30, 1864, Prowers and his family were released and the soldiers moved on. Later that same day, The Prowers were told of the atrocity that occurred the previous day at Sand Creek. It was an incredibly sad moment for Amache. She grieved over the death of her father, yet was relieved to learn her mother and two of her aunts had survived the massacre. John and Amache's oldest child, Mary, later recalled the time: "Mother, Father and I were out at Big Timbers when we heard of the massacre. We immediately hurried to Fort Lyon to be with Grandmother, and to be of what help we could to the stricken Cheyenne."[7] As Mary was not quite three years of age at the time of the Sand Creek Massacre, she most likely was recalling what her parents later told her of the incident.

An outraged John Prowers testified at the military investigation held at Fort Lyon in early 1865. Prowers also traveled to Washington, D. C. to take part in the congressional hearings. Again, Mary Prowers Hudnall recalled:

Father was called by the government to testify at the investigation held at Fort Lyon. Mother was always very bitter about the Sand Creek Massacre. A number of years later, while she was attending a meeting of the Eastern Star in Denver, a friend brought Chivington over to introduce him to mother, saying, "Mrs. Prowers, do you know Colonel Chivington?" My mother drew herself up with that stately dignity, peculiar to her people, and ignoring the outstretched hand, remarked in perfect English, audible to all in the room, "Know Colonel Chivington? I should. He was my father's murderer!"[8]

Unfortunately, Mary Prowers Hudnall does not recount Chivington's reaction. It must have been a very tense moment. On October 14, 1865, after months of political intrigue by both the United States government and heads of the various Indian tribes, yet another peace treaty was signed. The Treaty of the Little Arkansas promised many things to the various Indian tribes, including a 160-acre parcel of land to each of the survivors of the Sand Creek Massacre.[9]

And so it was that Amache, her mother, and Amache's two children, Mary and Katherine, were each given a 160-acre parcel of land as atonement for the Sand Creek atrocity.[10]

Amache Prowers chose her and her young daughters' land allocation wisely, and suggested that her mother do the same. The land chosen was along the Arkansas River, in an area then known as "The Meadows."

In a bittersweet turn of events, twenty-year-old Amache Ochinee Prowers, a Native American woman, became a landowner.

Many of the Sand Creek survivors who received the land reparations either had no interest in the land or were more interested in cash. In any case, Prowers was able to buy several of these claims, including those of George and Charley Bent.[11] Prowers became the largest landowner in the Big Timber area of southern Colorado, owning eighty acres along forty miles of river land, with nearly fifty thousand head of cattle. Today, much of this land is submerged by John Martin Reservoir.

However, in 1867, over a growing concern of Indian uprisings, Prowers moved his family and large cattle holdings to

Amache and John Prowers built this ranch house at Boggsville. *DPL*

the new land his wife had acquired, near the small community of Boggsville, established by his friend, Thomas O. Boggs.

Tom and Rumalda Boggs were happy to have them, and the children were thrilled to be reunited and meet the new members of both families, for there were many children. As Amache settled into a life she realized she had missed, her husband lost no time in reacquainting with old friends. Later that same year, Prowers' sister Mary and her husband, John Hough, arrived at the growing settlement.

Famed scout Christopher Houston "Kit" Carson, his third wife, Josefa Jaramillo, and their children were also living there, where Boggs and Carson operated a small sheep business. The Carson home, a modest stone and adobe structure, was located near the large barn, and faced the Purgatoire River. William Bent and his family also lived nearby. By this time, Boggsville had become the social center for soldiers and officers of Fort Lyon.

Prowers immediately began building a house for his family, just east of the Boggs' two-story adobe home. The house, built in two sections, was then connected by a single wall. One of the first two-story framed homes in the area, it was also the first to have glass windows, hauled by wagon from St. Louis, Missouri. The inviting entrance of the home faced the central courtyard, built in the New Mexican hacienda style. The Prowers' new home contained twenty-four rooms. A parlor, formal receiving room and large kitchen were among the rooms on the main floor, with bedrooms on the second level.

Amache put her own personal touches inside and outside the home. Inside were colorful Cheyenne blankets, along with rustic Victorian furniture, most of which were made locally. Outside, Amache built her own open courtyard which faced east, greeted by the rising sun each morning, a custom of her Cheyenne heritage. The courtyard included an *horno* (adobe baking oven.) Amache enjoyed the area's wildlife, bringing over a dozen prairie chickens onto her land.

Prowers built a trading post on the east side of Boggsville which his brother-in-law John Hough operated. Among the many items offered were Mexican saddles, guns and ammunition, bowie knives, clothing, shoes, boots and canned fruits. They also sold prime beef supplied by John and Amache Prowers' Hereford cattle, at ten cents a pound.

It was here at their new home in Boggsville that Amache gave birth to three more Prowers children, Susan, Inez, and their first son, John Wesley, Jr. Life at the Prowers house was always busy, yet full of joy. Amache loved spending time with her children. Many years later, Amache's children often recounted their mother's Cheyenne values and customs, and particularly remembered their fondness for the Cheyenne food. During the spring and summer months, Amache would gather wild herbs and fruits from the prairie and make delightful treats, such as prickly pear pickles. Mary Prowers Hudnall recalled:

Every season mother used to gather prickly pears for sweet pickles. She would burn off the stickers and cook up the pears in vinegar and sugar. They were delicious. She knew all the prairie herbs and their uses by the Indians; she gathered mint to make medicine; sage leaves were dried and steeped into sage tea which she felt was just good for everything. We always had preserves made with the wild plum, chokecherries, etc. And of course, we had our spring greens and wild lettuce.[12]

For several years following the Sand Creek Massacre, young Cheyenne Dog Soldiers, including George and Charley Bent, the sons of William Bent and Owl Woman, conducted murderous raids against many ranchers and homesteaders along the Arkansas River in retaliation for the massacre.

Largely due to Amache's presence at Boggsville, as well as William's Bent's affiliation with the settlement, Boggsville was spared Cheyenne retaliation. Mary Prowers Hudnall later recalled, "Father was always exceptionally good to mother's people, and they loved and honored him, paying heed to his advice as to their relations with the white people."[13]

In the year of 1868, tragedy struck the close-knit families of Boggsville. Following Christopher "Kit" Carson's return from a two-month absence, his health rapidly declined. Carson had been diagnosed with an aneurysm of the carotid artery, Carson nevertheless agreed to accompany Colorado Governor Alexander C. Hunt, who was also the acting Superintendent of Indian Affairs, on a trip to Washington, D. C. Carson headed the Ute delegation of chiefs and dignitaries, including his friend Chief Ouray, for a peace council with President Andrew Johnson and members of both the U.S. Senate and House of Representatives.

Upon his return to Boggsville, it was obvious to all that Carson's health was declining. John Hough, Prowers brother-in-law, later recalled, "Carson's health at that point was very bad. Not being able to ride about, he spent most of his time keeping me company, my trading store being only a few feet away from our quarters."[14]

Carson enjoyed the next two days being reunited with his children and his wife, Josefa, who was eight months pregnant. On April 13, 1868, Josefa went into premature labor. After giving birth to a healthy baby girl, a weak Josefa remained in bed for days. On April 27, forty-year-old Josefa Jaramillo Carson died.

While Thomas and Rumalda Boggs took care of the Carson children and comforted a distraught Kit Carson, John and Amache Prowers tended to the burial of Josefa. After a brief yet solemn service, Prowers, along with Thomas Boggs and John Hough, buried Mrs. Christopher Carson in the beautiful flower gardens just south and west of the Carson home at Boggsville.[15]

Carson, himself quite ill and devastated over his wife's death, died a month later at Fort Lyon, on May 23, 1868. Prowers and Boggs buried the body of Christopher Houston "Kit" Carson in the gardens of Boggsville next to his wife, Josefa.

At this time Prowers, along with Thomas Boggs and Robert Bent, the son of William Bent, built the first successful irrigation ditch in the area, a seven-mile ditch, from the Purgatoire River. The new irrigation system allowed the settlement of Boggsville the needed water for their crops.

While the men were devising and building their new irrigation system, Amache and Rumalda Boggs were busy raising their children, as well as caring for the Carson children. They must have done a fine job, for the children were also the best of friends. Not long after the tragic deaths of the Carsons, John and Amache Prowers suffered their own personal tragedy when their daughter Susan suddenly died in July.

In February 1870, the Colorado territorial legislature established Bent County. The new county, named for William Bent, encompassed 5,500 square miles, from approximately two miles west of Fowler to the Kansas border. Astonishingly for such a large county, the recorded county population was just under six hundred residents. The county seat was at Boggsville. John Prowers was elected county commissioner and Thomas O. Boggs was elected county sheriff. The two men each set up offices in their homes where they conducted the county's business. A school was built in Boggsville in 1871 and Prowers brought in a friend, P. G. Scott, as the area's first teacher. Within that first year as the county seat, Boggsville became the educational and social center of the county.

Prowers and Boggs were allowed to operate a post office to serve the area.

Amache Prowers and Rumalda Luna hosted many parties for the locals, educational events for the children, and dinners for the politicians. Along with hosting such events, the women were busy with their children, and tended to their husbands' livestock. The Prowers' cattle range was on the north bank of the Arkansas River, on land Amache had chosen from her government allotment. Thomas Boggs' sheep herd was on the south side of the Arkansas River, on land Rumalda had inherited through the Vigil-St. Vrain land grant.

Amache and John Prowers and their young family lived at Boggsville for three years. In 1873, the Kansas & Pacific Railroad extended their line from the town of Kit Carson, reaching the Arkansas Valley. A railroad town known as West Las Animas City was established. The new settlement was located upstream along the Arkansas River, approximately two miles north of Boggsville. In the fall of 1873, Prowers moved his family to the new town. Prowers and his brother-in-law, John Hough, established a freight station near the railroad. Known as Prowers & Hough, the freighting company not only received freight for the locals, it was also an economic opportunity for Prowers to ship his cattle east to the cattle markets of Kansas and Chicago, Illinois.

In partnership with W. A. Haws, Prowers opened a retail store in a large two-story building he had built near the railroad depot. In the back of the store a large warehouse held the freight delivered by rail and transferred the goods to wagons for deliveries. Not long after Prowers established himself as a businessman, he was elected to represent Bent County in the territorial legislature.

By all accounts, Amache enjoyed the change to city life. Prowers had built the finest home in Las Animas, at 715 Carson Avenue, for his wife and family. Becoming quite active in community service, church affiliations and the local school, Amache proved to be an effective leader in the town's social affairs.

In her home and among her family, Amache maintained

the Indian customs of her heritage. Every Christmas the children were given presents of homemade buffalo candy made of dried buffalo meat rolled in sugar.[16] Mary Prowers Hudnall recalled:

> Mother clung to many of the Indian customs and we children learned to like them. At Christmas she always prepared us an Indian confection made thus: she sliced dried buffalo meat very thin, then sprinkled it generously with sugar and cinnamon and rolled it up like a jelly roll. Then on Christmas day she would cut slices from the roll and pass it around; this was our Christmas candy. We kids just loved it, but father looked on rather askance, and would slip over to the store to return with a wooden pail of bright colored Christmas candies for us.[17]

Amache Ochinee Prowers truly embraced both cultures she lived in, and passed the traditions of each on to her children.

In 1875, the Atchison, Topeka & Santa Fe Railroad reached the town. With two railroads serving the area, businesses grew and the population soared. It was during this period that the town became known simply as Las Animas. That same year, Prowers organized the Bent County Bank. Prowers again brought his close friend, P. G. Scott, whom he had brought to Boggsville as the first schoolteacher at Boggsville, to Las Animas to be the bookkeeper in his new bank. Scott would eventually become cashier.[18]

In partnership with Charles Goodnight, Prowers built the first slaughterhouse in southern Colorado. Not only did the new business provide a local boost to the economy, it allowed Prowers and Goodnight an additional way to profit from their large cattle enterprises.

By this time John and Amache Prowers not only controlled more than forty miles of land along the Arkansas River due to Amache and her family's land allotments, Prowers enlarged the land holdings to over four hundred thousand acres, with eighty thousand acres fenced.[19] The Prowers cattle ranch shipped an average of ten thousand cattle per year to Pueblo, Denver and eastern markets.

Mary Prowers Hudnall recalled, "The Cheyennes were always welcome at the ranch; father saw that they were well treated and that they had a good present to take along when they returned to the tribe. Many a time I have seen father send out a rider on the range to select a riding horse for one of mother's relatives."[20]

Nevertheless, a prudent Prowers organized the Bent-Prowers Cattle Association in an effort to provide protection for the county's cattle owners. The new cattle association worked for range rights for their members as well as keeping non-members from encroaching on the grazing land. John Prowers was elected president in 1874 and continued in that capacity until his death in 1884. The minutes of September 7, 1876, recorded the following resolution: "...that we warn all persons who contemplate bringing in and turning cattle on the range occupied by members of this association, that steps will be taken to protect ourselves in our legal and long established rights. 'Self-preservation is the first law of nature,' and while we make no threats, we mean business."[21]

During those early years in Las Animas, four more children were born to John and Amache Prowers: George, Leona, Ida and Amy, named for Amache. Sadly, George died at the age of eleven. As the Prowers children grew older, John and Amache sent them to Westport or St. Louis, Missouri, to complete their formal education. It was a practice William Bent had begun with his children and had suggested to his friend and former employee.

In 1878, Prowers signed over the deed to the large two-story general store to Amache. By this time, Katharine Prowers had married her father's former business partner, W. A. Haws. Amache relished her new position as a business owner. While maintaining the standards her husband had established, Amache expanded the clothing line to include women's fashions, brought in more fabric, and added the latest canned goods and household necessities to the store's inventory.

During the winter of 1883-1884, Prowers began to feel ill. In February 1884, Prowers traveled to Kansas City to seek the best medical diagnosis. While in Kansas City, he was staying with his sister when he suddenly died on February 14, 1884. Prowers was forty-six years old. His body was brought back to Las Animas by train. Following a stately funeral service, John Wesley Prowers was buried in the Las Animas Cemetery.[22]

At the time of Prowers' death, he and Amache owned approximately forty miles of fenced river front and over sixteen thousand head of cattle. Just a few years prior to his death, Prowers had been offered $750,000 for his cattle and property. According to the Bent-Prowers minutes of 1884, the Prowers estate branded four thousand calves; Despite the handsome offer, Prowers declined to sell.

Now, at the age of thirty-eight, Amache Ochinee Prowers was a widow. Amache had inherited her husband's cattle enterprise and with that came new responsibilities. Prowers had always treated her as his partner and she had learned much from her husband in their twenty-two years of marriage.

In her own unique way, Amache carried on boldly and full of confidence. Amache oversaw the business of the cattle ranch while leaving the day-to-day operations to the ranch foremen. Amache also continued to operate the Las Animas retail store she had come to love. For the next fifteen years, with cultured refinement blended of two cultures, Amache became an accomplished and well-respected woman in a man's world of the nineteenth century.

During this time, Amache continued with her charity organizations, her church obligations and business affiliations. However, her grandchildren were her greatest joy. She enjoyed spending time with them and even participated with them in the popular activities of the era. Ida Prowers Horton later recalled that her mother loved to ice skate and ride a bicycle with her grandchildren.

In time, Amache Prowers remarried. Her new husband, Daniel Keesee, a local Las Animas businessman, would prove to be a guiding source in business matters as well as a comfort in her older years. The couple resided in the home that John Wesley Prowers had built for his wife and family.

Although Amache lived in the "white man's world," she remained proud of her Native American heritage, and never turned her back on her relatives. Curious neighbors watched through windows as Amache's relatives, Indians often wrapped in blankets, arrived for occasional visits with Amache.

Amache Ochinee Prowers died at the age of fifty-eight, on February 14, 1905. Ironically, it was the same month and day that John Wesley Prowers had died. She was buried in the Prowers family plot in the Las Animas Cemetery, next to her first husband.[23]

Amache Ochinee Prowers stands out as one of our unique Colorado ranching women. A Native American woman who suffered personal tragedy due to the Sand Creek Massacre, she nevertheless chose to live in the white man's world. Amache worked side by side with her husband, and with a true pioneering spirit, she realized personal triumph over both land and culture. And she did it with a grace all her own. Amache's granddaughter, Mrs. Frank Nelson, interviewed in 1954, said, "Amache lived a lot of years in the years she lived."[24]

Today, southeastern Colorado honors the pioneering legacy of Amache and John W. Prowers. Five years after the death of Prowers, Bent County, the county he had served both before and after statehood, was divided into additional counties. The Prowers name was given to one of these southeastern counties.

Shortly after the Japanese bombed Pearl Harbor in Hawaii, and America entered World War II, Japanese detention camps were set up across the country. One of these was erected in southeastern Colorado. It was named Amache, after the woman who had also been caught between two cultures.

# Notes

1. Halaas, *Halfbreed*, pg. 44.
2. The *Denver Post*, "William Bent's Life Saved by a Cheyenne Doctor," January 25, 1920.
3. Drumm, *Down the Santa Fe Trail and Into New Mexico: The Diary of Susan Shelby Magoffin*, pg. 61.
4. Sand Creek Massacre - Report of the Secretary of War, 39th Congress session, Washington, D.C., 1867.
5. "Sand Creek Massacre," pg. 151.
6. Howbert, *Memories of a Lifetime in the Pike's Peak Region*, pg. 121.
7. Hudnall, Mary Prowers, "Early History of Bent County." Interview in *Colorado Magazine*, Vol. XXII, November, 1945.
8. ibid.
9. Sand Creek Massacre, pg. 381.
10. The atonement of a 160-acre parcel of land was in keeping with the standards established in the Homestead Act, signed into law by President Abraham Lincoln in 1862.
11. Betz, *A Prowers County History*, pg.68.
12. Hudnall, Mary Prowers, "Early History of Bent County." Interview in *Colorado Magazine*, Vol. XXII, November, 1945.
13. ibid.
14. Simmons, *Kit Carson & His Three Wives*, pg. 134.
15. Christopher "Kit" Carson and his wife, Josefa, were later reinterred in Taos, New Mexico. Josefa's tombstone incorrectly gives the death date as April 23.
16. Clark, *Women of Boggsville*, Colorado History Center brochure.
17. Hudnall, Mary Prowers, "Early History of Bent County." Interview in *Colorado Magazine*, Vol. XXII, November, 1945.
18. Following Prowers death, Scott became president of the bank, a position he held until his death in August 1930.
19. Betz, *A Prowers County History*, pg.68.
20. Hudnall, Mary Prowers, "Early History of Bent County." Interview in *Colorado Magazine*, Vol. XXII, November, 1945.
21. Archives housed at the Big Timbers Museum.
22. Wommack, *From the Grave*.

*23.* ibid.

*24.* Boggs Scrapbook, Colorado History Center.

*DPL*

# THE EASTERN PRAIRIE

## Katherine McHale Slaughterback
**Snakes in the Grass**

## Christie Payne Merrell
**A Prairie Struggle**

## Mildred Montague Genevieve "Tweet" Kimball
**Colorado's Front Range Cattle Queen**

## Emily Louise Rood French Varney
**Reminiscences of Life on the Colorado Plains**

Kate Slaughterback Albert Moldvay was better known as Rattlesnake Kate. *DPL*

# Katherine McHale Slaughterback

## Snakes in the Grass

The Homestead Act of 1862, signed into law by President Abraham Lincoln, allowed for men and women over the age of twenty-one to file for a quarter-section (160 acres) of federal public land. This new law, which went into effect on January 1, 1863, required an initial filing fee of eighteen dollars. Clear land title was issued to the applicant after proof had been provided that the applicant had either resided on the land for five years and made improvements, such as home building or agriculture, or that the applicant had resided on the claim for six months, improved the land, and then paid $1.25 per acre to the government.

 The Homestead Act particularly specified that no land would be acquired if levied against creditors for debts owed prior to the issuing of the land title. The final requirement was that the applicant must not have raised arms against the United States government or given aid and comfort to the enemy, which was a significant requirement at the time of enactment, due to the ongoing Civil War.

 Katherine McHale was truly a woman of the Colorado prairie. She was born July 25, 1893, in the log cabin home of her parents, Wallace and Albina McHale. The McHales had a homestead nine miles east of Longmont. Kate, as she was called, was the couple's second child, their first child, James, having been born in 1891.

 Shortly after Kate's third birthday, her mother gave birth to a baby boy the couple named Francis Roy. Tragedy struck the McHale family five days later, when Albina died due to complications from childbirth. Wallace McHale, now a widower, had three children to raise on his own, as well as the farm to tend to. Kate's grandfather helped Wallace McHale when he could, while Kate's grandmother often cared for the children.

Kate was devoted to her father and he doted on her. However, as Kate grew older, her father expected her to complete her chores which included feeding the livestock, stacking hay, and cleaning the barn. "We earn our bread by the sweat of our brow," her father often told her. It would be a phrase she would repeat to her son years later.[1]

While the discipline and hard work McHale instilled in his children would prove to be beneficial in their adult lives, McHale also found time to teach his children how to ride a horse and handle a gun. As they grew older, McHale often took them on his hunting excursions. Again, discipline, as well as patience and concentration were taught, traits that would serve throughout Kate's life.

With her father's strict parenting, Kate acquired a strong sense of self-confidence. By the time Kate finished school, she had gained a reputation as a tough, no-nonsense woman, despite her petite physique. Following high school graduation, Kate enrolled at the St. Joseph's School of Nursing in Denver. Not long after Kate earned her degree, America entered World War I. Kate's nursing skills were invaluable, as were all nurses during the war. Due to the alarming number of returning soldiers suffering from the effects of chemical weapons used in the European theatre, the United States Army scouted the country for an effective location to build a medical treatment center to treat these war veterans. Because of Colorado's high altitude and the excellent reputation of the state's many sanatoriums for the treatment of tuberculosis, groups of Colorado citizens lobbied the army officials for the new medical facility. The site chosen was an open field in the town of Aurora, with a total population of just under a thousand citizens, which allowed plenty of room for future growth. The new medical hospital, first known as Army Hospital 21, was formally dedicated in the fall of 1918, just as the war was ending.[2]

It was at this medical facility that Kate continued with her nursing career. It was a trying time, as the Spanish influenza caused death all across the country. Kate healed the sick and cared for the dying in unmeasurable numbers. While Kate always maintained her kind demeanor, the experience of so much death took a toll on her otherwise good nature. In a letter written many years later, Kate related this experience and described her particular sadness at the deaths of so many babies from the epidemic.[3]

By the time Kate decided to leave her heroic nursing career behind, the facility where she saw so much pain, suffering, and death was formally renamed Fitzsimons Army Hospital in July 1920, after Lieutenant William T. Fitzsimons, the first American medical officer killed in World War I.

Although it is not known whether Kate's temperament was a factor in the failure of her first two marriages, it is known that by the age of twenty-nine, Katherine McHale Slaughterback found herself divorced for a second time when her marriage to Henry H. Slaughterback ended.

Kate was a very resourceful woman, which she demonstrated many times during her life. In 1923, Kate filed for a homestead of 640 acres. The land, which included a small irrigation pond, was located in the Four Way area approximately east of Platteville, and just north of Hudson.[4] Kate, a self-sufficient woman, built her own cabin and proved up her claim. As this was dry land, farming was difficult and water was very precious. Through irrigation, water was supplied from the South Platte River and various tributaries. Kate brought a few cottonwood saplings from the river which she planted near her cabin, hoping they would grow and provide shade on the hot, dry prairie. Kate was able to grow various vegetables, wheat and rye, raised chickens, and sold the vegetables and chicken eggs for income.

In time she was able to purchase a few milk cows. From the cow's milk, she made butter and sold it at the area market. It was a meager existence, yet Kate persevered. When they were able, Kate's brothers, James and Roy, helped their sister.

As hot and desolate as dry farming was on the eastern

Colorado prairie, the winters were also a trying time. The cold northern winds seemed to never stop and the blowing snow often turned into blizzard conditions. That first winter spent on her homestead, Kate experienced the force of winter weather in an uncharacteristic act given the teachings of her father. Despite the heavy snowfall, Kate chose to saddle her horse and attend to a few errands. Along the way, Kate's horse stumbled and Kate fell. Knowing she had broken her arm, Kate made a feeble attempt to grab the horse's reins, which resulted in the horse kicking her, breaking her collarbone. Miraculously, Kate managed to make her way back to her cabin. With the help of her neighbors, Kate was able to seek medical attention. One of those neighbors, a single father by the name of Adamson, who worked as a farmhand, offered to help Kate with her homestead as she healed.

Despite her own financial struggles, Kate remained a caring individual, often lending a helping hand to her neighbors. When her neighbor, Adamson, found himself in financial difficulties, Kate returned the favor he had granted her. Possibly remembering the many babies that had died during her nursing career, Kate offered to take in Adamson's youngest child, an infant boy named Ernie. In time Adamson, seeing that his son was loved and well cared for, allowed Kate to adopt him.

Early on the morning of October 28, 1925, Kate heard gunshots in the direction of the pond. It was not an unusual incident, as duck hunters often frequented the area near the pond, despite the "No Hunting" signs placed on posts Kate had staked around the pond. Kate's common practice was to saddle her horse and pack her .22 rifle after the gunshots ceased and ride to the pond to collect the dead fowl left behind by the hunters. This day was no different.

After Kate saddled her horse and packed her rifle, she put her three-year-old son, Ernie, in front of her in the saddle and rode toward the pond. Leaving her son in the saddle, Kate dismounted and tethered the horse to a bush approximately forty feet from the pond.[5] She grabbed her rifle and opened the gate to enter the pond area. At the gate, Kate saw a coiled rattlesnake, ready to strike.

Kate wasted no time in shooting the rattler.

Perhaps the report of firepower alerted the snakes in their nearby den, as three more emerged, slithering in Kate's direction. Kate didn't miss a beat and shot them all. Then, the rattlers began to appear from all directions. Kate thought quickly. With no time to reload, she pulled the fence post from the ground and began beating and stabbing the slithering reptiles. The battle went on for an unbelievable two hours. During the horror, little Ernie's cries must have been heartbreaking, but there was nothing Kate could do for her son but beat back the snake invasion.

Finally, when it seemed as if she had killed all the snakes, Kate cautiously retreated from the area. Kate rushed to comfort her child and gratefully patted her horse, relieved that the animal had not been startled and thrown the child from the saddle. Nearly exhausted, her hands bloodied and bruised, her dress splattered with blood, Kate slowly made her way back home. Along the way, she noticed a neighbor in his yard and stopped to tell him about the ordeal she had just endured. The man offered to go back with Kate to the site and collect the dead snakes. The neighbor's wife took little Ernie, while Kate and the gentlemanly neighbor rode back to the pond.[6]

At the gate area to the pond, Kate and her neighbor gathered all the snakes together. They counted one hundred and forty dead, bloody reptiles. Several were over three feet long. Then they were placed in three washtubs and transported back to Kate's homestead. There, Kate hung the snakes, one by one, on her clothesline to dry.

Meanwhile, as often happens in rural areas, the news of Kate's horrific ordeal quickly spread. A local newspaper reporter hurried to the area. Kate's neighbors directed the reporter to Kate's homestead. After interviewing Kate, the reporter asked to see the snakes. Kate led him to the yard where the reptiles hung, drying in the autumn air. Ecstatic over the photo possibilities, the reporter helped Kate hang the snakes over a nearby fence for a better photo opportunity. When this grisly task was completed, the reporter took several photos of the dead snakes and a few with

Kate spent hours killing these rattlesnakes. *City of Greeley Museum*

Kate Slaughterback standing next to them.

The photo of Kate and her snake kill was splashed on the front page of the newspaper. In the accompanying article, the reporter dubbed Kate, "Rattlesnake Kate." The moniker caught on, as did the sensational photograph, as it was picked up by the Associated Press and carried in newspapers as far east as New York City. From there, the photo and story made headlines in England, France Germany and Mexico.

Back at her Colorado home, Kate devised a way to capitalize on her newfound national fame. Kate took a few classes in the art of taxidermy. With this new skill, Kate was able to cure the reptiles until she decided what to do with them. In time, Kate painstakingly skinned the snakes and removed the rattle tails, carefully preserving both.

Kate created a flapper style dress, a popular fashion of the 1920s. In her bizarre contribution to cultural fashion of the day, Kate used four of the larger snake skins to make the bodice of her dress and forty-three more were used for the skirt. Then she carefully fitted the two pieces together, creating her snake skin flapper dress.[7] Kate kept the dress inside a trunk to preserve the reptile skin. Pleased with her new-found skill, Kate sent her design

74

to the United States Patent offices in Washington, D.C.[8]

Kate then used more dried snake skins to fashion a pair of shoes, a belt and a neckband. With the rattles of the snakes, Kate made jewelry, including earrings, necklaces, and bracelets.

With her local popularity as Rattlesnake Kate, she was a favorite guest at local functions where she always wore her trademark snake skin dress, matching shoes and belt.

Kate expanded her new popularity as Rattlesnake Kate. She began an active campaign to hunt rattlesnakes. The live snakes that Kate managed to capture were then carefully placed in a pen she built behind her home. While it is not known if Kate utilized the snake meat in her cooking, she did use the snake skins from those she killed in her various odd creations, including stuffed snakes, which would then be sold to tourists. Kate charged two dollars for just a snake skin and one dollar for the rattles. This was an incredible amount of money in 1925.

Kate managed to literally milk her rattlesnake reputation for more profit. With her nursing background, Kate knew of the need for snake venom in medical treatment. Therefore, Kate contacted a research laboratory in Los Angeles, California, who gladly agreed to purchase her snake venom. From the snake pen, which held up to thirty snakes at a time, Kate would milk the live snakes by poking them with a stick to which she had attached a sponge at the end. When the agitated reptiles put their fangs into the sponge, the venom was absorbed by the sponge. This action was repeated with a new sponge each time, until most of the snakes had bit into the sponge.[9] Then Kate would carefully squeeze the venom from each sponge into a container that would be sent to the California research lab. Kate repeated this routine once a week.

Not only was this dangerous, it was also time consuming. It wasn't long before Kate tired of the task and simply cut off the heads of the snakes and shipped those to California. She soon learned from the scientists that they were interested in the venom, not the heads. It made no difference to Kate. At two dollars per snake skin, she was making more money without personal risk incurred if she continued milking the venom.

Kate made several items from the snakeskins including this dress. *City of Greeley Museum*

The dry plains of northeastern Colorado were part of the Dust Bowl area, hard hit by the drought conditions of the early 1930s. There was no rain and crops died. What few crops did survive, the fierce winds blew to the hard, parched ground. Kate experienced the force of the wind on many occasions. During a severe windstorm, Kate's hay wagon was overturned, and her unbound hay blew across the prairie. During another major gust of wind, all of Kate's baby chickens, nearly fifty, were blown away and never recovered.[10]

In 1932, Kate, at the age of thirty-nine, received the shock of a lifetime. One day as she hurried to finish feeding her livestock before a storm rolled in, she opened the metal gate just as a lightning bolt struck the gate post. The jolt of electricity sent a shock through Kate, knocking her unconscious. Kate lay at the foot of the gate post for nearly five hours, while her eleven-year-old son Ernie did what he could. To Ernie's extreme relief, Kate awoke, seemingly with no severe injuries.

As the Dust Bowl years gave way to the Great Depression years, Kate, along with most Americans, felt the effects of a struggling economy. Without a steady income, Kate used her goat pen to hide a small still where she made "moonshine," which was illegal during the Prohibition era. Kate instinctively knew that the stench of the goat pen would not only keep authorities from inspecting the area, should she be caught in her bootlegging scheme, it would also conceal any alcohol smell. That is not to say that Kate was indifferent to her small goat herd. She was known to care for a sick goat in the warmth of her home.

Unfortunately, Kate's illegal foray with homemade booze did not generate the needed income. Eventually, Kate was forced to sell sections of her homestead, including a section she had to sell to pay back taxes.[11]

Now, with only eighty acres remaining of her original 640-acre homestead, Kate, at the age of forty-three, was faced with another economic struggle. America had entered World War II. Determined to hold on to her remaining property, Kate managed to make a living by again selling her garden vegetables, goat milk, and fresh eggs.

Following the war, Kate continued selling her farm goods and even managed to save money. By the end of the decade, she began saving money to begin the construction of a new home on her land. In 1952, Kate began the process of building her house. It was to be her new home and she would build it herself. It would be a five-year ordeal. During this building process, Kate lived in a converted chicken coop.[12]

Kate, weighing barely a hundred pounds, poured the concrete herself, erected the framing for the four-room house by herself, and roofed the structure by herself. Finally, in 1957, Kate's new home was finished. To celebrate the occasion, she bought a brand-new potbelly stove. Kate lived alone in her four-room house for the rest of her life. She was once asked in an interview by a reporter from the *Rocky Mountain News* if she was lonely. Kate replied, "I'm not lonely. I have a lot of people who drop in."[13]

In September 1969, Kate donated her famous flapper-style snake skin dress and her various snake-made accessories, as well as her rifle used to shoot the first four snakes, to the Greeley History Museum. Perhaps it was an act of nostalgia of days gone by, or maybe Kate knew her time was at an end.

Shortly after her generous gift to the museum, Kate was hospitalized at the Weld County Hospital in Greeley. Three weeks later, Katherine McHale Slaughterback, "Rattlesnake Kate," died at the age of seventy-six, on October 6, 1969. Several friends, admirers, and the curious attended her funeral. Following the service, Kate was buried in the Mizpah Cemetery in Platteville.

The *Greeley Tribune* ran Kate's obituary and a feature article recounting her rattlesnake massacre of 1925. The story brought new interest in Rattlesnake Kate. The City of Greeley's Centennial Village group bought Kate's four-room farmhouse with the intent to open it for tourists. However, the house had been neglected for years and needed costly repairs and refurbishing that was not in the budget.

In the summer of 2002, the Greeley Museum purchased Kate's house for four hundred and ninety-five dollars. The only item salvageable was Kate's potbelly stove. This was retrieved and placed in storage. The home was then disassembled, with each piece of lumber being numbered. Museum staff as well as volunteers moved the lumber to the Prairie Section of Centennial Village.

There, with photographs of the original house as an aid, the numbered lumber pieces were reassembled. Kate's prized potbelly stove was placed inside the completed structure.

Today, the home of Katherine McHale Slaughterback—"Rattlesnake Kate"—is opened to the public at the Centennial Village in Greeley. Her family still shares stories with the local museum visitors in Greeley.

# Notes

1. McNatt, *Kate Slaughterback*, pg. 1.
2. World War I officially ended on November 11, 1918, with the Treaty of Versailles.
3. The Greeley History Museum archives.
4. The *Rocky Mountain News*, "Rattlesnake Kate Earned Her Name," January 9, 1983.
5. ibid.
6. According to the staff at the Greeley History Museum, the name of Kate's helpful neighbors on that fateful day have been lost to history.
7. Kate's flapper snake skin dress is on display at the Greeley Museum.
8. McNatt, *Kate Slaughterback*, pg. 17.
9. Greeley History Museum.
10. McNatt, *Kate Slaughterback*, pg. 9.
11. The *Rocky Mountain News*, "Rattlesnake Kate Earned Her Name,' January 9, 1983.
12. ibid.
13. This quote was reprinted in the *Rocky Mountain News* article featuring Kate in the January 9, 1983 issue.

# Christie Payne Merrell
## A Prairie Struggle

When Christie May Payne left her family home in Nebraska as a young teenager, her intention was one of adventure and ultimate peace and prosperity. Arriving at her relatives' homestead in the small farming community of Abbott, in northeastern Colorado, it wasn't long before the opportunity to achieve her goals presented itself. Or so she thought.

With Christie's outgoing personality, she quickly made new friends and began to like living in the area. Her good nature, not to mention her beauty, also attracted the single young men in the area, who often called on Christie. Yet Christie was not interested in any of them.

But John Merrell was different, and although he was five years her senior, Christie was immediately smitten with him. Merrell was a ranch hand for one of the largest cattle ranches along the South Platte River Trail in northeastern Colorado, the JB Ranch, owned by Jared Brush.[1] Alice Merrell earned a business degree from Yale University, came west for adventure, just as Christie had. The couple courted for a little over a year and married shortly after Christie's eighteenth birthday. A year later the couple were blessed with their first child, Harriet, born in June 1891. It seemed as if those early dreams and plans that brought both Christie and John West, where the two were ultimately united, were about to come to fruition.

Shortly after the birth of little Hattie, John became the foreman of the JB Ranch. Christie was also hired as the cook for the ranch hands. The Merrell family moved to the main headquarters of the JB Ranch. During the first year at the ranch,

*81*

Christie worked tirelessly, cooking and cleaning for the ranch hands, as well as caring for her own family. In late 1893, Christie gave birth to her second child, a son she named Francis, but affectionately called him Frank.

With the good money both John and Christie were making, the couple remained with Brush and his cattle operation for the next two years. During that time the Merrells saved as much money as possible to obtain land of their own. Approximately a year later, the Merrells filed for a homestead claim along the south side of the South Platte River, in Logan County. After continuing with their employment for another year, primarily to continue with their savings plan, Christie and John Merrell resigned their positions with the JB Ranch early in 1894.[2]

The Merrells built a fine wood-framed home on their homestead, the first to be erected along the river between Sterling and Iliff. While Christie tended to the children and the household chores, to ensure the success of their venture, she also assisted her husband in the necessary work of breaking sod and planting crops. Through their hard work, the farm began to produce enough profit to sustain the family. But just barely, as the Merrells had two more children within those struggling years. Henry Augustus was born in 1895, followed by Carter Patrick, "Pat," in 1896.

Christie was a loving mother. She often sang to the children and taught them to play the organ. During those early years, despite Christie's hard work to make their farm prosperous, she always spent the evenings teaching the children their numbers and letters. On the other hand, John didn't seem to take much of an interest in his children.

In 1900, when Christie was pregnant with her fifth child, John made an extravagant purchase. John had several registered Belgian breeding horses shipped to the Merrell homestead from back east. Christie wondered how they could afford the expensive animals, not to mention the cost to care for them. Soon John was spending nearly all of his time with the horses, leaving the duties of the farm to a very pregnant Christie. Later that year, Christie gave birth to a baby girl she named Dorothy.[3] In 1902 Christie was again pregnant. When the baby Clark was born, Christie instinctively knew something was wrong, as the poor infant was very frail. Her husband seemed to be indifferent to the baby's condition or to his wife's needs.

John spent the days with his horses while Christie struggled with farm chores and caring for the children. After nearly a year of this routine, tempers flared. Then, John began spending nights in town. Early one morning in 1903, John Merrell returned to the homestead, packed his bags and, without a word, left his wife, his family and his homestead, never to return.

As was Christie's nature, she put her own emotions aside and concentrated on her children. Not letting on how dire their predicament was, Christie treated it as a sort of game of life with her children. She told her oldest son, ten-year-old Frank, that he was the new foreman of the Merrell farm. Twelve-year-old Hattie was given the duty of running the household.[4] The younger children were given such responsibilities as cleaning stables and milking the cows, gathering eggs and feeding the animals. With their mother's enthusiasm and happy nature, the children were delighted with their new-found importance. However, Christie knew there were hard days ahead. For weeks, after a long day of work, cheerfully encouraging and praising her children, she would go to bed and cry herself to sleep, if she slept at all.

Every morning as Hattie prepared breakfast, Christie and the boys would go to the barn, milk the cows, and gather eggs for the morning meal. Before she left the house, Christie always took a few minutes to rock her baby boy and sing to the ailing child. One morning, as Christie lifted little Clark out of his crib, she noticed he wasn't breathing. She did everything she could, but it was too late. Her baby boy was dead.

For the next several days, Christie barely seemed to function. The unbearable loss of her helpless baby boy was something she could not cope with. After the burial, Christie retreated to baby Clark's room. She stayed there for days, overcome with grief and despair. Christie's children let their mother be. They continued with their assigned duties and never complained.

Christie finally must have realized her other children needed her. One morning she cleaned out the baby's room, put away his baby clothes, and removed the crib. Then, as Hattie was cooking breakfast, Christie joined her sons in the morning chores of milking the cows and gathering the eggs for Hattie to fry.

It wasn't long before Christie was back to her good-natured self. She and the children worked together doing the farm chores and Christie never missed an opportunity to lavish praise on her children. For the first time since her husband left her, and death of her baby, Christie finally believed she and the children could make a success of the farm. Christie's optimism was short-lived. When Christie was informed that her husband had sold a portion of their land, she was devastated. Just recovering from the shock, Christie was then told that her husband had borrowed a large amount of money, using the Merrell homestead as collateral. Christie had always wondered where the money came from to purchase the expensive Belgian breeding horses. With that mystery finally solved, Christie made a trip to Sterling, the seat of Logan County, and filed for divorce.

Returning to what remained of her homestead, Christie rallied her children and worked like never before to pay off the debt and make her farm profitable. Along with the daily chores, Christie and all the children churned pounds of butter, made cream, jelly and jam, and gathered all the eggs they could. Then, every Saturday morning, everything would be loaded into the wagon and Christie would make the long drive into Sterling to sell her goods. A different child was allowed to go to town each Saturday. Then just before the return trip home, Christie would stop at the local mercantile where that child was allowed to purchase one special treat. It was hard work for all of them. Christie was particularly proud of the way her children helped with the added workload, all the while keeping up with their school assignments.

Years later, when the children were all adults, they often spoke of those trying years. They all agreed they were better people for the hard work and discipline instilled by their mother.[5]

The efforts of Christie and her children began to literally

pay off. Within a few years, Christie was able to pay the debt her husband had left her and have the mortgage reassigned in her name only.

Christie seemed to gain a new sense of pride. While continuing with the necessary work of the operation of her farm, she now began to turn her attention to her home. She rearranged and refurbished furniture and gave each child their own room. She planted flowers along the house and painted the outbuildings. With her self-esteem fully restored, in April 1909, Christie even applied for a patent for a shoelace fastener she had designed.

Occasionally, Christie was able to hire a man to help for larger jobs when the need arose. William "Will" Partridge was one who accepted Christie's employment offer. Partridge was a hard worker, but tended to drink too much. Despite her disdain for alcohol, Christie kept Partridge in her employ. He was good-natured and admired what the single mother had accomplished, and Christie felt relaxed in his company, a feeling she had not experienced in years. Soon the relationship between the two turned romantic.

Partridge encouraged Christie to take up playing the organ again, something she never seemed to have time for. Christie found a new sense of joy as she played and sang once again for her children, which she had not done since her baby boy had died all those long sad years ago. Christie encouraged Partridge as well. With her support and financial aid, Partridge filed for a 160-acre homestead claim approximately ten miles southeast of Christie's homestead.

The land Partridge filed on, situated along the south bank of the South Platte River, was the site of the Valley Station stage stop. This historic area was one of many places attacked along the South Platte River Trail during the Indian retaliation raids following the Sand Creek massacre in November, 1864.

In 1910, thirty-eight-year-old Christie Payne Merrell married thirty-five-year-old William Partridge.[6] Shortly thereafter, Partridge moved to his new land and began to "prove up" on the homestead claim. Meanwhile, as Christie was making preparations to join her husband at the new homestead, she received good news. An official letter of approval arrived from the U. S. Patent Office. Christie's design for the shoelace fastener received U. S. Patent number 948460.

By springtime, Christie and ten-year-old Dorothy had made the move to the new Partridge homestead. Christie left the Merrell homestead in the charge of her nineteen-year-old Hattie and her sons.[7] It would be the beginning of a sad saga in Christie's life.

When the school term ended, Christie's boys, seventeen-year-old Frank, fifteen-year-old Henry and thirteen-year-old Carter, joined their mother and stepfather at the new homestead. They helped in building a new house, broke the sod and planted crops. That summer, Christie and her boys settled into the new home and, for a time, everyone was happy. Christie helped her husband with the day-to-day operations of running the farm, just as she had at the Merrell homestead. During their free time, the Merrell boys enjoyed exploring the ruins of the old stage stop outbuildings on the property.

The Partridge couple were happy together, worked together, and were supportive of one another. Christie felt so sure that she and her husband could not only be happy together, but also make a success of the new homestead, that she sold the Merrell homestead. Christie and her children packed the remainder of their belongings and family treasures into the wagon and returned to their new home at the Valley Station site.

For whatever reason, Partridge's drinking began to increase. By the fall of 1910, Partridge would routinely leave the homestead in the late afternoon and ride into Sterling. He would then return home in a drunken stupor. Christie tried to reason with him, but it was no use. It seemed as if Christie was living this alcoholic nightmare all over again.

During one of the many confrontations between Christie and her inebriated husband, Partridge hit Christie. Her son, fifteen-year-old Henry, defended his mother. He tackled Partridge, grabbed him by the scruff of the neck, and shoved him out the front door of their home. A drunken Will Partridge stumbled to the barn where he slept off his alcoholic stupor in the piles of hay. The following morning, Partridge begged his wife to forgive him. Christie accepted the apology and hoped for the best. She and Partridge worked together improving the land claim and caring for the livestock. But it was not to last.

Rather than go into town to do his drinking, Partridge stayed in the comfort of his own home, despite Christie's pleas. Partridge's drinking escalated to the point that when inebriated, he would shout and curse at Christie and the children. One night as Partridge was in the midst of his usual cursing rant, he raised his whiskey bottle, and in a fit of drunken rage, hit Christie with it. As Christie fell to the floor, an out-of-control Partridge overturned furniture and threw various items at the walls. Then, Partridge staggered for a moment and fell to the floor. Thinking Partridge had finally passed out, Christie's boys came to the aid of their mother. Although Christie was pretty shaken by the blow from the whiskey bottle, she was otherwise fairly alert. Meanwhile, someone checked on Partridge. He wasn't breathing. He was dead.

The Logan County Sheriff was called and soon arrived at the Partridge homestead. The sheriff's deputies interviewed Christie and her children while the sheriff examined the body and collected evidence. When the sheriff and his deputies had completed their investigation, the body of thirty-five-year-old William Partridge was removed from the home.

Christie must have been embroiled in a mix of emotions. She had been married for less than a year to a man that caused so much heartbreak not only to herself, but her children as well. And now he was dead.

Meanwhile, following an autopsy, William Partridge was buried in Sterling's Riverside Cemetery, located two miles southwest of town. Neither Christie nor her children attended the services.

Shortly thereafter the results of the autopsy revealed that William Partridge died of poisoning. Evidence collected at the Partridge home included the whiskey bottle that Partridge drank from and then used to hit Christie with. This bottle contained traces of the poison compound. With this compelling evidence and the previous interrogations of the Merrell children, fifteen-year-old Henry was arrested for the murder of his stepfather. Possibly due to inadequate legal representation, the boy pleaded guilty to first degree murder. Henry Augustus Merrell was sentenced to life imprisonment at the Colorado State Penitentiary at Canon City. As one of his last acts as governor of Colorado, Governor John F. Shafroth pardoned Henry A. Merrell in 1913. The following year, Merrell, at the age of nineteen, joined the army. He would serve his country during World War I.

Christie's other sons, twenty-one-year-old Frank and eighteen-year-old Pat, also enlisted for the war effort. During this time, both of her daughters, Harriet and Dorothy, also left the family home to start their own lives.

For the first time in her life, Christie was all alone. Undaunted, she began a new venture. Christie applied for and was hired as an assistant game warden. She loved the work and felt challenged to learn all she could. It was during this time that Christie again married. Harry Jones had been hired to help Christie with the homestead after her sons had left to join the war effort. Shortly after the marriage, in a letter to her son, Pat, then away at war, Christie wrote, "I think I may have found some of the happiness I have longed for."[8]

The marriage lasted less than a year. Once again, reminiscent of her experience nearly fifteen years ago, Jones left the homestead one morning and never returned.

When her sons returned from the war, Christie turned the family homestead over to them and moved to a small house in Sterling. With her income from the farm's profits, Christie opened a store in town. She enjoyed the interaction with the community and met many wonderful people. Then, Christie was introduced to Ralph Baird. Baird owned a large ranch on Colorado's western slope. The two spent hours discussing the various aspects of land ownership and profitability. It wasn't long before the friendship turned romantic. When Baird proposed marriage in 1923, Christie accepted. The newlyweds moved to Baird's ranch on the western slope. By all accounts, including weekly letters she wrote to her children, Christie was happy and marveled at the beauty of the Rocky Mountains, which were the backdrop of her new home. Rejuvenated by the natural beauty of the area, Christie reveled in the day-to-day operations of the ranch.

Christie's children always looked forward to their mother's weekly letters. In 1925, suddenly the letters didn't arrive. After a few weeks, Christie's oldest son, Frank became concerned. Taking a leave of absence from his employment as an executive with the Chrysler Corporation, Frank Merrell booked a flight to Colorado's western slope.

Arriving at the Baird ranch, Merrell was greeted by Baird. After a very brief conversation, Baird informed his son-in-law that his mother had left him. As Merrell made his way through the house, he noticed that the bedroom closet was full of her clothes. He also saw that her makeup and various personal toiletries were present.

Alarmed at his discoveries, Frank Merrell left the Baird ranch and immediately notified the authorities. An investigation ensued and Ralph Baird was arrested on suspicion of murder. After a few days of intense interrogation, Baird finally confessed to the murder of his wife. In his confession, Baird stated that during a heated argument, as Christie reached for a gun, he grabbed a skillet and hit her over the head with it.

After Baird revealed the location of Christie's body, and Baird was officially charged with murder, the authorities recovered the body. Frank Merrell sent a wire to his siblings in Logan County, notifying them of the death of their mother, which read in part, "Will bring Mother home this week."[9]

Following funeral services, held in Sterling, Christie's children buried their mother in the J. H. Merrell plot at Riverside Cemetery. Finally, Christie was at peace.

Following the death of their mother, the Merrell children eventually resumed their lives. Frank returned to his employment with the Chrysler Corporation. Dorothy returned to her husband and family, while Hattie became a fashion designer in New York City. Hattie later moved to Los Angeles, California, where she remained for the rest of her life. She never married and died in 1988.

Both Henry and Pat remained on the homestead at the Valley Station site. In fact, Pat managed the day to day functions of the farm, eventually taking over the operation, which he managed for most of his life.

The Logan County Historical Society, in conjunction with the Overland Trail Museum in Sterling, began a project of developing the historic Valley Station site as a site for visitors to explore.

Carter "Pat" Merrell was instrumental in this plan. Through his maps which he drew from his memories of exploring the historic ruins as a young boy, Merrell was able to provide the historic detail that visitors are able to witness today.

# Notes

1. The new town of Brush, Colorado would be named for Jared Brush.
2. Propst, *Those Strenuous Dames of the Colorado Prairie*.
3. The 1900 U.S. Census records lists Christie's age as twenty-five.
4. ibid.
5. Merrell, Pat and Jim. *The Merrells*.
6. 1910 U.S. Census records lists Hattie as the head of the household.
7. ibid.
8. Merrell, Pat and Jim. *The Merrells*.
9. 9. ibid.

Tweet Kimball revolutionized cattle ranching in Colorado and was the first woman elected to the Board of the National Western Stock Show. *DPL*

# Mildred Montague Genevieve "Tweet" Kimball

## Colorado's Front Range Cattle Queen

Mildred Montague Genevieve Kimball was born into a prominent Tennessee family at Fort Oglethorpe, in Catoosa County, Georgia, on June 18, 1914. Her parents, Richard Huntington and Mildred Montague Kimball, both came from strong military families. During the Civil War, her maternal great-grandfather had purchased nearly a million acres of land in Texas. Fearful of how the war would end, a victory for the north or the south, he had his land surveyed by two separate assessors, one from the North interests and one from the Southern interests. With each granting titles to his land, he was assured of retaining his land despite the outcome of the war.

Tweet's father followed the family military tradition. A graduate of West Point with the class of 1907, Richard Kimball became a career soldier, eventually earning the rank of Colonel. Thus, the family moved often. Young Mildred, the couple's only child, adjusted to the many moves with ease and her proud father gave her the endearing nickname of "Tweet," a name she cherished and would proudly claim the rest of her life.

Tweet attended the public schools of Chattanooga, Tennessee. She later attended Pennsylvania's Shipley School, and then went on to graduate from Bryn Mawr College, where she earned a degree in the history of architecture and art. She and her mother, also an avid art lover, enjoyed trips to Europe together where they collected china, paintings, Venetian glass and first editions of classic books.

An avid equestrian, Tweet's father taught his daughter how to ride at a very young age. With proper training, Tweet soon became an accomplished equestrian in her own right. In 1938 her father invited his twenty-four-year-old daughter to accompany him to a thoroughbred horse sale held at the famous King Ranch, near Kingsville, Texas. It would be the first of three events in the year 1938 that would change Tweet's life forever.

Despite the many beautiful racehorses at the ranch, it was the magnificent Santa Gertrudis cattle, grazing in a meadow beyond the setting of the horse sale, that caught the eye of Tweet Kimball. Pointing them out to her father, he too was also impressed. "We thought they looked marvelous," she later recalled. This breed was the first distinctive American breed ever produced and was developed by Richard King on his King Ranch in 1938. Named for Santa Gertrudis Creek that ran through the King Ranch land, the cattle were a crossbreed of an Indian Brahman bull named Monkey, and a British Shorthorn cow. The result was a quality animal that was five-eighths Shorthorn and three-eighths Brahman. This new breed garnered the attention of ranchers all over the south. In 1940, Santa Gertrudis cattle were recognized by Texas cattlemen as the only breed solely of American origin. This experience became ingrained in Tweet's mind and she dreamed of the day she would have a cattle ranch of her own.

Not long after father and daughter returned to Tennessee, where the retired colonel was running his father's businesses, he received a call from the War Department. World War II had broken out in Europe, and the United States military forces were stepping up security. Colonel Kimball was asked by a group of generals at the Pentagon to join the senior commanders. Kimball agreed and was to become commander of Fort Oglethorpe, the very fort that he was stationed at when Tweet was born. Tweet later said, "He wanted to go back and 'kill the Germans.' It was 1938 and the Army made him the commandant of Fort Oglethorpe."[1] Unfortunately, before the colonel was to leave Tennessee for his new post, he suffered a fatal heart attack. Tweet greatly mourned the loss of her father.

For whatever reason, for Tweet herself never said, later that same year Mildred Montague Genevieve "Tweet" Kimball married Merritt Ruddock. The Ruddock family were well-established among the elite of Tennessee. Their plantation, Curl's Neck, was located between Richmond and Williamsburg, along the James River.[2] Ruddock was a product of high society living and little practical sense. Mrs. Ruddock, acutely aware of her son's shortcomings, took Tweet aside on the very morning of the wedding to inform her future daughter-in-law of Merritt's lack of financial understanding and responsibilities. When Ruddock was appointed to U.S. Diplomatic Corps, he took his wife as he traveled the world, where Tweet, following her passion, purchased many works of fine art. The couple lived in a country home just outside of London for four years, where they adopted two boys, Kirk and Richard. The new happy family often spent time at Buckingham Palace, where the Ruddock boys enjoyed playing with young Prince Charles.

The well-educated, charming, southern-genteel Mrs. Tweet Ruddock was instrumental in her husband's political career, as Ruddock was later appointed, following the war, as the secretary of the American Embassy in London.

When Ruddock's term as the secretary of the American Embassy ended, the couple closed their rental home and prepared to return to America. However, just before they were scheduled to set sail for home, the Cunard shipping office informed Tweet that the state rooms which Merritt had booked had not been paid for. An embarrassed Tweet took care of the problem and the Ruddock family boarded the ship on time for their return to the United States.[3]

Back home, the Ruddock family lived in California, where their marriage began to fall apart. After ten years of marriage, Merritt and Tweet Kimball Ruddock divorced. Not only did Tweet gain sole custody of the boys, her ex-husband offered to buy her anything she wanted west of the Mississippi River as part of the divorce settlement. Kimball, a vibrant, energetic and independent woman, gladly accepted the offer. "When I divorced him, he said I'd probably go back to Tennessee and talk about him. He said 'If you'll buy property west of the Mississippi, I'll help you.' And that's what I did."[4]

Tweet Kimball, with her independent nature, took back her maiden name and moved on with her life, a new independent life in the West. As Kimball set out on her adventure in the West, she spent time in several states before visiting Colorado. Enlisting a realtor's services, who showed her several ranch properties for sale, soon became a time-consuming process, as Kimball would later say in an interview: "...a very nice agent showed me places all over the state." However, she did not care for the eastern plains of Colorado. "There weren't enough trees," she said. When the realtor took her to the western slope of the Colorado Rocky Mountains, she later recalled her first thought was, "Too much snow for a Southerner."[5] As Kimball became discouraged, the realtor showed her one more property. It was a place in the South Platte River Valley close to the Rocky Mountains, with the Rampart Range to the west, but not too close, with plenty of sprawling land, yet less than an hour's drive to Denver. It was exactly what Tweet Kimball had been looking for.

It was the spring of 1954 when Tweet first saw the sprawling ranch lands of early Douglas pioneers Charles Alfred Johnson and his Charlford castle, and his neighboring rancher Ray Blunt's Sunflower Ranch. As she walked around the area with the realtor, she thought of the possibilities of her dream coming to fruition and learned of the history of the area.

The historic Cherokee Trail, so named for one of the many Native American tribes who once roamed through the eastern plains of Colorado Territory, ran through the very area she was considering purchasing. The Cherokee Trail was established by a group of gold seekers headed west to the California gold rush of 1849. It was a trail that stretched west some six hundred miles from Bent's Fort on the Arkansas River, and then turned north, at Fort Pueblo, to the Wyoming border.

At Fort Pueblo, the trail followed Fountain Creek, the largest tributary of the Arkansas River. At the small settlement of Fountain, the trail left the creek and crossed the Arkansas-Platte Divide, where the South Platte and Arkansas rivers divide in their drainage. This area was later renamed the Palmer Divide. Good, clear water was found throughout the area and made for an excellent rest area for the travelers and their animals. Among the many areas to benefit from the South Platte River drainage was the area later known as Russellville Gulch.

It was here in June of 1858 that a gold prospector from Georgia, William Green Russell, along with his brothers Levi and Oliver, having followed the Cherokee Trail, stopped to rest their animals. It was a spot near the east branch of Cherry Creek. Luke Tierney, who was with the Russell brothers, recorded the following in his journal: "On the morning of the twenty-second the weather was excessively hot. After traveling three-quarters of an hour, the road led us to cross the creek. One of our men, taking a pan full of gravel from his bed, washed it and found several particles of gold."[6] The elated group of men immediately set up a campsite. W. G. Russell, along with a few men in the group, staked several claims in the area. They name the site "Russellville."[7]

As a small mining settlement on the plains, Russellville was overshadowed by the discovery of gold near Denver City. Nevertheless, the settlement grew slowly. News of the gold discovery was reported in a few newspapers across the region, such as the *Kansas City Journal*. Prospectors flocked to the area and staked out claims. Soon, little log cabins were built, replacing the temporary tents. One of the many prospectors to arrive at Russellville recorded his experience in his journal:

Friday, June 10, 1859: In camp at last on the headwaters of the long sought, anxiously looked for Cherry Creek. Saw three men working a tom. They were washing only the surface sand, and as a result of their day's labor took out about five dollars. Not very encouraging. Washed out a pan myself and got three cents. This would pay. All about us is another grand pine forest, and in the midst of it a new town called Russellville. Here there is a steam sawmill in operation, which cuts about 4,000 feet of wood a day. Since the first of April when they commenced operations, they have sold 60,000 feet of lumber, at $8 per hundred, which, considering the abundance of material, and

*97*

its convenience, is a pretty tall figure. Have prospected pretty thoroughly, and found gold in every instance, but it is very fine. Wages, say $2 to $3 per day, can be made here.[8]

As the Russellville settlement grew, businesses were established, and farmers and ranchers claimed land in the area. Buildings and homes were erected with lumber provided by the first sawmill business. In April 1859, N. S. Wyatt and Hiram P. Bennet brought their sawmill west from the Missouri River, where they set up their operation along Running Creek, with a good supply of timber, not far Russellville.

More towns sprang up within a few miles of each other: Oakes' Mill, Frank's Town, and Round Corral. Oaks' Mill, located on the banks of Plum Creek, was so named in 1859 for D.C. Oakes, who started one of the many sawmill operations in the area. The area was later known by the locals as "the old Coberly place," where Oakes' in-laws had a home. Frank's Town was named by the founder, James Frank Gardner, in 1859. The name was later changed to Franktown. Round Corral, established in 1859, became an important junction along the first territorial road of 1861, allowing for stagecoaches, freight wagons, and westward pioneers to travel into the Colorado Territory. The settlement of Round Corral later became the town of Sedalia.

Another man who chose to settle in this vicinity was John Blunt. Following his service as a Union soldier during the Civil War, Blunt brought his family west for a new beginning in 1868. First settling on land along East Plum Creek near Round Corral, the family eventually homesteaded on land a few miles southeast. Here, in 1873, Blunt plowed the land for crop planting, and brought in his cattle to graze on the open range. He named his homestead Sunflower Ranch, where they planted sorghum and wheat and raised cattle. Apple seedlings, acquired by the family as they crossed the Kansas prairie, were planted in a special area set aside for an apple orchard.

Blunt built a fine home for his family. The 1,370-square-foot house, with its unique design, was the product of John Blunt's inventive common sense. While practical for life on the Colorado prairie, it was also the most elegant home in the entire area. In this home, John Blunt would raise his family and three generations would carry on the family business of the Sunflower Ranch. By 1897, the land holdings of John Blunt's Sunflower Ranch had increased to two thousand acres. It was also in that same year that Blunt created a bit of controversy among the cattle ranchers when he began using the dehorning process with his cattle. Many claimed it was an inhumane act.

Frederick Gerald Flower, a colorful immigrant from England, arrived in America and promptly renounced his English citizenship in 1892. Making his way west, he settled in Douglas County, where he filed on a homestead on land adjacent to Blunt's Sunflower Ranch on August 6, 1894. Here, he built a home constructed of local stone, for he and his wife, Amy. When the home was completed, he and Amy, along with Flower's sister, Beatrice, moved in on January 18, 1895. This magnificent home sat on the edge of a high plateau in the prairie which offered a fabulous view of the Front Range of the Colorado Rocky Mountains. A long trail to the house began at the old territorial road, and gradually wound its way around the plateau to the Flower home.[9] When Flower filed his homestead claim form, he stated that he had strung approximately a half-mile of barbed wire to contain his livestock. Over the years, Frederick G. Flower built a sizable herd and also added to his original homestead, which by the turn of the century was nearly twenty-four hundred acres.

In 1920, Charles Wilcox, a wealthy Douglas County landowner, donated forty acres of his land to the county for a natural park. The donated land included the ancient Indian landmark known as Wildcat Mountain, which became a favorite spot for tourists. By 1924, the city and county of Denver had taken over management of the park, as part of the Denver Mountain Parks System. The popular area was named Daniels Park in honor of Major William Cooke Daniels, co-owner of the famed Denver business the Daniels & Fisher Department Store, who also owned a home nearby at Wildcat Point.

On a warm sunny weekend in the summer of 1924, Wilcox welcomed his friend and business associate, Charles Alfred Johnson (known as Carl by his family and friends), to his summer home at Wildcat Point, near the newly-designated Daniels Park. The two spent a glorious weekend touring the area on horseback, with Wilcox showing Johnson around the area and pointing out the fabulous vistas of the Rocky Mountains. Johnson left his friend's home and returned to Denver filled with glorious dreams for his future. (Johnson, a native of Boston, Massachusetts, had already spent some time in Denver during a trip with his cousin.) Enamored with the culture of the West, he moved to Denver in 1891, where he set up a successful real estate business, and became quite wealthy in the process. He was instrumental in the early planning and developing of Denver's Park Hill neighborhood.

When Johnson returned to Douglas County later in the summer of 1924, he and his wife, Alice (the former Alice Gilford Phillips), traveled around the area of Wildcat Point, looking for an ideal spot to build a summer home of their own. They found the perfect site complete with a fabulous hill upon which they could build their dream home. There was just one small obstacle they needed to overcome: the land was owned by Frederick G. Flower. After negotiations, Johnson purchased the entire Flower landholdings, including his home, for five dollars an acre.

Not long after the land purchase, Johnson hired his long-time friend, Denver architect Burnham Hoyt, to build his summer home. Hoyt presented a design with architectural details resembling European castles from the fifteenth century found in England and Scotland. Construction of the castle-like mansion began before summer's end of 1924. Hoyt hired thirty local Cornish stonemasons to construct the edifice, using native rhyolite stone quarried on Johnson's land.

The construction of the Johnson home was completed in two years. The original trail that Flower had built to his house along the old territorial road was improved to accommodate Johnson's automobiles. The new, improved road gradually led uphill to the Johnson's new home on the hill. When the Johnsons finally moved into the mansion in 1926, they named their elegant home "Charlford." The name was in honor of the couple's sons, combining Charles' and Alice's son, Charles, Jr., with Alice's son from a previous marriage, Gilford.

The *Rocky Mountain News* ran a detailed account of the Johnson home in the August 29, 1926 issue. The headline read, "Wonder House on Promontory Near Sedalia Realizes Day Dream of Denver Business Man."

When Charles and Alice Johnson moved in 1926, they were so impressed that their summer home would eventually become their primary residence. A series of garages would be built to house Johnson's fleet of Packards, and large pool was constructed.

Charles Johnson established the Johnson Dairy Company, supplying milk, eggs and other dairy products to residents and businesses in Sedalia. As the dairy farm prospered, Charles acquired additional land. His land holdings would eventually reach to the edge of the land owned by Frank E. Kistler, another wealthy Douglas County landowner. Both Charlie, Jr. and Gilford would have fond memories of growing up at Charlford. The Johnson family lived at Charlford for the next twenty-five years. That was when Tweet Kimball entered into negotiations to purchase the land.

After negotiations with Charles Johnson, Jr., Kimball purchased Charlford and the Johnson's family landholdings, as well as the adjacent land of the Blunt family's Sunflower Ranch from Ray Blunt, in May of 1954. With the purchase of the historic Blunt and Johnson homesteads, Tweet Kimball now became one of the largest ranch owners in Douglas County.

The Blunt and Johnson homesteads, along with Charlford, appealed to Kimball for a variety of reasons. With her Scottish ancestry, as well as her keen interest in architecture, she was particularly intrigued with the fifteenth-century Scottish style castle. Yet, it was the land, the buildings and the barns that brought a sparkle to her eye. For this was where she could finally fulfill a lifelong dream, a vision of a mighty cattle ranch.

After moving into the enormous twenty-six-room Charlford

castle, Kimball began work on her plan for making her dream of a cattle ranch a reality. First, she renamed her land Cherokee Ranch, in honor of the original Cherokee Trail and the Indian tribe that had once inhabited her native homeland. She then followed up by renaming all the buildings on her land. The Charlford castle became the Cherokee Castle, the Flower Homestead became Chickamauga, the Johnson Farm became Wauhatchie, and the Blunt Homestead became Amnicola.

It was also around this time that the Montague family home in Chattanooga was being demolished for a new highway. Tweet had her mother's family possessions, art and heirlooms packed up and shipped to Cherokee Ranch, where her mother came to live with her.[10]

When Kimball began to inquire about the purchase of Santa Gertrudis cattle, she was met with resistance by cattle ranchers from Kentucky, Tennessee, and Texas. The reasons for this lack of cooperation were twofold. First, she was a woman, dealing in a man's world. Second, she was told that Santa Gertrudis cattle were accustomed to warm weather and could not survive the cold climate of Colorado. The ever-persistent woman that Kimball was eventually found a Texas rancher who agreed to sell her a few of his animals. With this purchase of two bulls and twenty-nine cows, Kimball began her herd of Santa Gertrudis cattle.

However, her battles were just beginning. Rumors spread quickly among the Douglas County ranchers that Kimball was bringing "those damned red Bremmers" into the county. Once the Texas animals arrived at Cherokee Ranch, Kimball's ranch foreman refused to unload the cattle. According to Kimball's own account of the incident, the foreman was immediately fired, but because he had a family and was their only means of support, she allowed him to stay at the ranch for two weeks. "But he was to have nothing to do with the cattle," she said. Evidently the foreman did not fully grasp the kindness extended by his former boss, as he later intentionally left the pasture gate wide open. Fortunately, it was early in the morning when Kimball discovered her cattle wandering along the road leading to her ranch. After gathering the cattle and returning them to the pasture, Kimball then ordered the foreman immediately off her property. The man refused to leave. Kimball later stated, "Things were different then. I called the sheriff and he came out and got the man off the ranch. Today, you'd have to give the man thirty days' notice and probably take him to court, and all the while he'd be wreaking havoc on the ranch."

Tweet Kimball would not be deterred from her dream of a quality cattle ranch. She once said, "I'm an optimist and a planner, and I was always really interested in animals." She had spent years studying this breed, their offspring and the genetics. She believed in the superiority of these animals. Tweet worked constantly at improving both her herd and the operation of the ranch. Although she had a large ranch crew, Tweet insisted on a hands-on approach in all aspects of the ranch. She personally inspected the cattle daily, determined to produce only the finest of good breeding stock. Tweet continued with her research, determining that the only way to study the breed and improve the quality was to know which bulls had sired the calves, keeping meticulous records. Her theory proved out and eventually was adopted by ranchers around the state. She even named her prized bulls: Cherokee Commander, Cherokee Minotaur, and Cherokee Governor.

Tweet handled the bulls to attract buyers. She even held a series of public events, showcasing the Santa Gertrudis bulls. She held an essay contest, with a first-class bull being awarded to the winner. With her careful planning and effort, Tweet's sales increased substantially. It took time, yet eventually the ranchers of Douglas County were persuaded. She soon gained recognition as the first rancher, not to mention female rancher, to introduce the Santa Gertrudis breed into Colorado. Kimball later said, "People changed their minds when they saw what that bull could produce."[11]

Next, Kimball approached the National Western Stock Show in an effort to show her Santa Gertrudis cattle. As there was no class for such a breed, Kimball was denied. She later recalled,

"They were very narrow-minded. They claimed the cattle weren't purebred." Undaunted, Tweet formed the Rocky Mountain Santa Gertrudis Association in 1961, with the intent to further the breeding program. Kimball's breeding program proved so successful she soon began receiving awards and national acclaim for her superior cattle breed. Eventually the board members of the National Western Stock Show relented, and Tweet Kimball's prized bulls were allowed to compete. For the next twenty years, Kimball's quality cattle and bulls would continue to win awards, culminating with the Grand Champion Bull award in 1981. She also sponsored the Santa Gertrudis Breeders International Conventions at her Cherokee Ranch.

Kimball once again raised the ire of local ranchers with her innovative approach to cattle breeding. She was the first in the state of Colorado to introduce the concept of single-sire herds. The common practice was to allow several bulls into a pasture with hundreds of cows. Kimball's inventive breeding program produced calves year-round. Thus, she was able to sell her calves to ranchers during any season. Tweet's cattle sales soared. She was shipping her calves to Texas in the winter and to Canada in the summer. For the next forty years, Santa Gertrudis cattle would be sold all over America and even world-wide, for as much as thirty-thousand dollars, to countries including Canada, Russia, Tasmania, South Africa, South America and Taiwan.

Tweet's life as a rancher was not without hardship and tragedy. In 1965, heavy flooding from the South Platte River devastated the area for miles along the river from Denver, and as far as Fort Morgan and Sterling to the northeast. Devastation lay in the wake of the flooding waters. Tweet Kimball later recalled the havoc left behind with four bridges destroyed and the dead animals laying across the plains:

> That storm took twelve feet of topsoil from the fields. The Santa Gertrudis cattle during the storm were in single sire herds along the creek. Due to the commanding leadership of the Santa Gertrudis bulls who shepherded their cows and calves

Tweet Kimball joined two ranches to form her beloved Cherokee Ranch estate.
*DPL*

to high ground, not one animal was lost when an adjoining
ranch lost forty cows and all their calves. The Santa Gertrudis
have shown an extraordinary ability to accept new climate and
rugged terrain.[12]

As busy as Tweet Kimball was with her ranching enterprise,
she managed to find time for a personal life, but it never worked
out. She married three more times with all ending in divorce. Each
time, she threw herself back into her life's passion, her dream

ranch and the Santa Gertrudis cattle. Although she always reverted to her maiden name, she was often referred to as "Mrs.," a title she didn't mind at all. In fact, she once said, "After being married four times, I *am* Mrs."[13]

Tweet Kimball had spent years developing her cattle enterprise. With her prize-winning Santa Gertrudis being sold and bred all over the world, her Cherokee Ranch was recognized as one of the leading cattle breeding ranches in the world. By the turn of the century, it was also recognized as one of the finest and best-preserved ranches in Douglas County.

With such acclaim came social notoriety. The Cherokee Ranch castle became the scene of many social events, charity causes and public events, hosted by Tweet Kimball. Tweet took pride in her Southern heritage and upbringing. She personally typed out the invitations to her many events at the ranch and followed up with hand-written thank you notes to the guests.[14] Notable guests included Prince Bernhardt of the Netherlands, Princess Anne of England, and Winthrop Rockefeller, to name a few. One of her favorite events was the annual Calcutta where guests bet on each rider, horse and hound. This and other significant events are often recounted by her faithful butler of over twenty years, John Lake.

Kimball adorned the mansion with the many works of art and antique pieces she had collected over the years. Several smaller pieces are showcased in the niches of the stone castle walls, including pieces from China and Europe. She also graced the mansion with her eclectic collection of fine paintings and drawings, including exquisite drawings by Sir Christopher Wren, the architect of St. Paul's Cathedral in London. The twenty-six rooms were filled with seventeenth- and eighteenth-century furniture, many pieces of which Kimball had purchased on her European travels following World War II. For example, a second-floor bedroom featured an elaborate four-poster bed with the numerals "1674" carved into the frame. It was believed this bed was commissioned by a relative of King Charles II. The massive bookshelves in the library hold several hundred first-edition works of literature, also collected during her time in Europe.

Tweet Kimball's favorite form of recreation was long rides across her land, just her and her horse. "I love it best," she once said. During these quiet rides she was alone with nature. She often observed several species of birds, including falcons and eagles. She saw bears, coyotes, elk, deer and mountain lions.

With her love of wildlife, she created a natural wildlife preserve on her land, working in conjunction with the Birds of Prey Foundation headquartered in Boulder. Kimball served on the board for a time, and through this partnership, many injured birds, including owls, hawks, eagles and falcons, that had been rehabilitated at the Boulder facility were released at Cherokee Ranch. The birds that were unable to fly or hunt their own prey were cared for at the Cherokee Ranch facilities.

The urban sprawl of the 1990s brought an influx in population and home building to Douglas County. "They ruin the view," said Kimball. It was this encroachment of the land and the effect on the wildlife that she had so doggedly worked to preserve that really spurred her to action. Her plan was to preserve the ranch as open space; in effect it would create a buffer between the urban growth of Denver from the north, and Castle Rock from the south. In 1996, Kimball worked with Douglas County to protect her Cherokee Ranch. Her intent was to preserve her land and create a buffer against encroachment of the Cherokee Ranch land and wildlife preserve. She named her new effort the Cherokee Ranch & Castle Foundation. Kimball then donated her mansion, her art, book, and furniture collections, along with the working cattle operation and the land, to the foundation. As president of the foundation, she would live on the ranch for the remainder of her life. She then offered the development rights of her ranch to the county for two million dollars, with the contingency that her foundation administer the property as the wildlife sanctuary and open space she had developed. Douglas County officials enthusiastically accepted the offer, as the three thousand acres of land was worth considerably more. Through a conservation easement land negotiation, the county would pay Tweet's foundation in installments of $200,000 over a ten year period.

However, during the negotiations her sons brought a lawsuit, suing her for the land development rights. Kimball was so outraged that she later said, "They've queered their mother on them forever." She settled the lawsuit with her sons, one a county deputy sheriff, the other a Denver jeweler, by giving them each five hundred and fifty acres of her beloved Cherokee Ranch. With the lawsuit settled, despite the heartbreak it brought, Tweet Kimball went on to serve admirably as president of her newly created foundation and worked tirelessly to improve the wildlife sanctuary. She was once quoted as saying, "I have more to do than I'll have time to do." This was certainly true of Tweet Kimball. Not one to let the grass grow under her feet, despite running a nationally acclaimed ranch and hosting lavish parties in her spectacular stone castle, she still found time to be very active in the community. She remained president of the Rocky Mountain Santa Gertrudis Association for several more years. After years of in-fighting, she was finally accepted as a respectable rancher and eventually served on the board of directors of the National Western Stock Show, the first woman ever to do so. Tweet also found time to serve on the Douglas County Water Advisory Board, the county's Educational Foundation, and as a trustee of the Denver Art Museum.

Tweet Kimball was loyal to her employees. One of many accounts reflecting the character and diligence of Tweet Kimball is often related by Meg Anderson, an employee who spent twenty-three years at the ranch until Kimball's death in 1999. The two women became close friends over the years. In 1991, as Anderson's daughter was planning her wedding, Kimball insisted hosting a portion of the wedding event. The bride and groom settled on a brunch at the mansion the day after the wedding. Anderson and her husband, who worked as a butler in the mansion, arrived at the ranch the morning of the brunch. There was seventy-seven-year old Tweet Kimball, with a five-gallon bucket of water in each hand, carrying them up the two-mile long road to the mansion. When asked what she was doing, Kimball casually replied, "Well, the water went out at the castle and you must have water."

As Tweet Kimball celebrated her eighty-second birthday, she began the plans for her wish for the future of her mansion at Cherokee Ranch. She wanted her home to eventually become a museum, open to the public to view her art collection as well as learn of the history of her land. "Everything in this house has a story, and it all must be recorded," she said. And so, she set about cataloging all the works of art, paintings, prints, sculptures, artifacts, and furniture, as well as the extensive book collection, in the mansion. She did this by hand, as she was leery of computers. She also worked tirelessly with the National Historic Preservation Commission providing comprehensive land documents, deeds, and historic information. Her work paid off when the United States Department of the Interior declared her ranch land the "Cherokee Ranch Historic District," as part of the National Register of Historic Places. She was also recognized with an award from Colorado Preservation, Inc. In March of 1997, the Cherokee Ranch & Castle Foundation received a $24,000 grant from "Great Outdoors Colorado," which allowed the foundation to construct walking trails around the property, and a visitor's center. Shortly after her death, the Castle Rock Chamber of Commerce bestowed upon Kimball and her foundation the P. S. Miller Award, recognizing her philanthropic gesture to county residents.

Mildred Montague Genevieve "Tweet" Kimball died nearly three years later of a heart attack, on January 14, 1999, at the age of eighty-four. A fine stone memorial on the ranch marks her final resting place.

Tweet's tireless work, extraordinary energy and her devotion to her land and the wildlife is her legacy that lives on at the Cherokee Ranch and Wildlife Preserve.

Today, The Cherokee Ranch & Castle Foundation welcomes guests to experience the many amenities the foundation has to offer. Guided tours of the mansion are scheduled throughout the year, featuring the extensive collections of Tweet Kimball, which the foundation says is the most complete collection of seventeenth- and eighteenth-century art in the country. Afternoon tea events are held monthly and are a wonderful way to enjoy the history and highlights of the mansion. The foundation also hosts weddings at Cherokee Ranch, both indoors and outdoors, with a breathtaking setting against the Front Range of the Rocky Mountains. The Performing Arts Series, held from June through December, includes a wide variety of talent from the Colorado Symphony Chamber Music, the Denver Brass, Denver Center Theatre Company, and the Lamont School of Music at the University of Denver.

A small herd of Santa Gertrudis cattle are still bred on the ranch, and the 31,000 acres of land is now completely protected as a wildlife sanctuary, the true legacy of Tweet Kimball.

# Notes

1. Casey, Susan, "The Lady of the Castle." Interview with Tweet Kimball, *Douglas County News Press*, May 8, 1996.
2. John Lake and Meg Anderson, Cherokee Castle historians.
3. Anderson and Lake, *Castle Entertaining From Ranch Hands to Royalty*, pg. 2.
4. Casey, Susan, "The Lady of the Castle." Interview with Tweet Kimball, *Douglas County News Press*, May 8, 1996.
5. ibid.
6. Hafen, *Pikes Peak Gold Rush Guidebooks of 1859*, pg. 105.
7. The *Douglas County News* of July 8, 1876 recalled the historic event.
8. *Diary of a Journey to the Pike's Peak Gold Mines in 1859*, Denver Public Library.
9. This road is now known as Daniels Park Road.
10. Anderson and Lake, *Castle Entertaining From Ranch Hands to Royalty*, pg. 4.
11. Casey, Susan, "The Lady of the Castle." Interview with Tweet Kimball, *Douglas County News Press*, May 8, 1996.
12. *Livestock Magazine*, September, 1981.
13. Casey, Susan, "The Lady of the Castle." Interview with Tweet Kimball, *Douglas County News Press*, May 8, 1996.
14. Anderson and Lake, *Castle Entertaining From Ranch Hands to Royalty*, pg. 4.

# Emily Louise Rood French Varney
## Reminiscences of Life on the Colorado Plains

By the turn of the century, women were exerting a sense of independence. Indeed, within a decade the Suffragette movement would sweep the nation. In 1915, the *Denver Times* issue dated March 16 reported on the increase of female ranchers and homesteaders. Under the headline, "Women are Taking Up Much Land in Colorado," the reporter wrote, "Many Teachers, nurses and stenographers are taking up claims and expressing themselves as delighted with the restful atmosphere."

While this was true of many, it was not the case for Emily Rood French Varney. Personal, family, and financial struggles led Emily to take up a claim in Elbert County.

Emily Louise Rood was born in Calhoun County, Michigan, on August 14, 1843, to Morgan and Anna Rood. Emily's father followed many others to California during the gold rush of 1849, leading the famous group known as the "Wolverine Rangers." Sometime prior to this, Rood had divorced his wife. Ten years later the desire for gold riches led him to Colorado during the Pikes Peak gold rush.  Returning to Denver, Morgan Rood seemed to have given up the miner's life and opened his own gun shop in 1860.[1] It was during this time that Rood met a widow, Anna Bickford. The *Rocky Mountain News* carried news of their wedding in the February 7, 1868 issue of the paper: "On Thursday evening, in St. John's church by Rev. Mr. Kehler, Morgan L. Rood, esq., and Mrs. Anna Bickford, both of this city."

On March 17, 1858, Emily eloped with Marsena Hamilton French. He was twenty-three, she was fifteen. There were nine children born to the couple: Ada, 1860; Helen, 1862; Marsena B., 1864; Emily A., 1867; Chauncey Morgan, 1869; Abigail, 1871;

Olive, 1875; Daniel, 1877; and M.K. in 1880.

In 1870, Marsena enrolled in medical school and Emily took on domestic jobs for added income. It would be a needed financial requirement periodically throughout her life.

In the spring of 1876, the French family were living in Golden, Colorado, where Marsena set up his medical practice. By the time of M.K.'s birth in 1880, the family were living in Denver.

On May 11, 1885, Marsena and Emily filed on a homestead in Elbert County. Emily's younger sister, Annis (sometimes referred to as Annie, after her mother), took a homestead next to the Frenches on May 14, 1885.[2] It is not known why Annis moved to Colorado, other than to be near her sister, as she had suffered a spinal injury a decade earlier and could not stand erect. Because of Annis' disability, Emily was forced to run both households, including daily chores such as retrieving water from the nearby South Platte River, caring for the animals, plowing, gardening, and tending to her children's needs. It was Emily who did all of this while Marsena practiced medicine in the town of Elbert.

Tragedy struck the French family with the death of four-year-old M.K. from accidental poisoning on May 31, 1885. The child was the first burial, lot 70, block 5, in the Elbert Cemetery.[3]

A distraught Emily persevered through her grief and managed to prove up on both pieces of property. With the help of some of her children (Ada, Helen and Marsena B. were grown and living their own lives), she managed to raise alfalfa, corn, potatoes, and oats which were sold in town. In 1889, this income literally dried up. It was the beginning of a severe drought that would last for years. This was also the year that Emily's life changed forever.

After thirty years of marriage, Emily and Marsena divorced. It was a nasty dissolution of marriage with Marsena seeking not only sole possession of their land, but custody of the minor children as well. He even petitioned the court to turn over Annis Rood's land claim to him. The sisters united and fought Marsena in the Denver courts. It was a fight that went on for years and would cost Emily dearly. By 1890, Emily was alone on her property. She had built a four-room house for her sister but soon found herself caring for Annis as much as she was caring for her own place. It became a hardship which Emily sometimes resented, but she carried on, confiding only to her diary.

It is through Emily's unedited diary writings for the year 1890 that we get a real sense of time and place and the struggles she endured on the isolated eastern prairie. Emily's writing, with its shaky spelling and grammar, perhaps a result of her troubled spirit, is repeated verbatim.

January, Wednesday 1, 1890 Emily L. French Elbert, Colorado
Let me only in the fear of God put on these pages what shall transpire in my poor life. Pure truths are only of value. I seek not the applause of the people only that I may deserve the epitaph - She hath done what she could…God be with me through this year.
Had a good night rest - did not wake till I heard Annis making the fire. I fell asleep & did not waken till she came to the door & flung it open, wishing me a happy new year. I thanked her and got up.

January, Sunday 5, 1890
Up before daylight, I must take A to her Ranche, it is quite a while since she was there. They are bound to take it from her if they can - I took some bread, potatoes, rice, meal, sugar, dried apples, onions, Bacon, milk and 2 quilts, a pair of blankets & a pillow so she can be comfortable. We met Mr. Waldo, had a talk with him, he seems all right - we have to trust someone. I made a fire, thawed out the kettle & pail so to go to the spring & get her some clean water. I never stopped once. When I got there he [Marsena] sprung on the platform, had a pail, said I could have no water. I told him I should. He commenced his low talk. I told him I came for water, not to see or hear from him. I told him he ought to be ashamed, he took a young, virtuous girl from her fathers house. He said I was as good as I was then. I told him he had just told the truth he never meant to. I took my

pail and started for home. Annis with her fire & supper most
ready now. She all right.

January, Tuesday 14, 1890
The true measure of faith for us oh Lord
I coughed and shivered all night. Arose at 7, Annis had a fire
& my oatmeal cooked. I nearly froze getting the rest. It is one
of the coldest days. She combed my hair. The stove smoked so
we had to go in at the fire place and let the fire in the stove go
out. I took down the stove pipe and cleaned the soot out, so if it
would burn it could, but no use, it drew into the kitchen.

January, Sunday 19, 1890
Shall I & my dear children be of his chosen…How I do long
to be near my children. God only knows the real desire of my
heart. How unhappy I really am, will he bring me a home? I
trust him in all things. I got up, dressed in my black dress, took
my good old horse Ric her oats. She waits at the gate for them.
I came home, swept up the front room and kitchen. Annis had
burned up the bread I put on to steam. She seems to forget
so easy. She combed my hair, washed my neck. I made a fire
in the fire place. How I do wish I could have a nice cheerful
companion to sit opposite me.

February, Monday 10, 1890
Up at 1 A.M., fed the horses grain and hay, caught the chickens
and tied them so they can be safe in the basket & box, had my
breakfast at 3, oatmeal & tea, started at 4 1/2. On the way
tried to hitch Ric beside Fanny, no go. She will not lead good.
I had one stand, 2 chairs, 1 rocker, my feather bed, a few tins,
the chopping bowl. I turned into the road leading out by the
sheep ranch, 2 of the chickens got away. Was going along, the
sun shining so nice, suddenly it grew dark, the wind blew oh so
hard. Mon the 10th, went by way of Elizabeth, got caught in
that awful storm, a man perished 3 miles out on the way to his
home. God save poor me. I went in to the old Reynolds house, I

had been there before, knew where I was.

February, Monday 17, 1890
Got up at Mrs. Brooks, she so poorly. I did all that I could
to help her, swept the whole house, cleared and washed the
breakfast dishes. He watered and hitched up Fanny and Ric. At
9 I started, the wind is always tearing this terrible Colorado. I
drove straight towards home, inquired on the way for the right
roads. I had a fearful time going down the roads fenced up. On
the road that goes by the Merino sheep farm I did not know it,
so I had a bad drive. Led old Fanny - Ric hitched behind, down
I go into a gully. Got to my poor home 2 P.M., Annis hard at
work on the buggy rug. She does at times seem to try. What
can I do, must I go on liveing this way, no use to try to make
a companion of her, she is so dull. Blackberries, bread, tea, I
brought a basinfull home.

February, Wednesday 26, 1890
I up but so sick I could not eat. I had a chill, in about 1 hour I
had to lie down. I slept on the lounge. I coughed so hard she
fixed me some ginger tea, done all she could.[4]

March, Sunday 2, 1890
I lay still for fear of having a coughing spell. I am so sick &
sore. Annis sleeping sound, she is a careless nobody. Oh why
am I left with only her for a companion. I called her, then had
a hard coughing spell. She made a fire in the grate or fire place,
it smokes so in the stove. The wind no blowing for a wonder. I
called old Ric & gave her a feed of oats. She looks much better,
the sore on her back nearly healed, has one now on her neck.
I crawled to bed, oh dear I am so sick, wont someone come,
I fear not. My feet are cold. Oh why cannot I have some care
when I always have done all in my power for others, must I
suffer here alone & make no sound. God send me relief.

March, Thursday 13, 1890

My head aches, I am sick, did not get up till 8, Annis called to breakfast, I did not want any. I got up, she combed my hair. Will I ever be so I can rest. God hasten the time, I pray. We got the three buildings moved all right. Got nine sacks potatoes.

March, Sunday 30, 1890

I up at 5:30, sister slept in her chair last night. I had covered up the potatoes with new rug & carpet - it so bitter cold & storming. We got breakfast by the Fire place & eat there cozy any way, if the storm does rage outside. Sister combed my hair, I am getting gray so fast. Oh how bitter cold it is, I cleared off the lounge and lay down, Annis reading out loud Phillida - in my Ladies Home Journal. I went and changed the pail in the well, then I got the horses watered - they drank both of them, Ric & Roney, 9 pails in all. Then I sat me down to again to write in my dear little diary, the holder of my poor thoughts and actions - may I yet record successes - God be with & bless for Jesus sake.

April, Thursday 3, 1890

Made the great mistake of my life, I feel it so clear, let Ric & Roney go for $75.00 for a small I guess part poney. Oh dear, I feel as if it was a big mistake now & I never have rode behind him till today.

May, Sunday 25, 1890

We are still not feeling well. I got a lunch for us, then set down to write up a week in this dear little book. How I can remember and always could, will it always be so? She grows more kind as the days go by, there may be rest for me yet. Now I must do a little to prepare for evening service, I think we will go to night, why not? God be with us & bless us this service to our good, will he help me do?

May, Thursday 29, 1890
I up early, so much to do, something all the time, even tho it is
to pay my debts. I have the shirt to wash, made a fire & some
starch as I got the breakfast, bread, cookies & coffee, may we
always have so much. Worked as hard as I could all day.

May, Saturday 31, 1890
Went first to get the stuff to add to what I already had to put
on a small room for the hay & tubs & c, got 1 door painted,
so nice, I put in the tent for the horse to bruise, I dont seem to
think anymore.

June, Saturday 7, 1890
Up early, I am feeling so very bad I can scarcely get up. We had
coffee, fried bread, rice. I swept off the floor, it is so nice now
that we have it oiled with linseed. We can keep so nice. The
flies have got in so thick since McBride began to paint, I glad it
is all done. Now when I get all the little bills settled we can get
something ahead to live on. I got 5c meat, 10c broken crackers.

June, Thursday 12, 1890
Being dead to sin, we put on the new.
Mr. Huntington came for me to go help his wife, she sick all
night. I done the work - such a dirty hole, food thrown every
where. I could live so nice out of what they waste. He came
again tonight, why?

June, Wednesday 25, 1890
Carried 7 lbs nice butter to Mrs. Sorrells, let it go on what I
owe her. I got my envelopes for 6 mo, 10c per week.

August, Sunday 17, 1890
Such a long hard night with Mrs. OBrian, her labor so
protracted. Dr. Bradley a nice man & a No 1 physician, he so
careful of her. The labour slow, she 30 past, no wonder she
has a hard time. It is her first child, it had to be born on the

floor, he did not want to use instruments. It such a nice plump thing, but cried while being dressed. She wanted it christened Marguirett Agnes. I dressed it in its christening robes, very nice & sent to it from N Nersey.

September, Tuesday 2, 1890
I was too tired to get up, could not eat, went to work. Mrs. Anna OBrian sent last night for me then Dr said it would not be for the best.

September, Sunday 7, 1890
I am poor & needy! the lord pitieth me
I lay long dreading to get up, nothing in life for us. I read after I got my poor work done, such a long lonesome day. If I had lots of money I would be all right.

September, Tuesday 30, 1890
Oh Dear, so hard, washed all day. Ironed & a pot roast. I went to prayer meeting. Baked bread, finished ironing, cleaned the stove, burned myself.

October, Sunday 12, 1890
Thy will be done on earth as it is in heaven…I let the children [Olive and Daniel] stay in bed, they love so to sleep in the morning, nothing to hinder them from rest. Oh how I do wish I could have a little help in maintaining my home. I shall dread the cold winter so much. I went with Dannie to morning Church Baptism.

October, Wednesday 15, 1890
It snowed hard. I got up, took the broom, swept off the doorway. Dannie hitched Fanny so I could go see about Annis advertising her land. She lost the paper I had got ready, so I have to see to getting another. I got it, went to Lindell, got a check for $5.00, he see's I have a hard time to live, went to prayer meeting.

November, Saturday 8, 1890 Another day, oh when when will I have my time all to rest, will it ever come. I never combed my hair or sat down all day. I lay, for I am not feeling well enough to get up, yet I must. I come unwell last night, I am verry bad of late, my age must be. I am so glad no more babies for me.

December, Wednesday 3, 1890
Lord shall enter into rest…We at work hard to get fired, the wind awful, seems as if it would blow the house down. We could scarcely keep warm. I am bad with my monthly sickness - yet I must do for the rest.

December, Friday 5, 1890
Up early, breakfast, tea, cake, potatoes, salmon that we brought all the way from Dake. We are nice but it is so cold. Drove over to see if Wm. Green would not come to see Annis at the ranch, since the buildings were moved, yes he would come and sure he came while I was gone, told her that she was all right, had $500.00 improvements. Drove old Fanny to Kiowa, 9 oclock. My brand not recorded.

December, Sunday 7, 1890
Such a cold raw morning, we can never get down to Church in time for service, so bitter cold. We put the sled, in buckboard, sack potatoes, baskets & c. I will never drive to Elbert, no we turned Fanny's head toward Elizabeth, will put the things with Nan West. We was nearly frozen, Mrs. West got dinner for us, at 1 fed Fanny started on 2 30. Have to go to ranch forgot axe & affidavit I got Lee Ramsey to make last Friday. On to the ranch, Annis Ranch, 6 years of hard life she has been there, the old heathen [Marsena French] he wants everything. We have good bye, not sorry to go, everything speaks plain of long and fearful suffering. To Elbert, we got her in the buggy, started over to Fricks when tipped over by crick.

December, Monday 8, 1890
Annis so bad sick, 11 at night. Up, combed, washed before breakfast, Annis bound to go to table, Annis eat good, then dropped off to sleep at the table. We, Dan & I, got her to the lounge, then suddenly she had 2 more of the strangest spasms I ever saw. I sent quick for the Dr, he gone.

December, Monday 15, 1890
I sat and wrote in this till I was so cold & sleepy last night. We was eating, in come an Insurance man. I say no to everything.

December, Monday 22, 1890
We shall not trust in ourselves, but in God which raiseth the dead...Amen. Up at 5, must hurry to work, everything in the house dirty. I shall carry a sheet, some pillow cases for Annis, the tea towells &c so verry dirty.

December, Thursday 25, 1890
Thanks be unto God for his unspeakable gift
I sat down to put the pages in this from the 21st - this is the night I have had to myself. We had a baked rice pudding, boiled beef, tea, milk, thanks to Mrs. Wier that lives on the hill we can have skim milk at the house we want. A neighbor brought another gift of mush, beef and some red & white knittings. The wind at 9 oclock is rageing wild but I know we are all right at home.

It was as if the financial and personal issues were constant for Emily.

On February 15, 1892, Emily's ex-husband, Marsena French, once again appealed to the courts to acquire both Emily and Annis' land. Emily contested the action, citing the Married Women's Property Act of 1840, which legalized female ownership of land and property. Emily finally won this ongoing battle on July 16, 1894.

However, on October 19, 1892, Emily married George

Varney, Jr. Her new husband was a businessman and the couple relocated to Castle Rock, Colorado.[5] A son was born to the couple on July 16, 1893, but died at the age of two weeks and five days on August 4, 1893, from cholera infantum.[6]

When Marsena French learned of Emily's remarriage, he refiled his claim to his ex-wife's land. The affidavit claimed: "Emily L. Varney is a married woman, living with her husband, is not the head of a family, and is not qualified to make entry for said land."

This time the judge ruled in favor of French, and on October 25, 1894, Emily lost her land claim and all that she had spent nearly forty years working for.

On August 8, 1898, Emily Louise Rood French Varney died, possibly from the early onset of dementia or Alzheimers. She was fifty-two. Emily was buried in the Varney family plot in Cedar Hill Cemetery in Castle Rock.[7]

## Notes

*1.* Lecompte, Emily, *The Diary of a Hard-Worked Woman*, page 147.

*2.* Homestead Applications filed in Arapahoe County, Colorado, described as W2 NW4 Sec. 32, and E2 NE4 Sec. 31.

*3.* Elbert Cemetery records. Also see Wommack, *From the Grave*, pg. 249.

*4.* Emily seemed to have caught a cold in January she never really got over. By March it had worsened; she became weaker and caught "La Grippe" or "catarrhal fever," a dangerous stain of influenza which became an epidemic worldwide.

*5.* Genealogical records of George Varney, Jr.

*6.* ibid.

*7.* Cedar Hill Cemetery records, Douglas County, Colorado.

DPL

DPL

124

# THE CONTINENTAL DIVIDE

## Florence McIntire
**First Lady Turns Rancher**

## Adeline Hornbek
**Florissant's First Female Rancher**

## Annie and Kitty Harbison
**Devoted Sisters to Family Ranching**

Florence McIntire championed women's rights long before the Suffragette movement. *Sanford Museum*

# Florence McIntire

## First Lady Turns Rancher

Florence Johnson was born in New York on August 15, 1858. Florence spent a good deal of her childhood in New York City before moving with her parents to New Haven, Connecticut. It was in New Haven that Florence met Albert McIntire, her future husband.

Albert Wills McIntire was born in Pittsburgh, Pennsylvania, on January 15, 1853. He was the son of Joseph Phillip and Isabel Wills McIntire. In 1869, at the age of sixteen, McIntire enrolled at Yale University and graduated from the academic department in 1873.

While attending classes at Yale, McIntire found time to court Florence Johnson. Shortly after completing his academic studies, Albert and Florence were married in New Haven on July 16, 1873.

Two years later McIntire earned his law degree from Yale Law School at the age of twenty-two. The couple remained in New Haven where McIntire practiced law. On December 1, 1874, Florence gave birth to their first child, Joseph Phillip.

In 1876, the year Colorado became the thirty-eighth state in the Union, the McIntire family came west to settle in Colorado. The couple spent the next four years in the Denver area, where Albert opened a law practice. Learning of the rich silver strike in Leadville and seeking new opportunities, in the summer of 1879 the couple made the trip over Mosquito Pass to the bustling mining town of Leadville. While in Leadville, McIntire met and became friends with Leadville's first mayor and first millionaire, Horace A. W. Tabor. Tabor showed McIntire around the mines and encouraged him to invest in Leadville's newest industry.

However, Florence had other ideas. She had been hearing of the lush meadows and rich farmland in the San Luis Valley in southern Colorado. McIntire agreed to travel to the area, and in the fall of 1880, the McIntires purchased three thousand acres in Conejos County. The land lay on the south side of the Conejos River at a natural spring that would be named McIntire Spring, just northeast of the small settlement of Sanford and north of present-day La Jara, Colorado.[1]

While Albert spent much of his time visiting area ranches and purchasing cattle, Florence oversaw every aspect of the construction of the couple's new home, employing local Hispanic labor. The main house was built of adobe with brick and wood enhancements, thus blending the Territorial adobe style with Anglo building traditions. The L-shaped two-story house consisted of three-brick-wide molded adobe walls approximately twelve feet high. The center of the main house sat on an elevated foundation flanked on each side by smaller wings at ground level. Italianate door overhangs and window openings included decorative wood moldings. Wooden rafters were used in the roof construction and were covered with small branches in the traditional adobe style. The roof was then covered with tar paper which was water resistant and capped with dirt. Large, arched doubleheaders marked the main entrance for the house on the north side.[2]

Inside the home there were eight rooms and a large cellar with access from the kitchen area. The flooring consisted of 1 x 4-inch, tongue-and-groove hardwood pine. The main portion of the house included a parlor, large hallway, and kitchen to the back. A large double-sided fireplace, made of nine-inch adobe blocks, graced the parlor. A fireplace was also located in each wing of the house. An open hearth, as well as a coal-burning stove, were located in the kitchen.

When her new home was completed, Florence named her ranch "Los Ojos," Spanish for "the eyes." Florence planted several trees near the house, hoping they would one day provide much-needed shade from the hot summers on the prairie. A fine vegetable garden was planted at the rear of the house. Florence's husband Albert was purchasing fine Black Angus cattle on a grand scale. As a result, the couple purchased an additional thousand acres of land.

Possibly due to their increased land holdings, as well as their large cattle operation, both Florence and Albert became well-respected in the San Luis Valley. As a result, Conejos County officials encouraged Albert McIntire to enter politics. In 1883, McIntire was Conejos County Judge, a position he held for three years.

During this time, the McIntires entertained their powerful guests at the ranch with fine food and drink. Possibly due to the disdain many in the local community held toward the use of alcohol, the McIntires concealed a depository or dump for the many liquor bottles under a subfloor of a separate outdoor structure.[3]

As the McIntire couple became more popular across the state, the social gatherings increased. Albert even built a large pond at the spring that would bear his name, and stocked it with trout so that his colleagues could enjoy fishing.[4] He built a separate structure where he and his friends could play poker and freely imbibe in alcoholic beverages.

In 1884, the couple welcomed their second child, a girl, which Florence named Mary Elizabeth. Meanwhile, Los Ojos was flourishing with Florence and Albert working side by side. Albert soon looked to improving the irrigation on the ranch. Because of this, Albert became very familiar with the practice of water law. With Albert's legal abilities with water law, his law practice quickly picked up. Soon, Albert began spending more and more time away from the ranch.

Florence did not mind this new development at all; in fact, in time she grew to enjoy it. And at the age of twenty-four, Florence was a quick study. Rather than focusing on the traditional realm of the household where women's responsibilities revolved around domestic life, Florence chose a nontraditional female management role where she was the sole person involved in the management and success of the ranch. She took on all the duties of the ranch operation including the daily workings of the ranch, business and financial concerns, as well as taking care of her two children. It was a role she came to relish and a position she refused to relinquish once her efforts began to be profitable.

While Florence enjoyed her newfound independence, it was not without challenges and sacrifices. In early 1887, three-year-old Mary Elizabeth died. Florence must have persevered through her grief. It is not known if Albert was at the ranch during this time, however. It was during this time that his term as Conejos County Judge came to an end and he chose not to run for reelection. This could be because of the death of little Mary Elizabeth and the fact that Florence was about to give birth to their third child. On April 2, 1887, Dorthea Lord was born at the Los Ojos Ranch.

By 1891, Albert was a strong leader in the state's political arena. When a vacancy in the Twelfth Judicial District opened, Albert was appointed by Governor John L. Routt. It was a position which again took him away from Florence and the ranch for long periods of time.

In 1894, McIntire was nominated for governor by the Colorado Republican Party. The slogan for the campaign was, "redeem the state," a reference to the economic silver panic of the year before. McIntire went on to soundly defeat the incumbent populist Governor Davis Waite, who had become quite unpopular, by more than 20,000 votes. With his election, Albert McIntire became the ninth governor of Colorado.

The Colorado gubernatorial election of 1894 marked the first time that women were given the right to vote in a Colorado state election. This was a direct result of the American Female Suffrage Movement. As a social, economic and political reform movement aimed at extending suffrage to women, this was something Florence would have fully supported. It was also during McIntire's term that the tenth general assembly, which convened on January 2, 1895, was the first to occupy the legislature chambers in the new capitol building.

Governor McIntire's old Leadville friend, Horace A.W. Tabor, now Colorado's "Silver King" millionaire, opened his

Florence McIntire ran a very efficient ranching operation from her adobe ranch house. *Sanford Museum*

majestic Tabor Grand Opera House for the inauguration ceremony and festivities. McIntire chose to have his public reception at Denver's finest hotel, the Brown Palace Hotel. The evening's inaugural ball was held at the popular Broadway Theater. Florence McIntire accompanied her husband to all these events, the one and only time she was in Denver during her husband's term as governor.

During his administration, and at Florence's urging, Governor McIntire was instrumental in strengthening the voice of women through legislation he enacted. There is no question that Florence achieved a level of self-sufficiency that allowed her to gain self-respect and successfully operate the ranch on her own.

To that end, during her husband's term Florence remained at Los Ojos Ranch in the San Luis Valley. Curious, a reporter for the *Rocky Mountain News* ventured south to visit Colorado's First Lady at her ranch. In the front-page article of the issue dated November 18, 1895, the reporter extolled the virtues of the First

Lady, stating that she was in charge of "all the buying and carried on the ranch chiefly alone."

The article also featured elements of the main house at Los Ojos, stating in part, "the building had an irregular crossing pattern comprised of a square arrangement of eight rooms and a small hallway." There was a photograph of the parlor with the double fireplace and a photograph of the exterior main entrance. In an interview, Florence McIntire told the reporter that she was against her husband's foray into politics and further stated that she abhorred politics on every level. Florence is quoted as saying: "I have a disinclination to put on the bonds of social life, rendered the more trammeling by an official position."

This clearly showed a reluctance on Florence's part to maintain the conventional duties of a wife but displayed her increasing level of confidence and independence from her husband.

Not long after this, Florence expressed her desire for a divorce from Albert. She actually filed divorce papers in Conejos County during her husband's term as governor, but was persuaded to drop the suit at least until the end of her husband's term. During his term in office, McIntire helped guide the state out of the economic depression of 1893, caused by the silver panic which ruined many including his friend, Horace A.W. Tabor. Governor McIntire also backed the Western Federation of Miners during the Leadville miner's strike, eventually sending the Colorado Militia where they set up a tent city called "Camp McIntire." [4]

During his two years in office, he worked to increase medical care for the insane, established a state home for girls, and called for legislation that would ensure equal suffrage, supporting women's causes such as the temperance movement. These measures increased his popularity with his female constituents despite it being overwhelmingly unpopular with his male supporters and friends.

As New Year's gifts and perhaps a show of appeasement with his friends, Governor McIntire handed out silver whiskey flasks.[5] The governor served one term, from 1895 to 1897. When it was over, he returned to Los Ojos. But not for long. Florence promptly divorced him.

It appears that Florence had been planning this divorce since her first filing two years earlier. She had educated herself on the recently enacted laws of female land ownership and presented her proposal to Albert. When she was granted her divorce in June 1898, Albert deeded all his interests in the ranch as well as the land to Florence.

Not only was the divorce of the former governor front page news in all the papers; it was a wonderful testament to the woman's movement that was beginning to take on a large momentum in Denver and across the state. The *Denver Times* devoted an entire page of their July 14, 1898, issue to the McIntire divorce and Florence's newfound financial independence.

Now with Florence in full control of Los Ojos Ranch, she wasted no time making improvements and increasing her land holdings. She built new outbuildings, including a second livestock pen and a tool shed. She made improvements to the main house as well, and added a circular driveway in front of the house.[6]

It was during this time that Florence took an active role in the suffrage movement and female activism. The newly expanded homestead laws were aimed at women to promote economic opportunities and further settlement. Florence exercised her newfound freedom by taking full advantage of these new laws.

In October 1903, Florence acquired a large section of land adjacent to Los Ojos. This was an isolated tract consisting of forty acres and was adjacent to the southwest section. Florence purchased the property through a public land sale. According to the homestead records for the property filed at the National Archives offices in Washington, D.C., Florence filed a Cash Entry on the land parcel stating that she was a single woman, which allowed her to meet the criteria for filing under the expanded Homestead Act.[7]

Both of Florence's surviving children remained with Florence following the divorce, grew to have families of their own, and stayed in the San Luis Valley. Joseph married Caroline Marie Rasmussen in 1897 and gave Florence her first grandchild, Helen Frances, in 1898. Dorthea lived with her mother until her marriage to Edward Cortez. Dorthea and Edward Cortez homesteaded land adjacent to Los Ojos. Dorthea gave Florence her second grandchild, Elsie, in 1909.

Florence continued to successfully manage the day-to-day operations of her ranch, although with some difficulty. As with many ranchers and homesteaders, finances were tight during the lean years, or due to unforeseen circumstances brought on by weather or economic downturns. It was no different for Florence McIntire. However, Florence managed to sell livestock to pay her debts and make ends meet with the sale of fruits and vegetables grown in her gardens. Florence was able to maintain a steady, although somewhat meager income from the ranch proceeds for her livelihood.

This changed when tragedy struck in 1911. Florence, who had been ill for some time, was diagnosed with cancer. Then, in August, Florence's son-in-law Edward Cortez drowned in an accident while cutting hay next to the Conejos River. While Dorthea grieved over the death of her husband, she also had to help her ailing mother with her needs and assist with the operations of Los Ojos.

Mother and daughter worked together for the first time as they struggled to hold on to both properties. Perhaps because of large medical bills, Florence took out loans against her property. When this money ran out, Florence was truly in debt.[8] In the fall of 1911, Florence began to sell off small sections of her landholdings.

On April 22, 1912, Florence Johnson McIntire died. She was fifty-three years old. Florence was buried in the family plot at the La Jara Cemetery. Her children, Joseph and Dorthea, had a fine granite stone placed to mark the burial site. On the other side of the marker, the name of their father, Albert Wills McIntire, would be added in 1935, following his death and burial next to their mother.

Florence bequeathed the main house and cattle operations to her son, Joseph. Although he did not live in the house, he did maintain it until his death in 1929.

Following the death of her mother, Dorthea remarried and

was again able to add to the land holdings of both properties. She and her new husband, Jose Samuel Cortez, filed for and proved up on a homestead of 120 acres adjacent to Los Ojos. Interestingly, it was discovered that ruins of Zebulon Pike's 1806 stockade were laid in the northern section of the land. In November 1926, Dorthea sold this land to the state of Colorado.[9]

Following Dorthea's death in 1975, Florence McIntire's Los Ojos ranch was also sold to the state. Today the property is in the hands of the National Park Service. It was designated a state and national historic property on March 26, 2008.

The site encompasses a section of land approximately six hundred fifty feet by fifteen hundred feet and includes visible remains of the McIntire Ranch. The site consists of the ruins of the main adobe block house, an L-shaped foundation depression partly enclosed with a rock alignment, a raised foundation of an outbuilding, a depressed foundation, a masonry spring enclosure, a livestock pen, three foundations of unknown purpose, and seven artifact concentrations.[10]

Over the years there have been several archaeological studies of the property. Artifacts have been found in the potato and fruit cellars as well as the foundation of the main house, including the bases of the three fireplaces. Several liquor bottles have been found in one of the concentration sites. This is believed to have been constructed by Albert as a discreet disposal for the liquor bottles, as it is located separate from the house by a considerable distance. Here, maker's marks include the Millgrove Glass Company and the Modes Glass Company. Curiously, there were no liquor bottles found in any of the other concentration sites. Archaeologists believe further examination may reveal clues about Florence's habits and behaviors practiced during her sole occupation of Los Ojos in the 1900s.

There is no doubt that Florence Johnson McIntire exhibited a level of self-sufficiency which led to her success as a woman rancher and a leading role model for those who were just entering the suffragette movement.

Indeed, Florence was a woman ahead of her time.

# Notes

1.  The *La Jara Gazette*, June 24, 1942.
2.  Archives of the United States Department of the Interior National Park Service, who now oversee the property.
3.  McIntire Ranch, Conejos County, Colorado, National Register of Historic Places Continuation Sheet, page 21, Section Number Archaeological evidence shows that the lack of other types of artifacts in the dump site would suggest that it was used strictly for the disposal of liquor bottles.
4.  *Alamosa News*, "Rabbitbrush Rambler: Governor McIntire," by Virginia Simmons, August 1, 2017.
5.  ibid.
6.  Archives of the United States Department of the Interior National Park Service and the National Register of Historic Places Continuation Sheet, McIntire Ranch, Conejos County, Colorado, page 4.
7.  National Archives No. 2883.
8.  Conejos County Courthouse, County Clerk's Office, Book 84, page 399, and Book 88, age 325.
9.  Today, according to the National Park Service, the ruins of the Cortez Ranch may lie somewhere in the overgrown bottomlands around Pike's Stockade, as at least one building foundation was discovered near the present-day restroom facilities.
10. Archives of the United States Department of the Interior National Park Service, who now oversee the property.

# Adeline Hornbek

## Florissant's First Female Rancher

Adeline Warfield Harker Hornbek Sticksel faced unbearable odds as a single female rancher with determination and the sheer will to survive and provide a life for herself and her four children.

Adeline was born in 1833 in Massachusetts. The adventurous young fiery redhead left her New England home, following her older brother, Alexander, to the faraway Creek Nation in the Oklahoma Territory. Alexander Warfield's successful Indian trading post had helped to establish him as a well-respected trader and merchant. By the time his sister arrived, Warfield had expanded his business and appointed his friend and fellow trader, Simon A. Harker, as accounting clerk at the trading post. Harker, an emigrant from England, succeeded in overcoming the cultural transition with ease and learned to deal with the Native Americans in sign language, and eventually was able to speak the language.

Harker and Adeline were soon smitten with one another. In 1858, twenty-five-year-old Adeline Warfield and thirty-three-year-old Simon A. Harker were married. They lived near the trading post in Oklahoma, where Adeline gave birth to a son, Frank, followed by a daughter, Annie, ten months later. Shortly thereafter, in 1860, Simon's health began to fail, and he fell into a lingering illness he attributed to the climate.

Whether it was due to Simon's health or the likelihood of an impending Civil War, the Harker family left Oklahoma traveling by an ox-drawn wagon, headed northwest for the arid plains of Colorado Territory and a healthier climate. In the spring of 1861, just as Civil War was erupting in the East, the Harkers arrived in Colorado Territory.

The Colorado Territory had been established that same year of 1861, following the discovery of gold in the Rocky Mountains, at Russell Gulch. In 1859, the new mining supply town of Denver City was formed. It was near this area of the Colorado Territory that the Harkers chose to make their new home in the West.

They settled along the South Platte River, just northeast of Denver City, where they farmed and raised cattle. This would be the beginning of a forty-year ranching career for Adeline.

It was a good choice for the Harkers. Fresh food and produce were rare in Denver City. When available, they were brought to the supply town by wagon train, and even then, were not fresh. Because the goods were so rare, they sold for very high prices. Thus, the few nearby farmers could offer their fresh produce at far lower prices than the wagon train traders and still make a handsome profit.

During this gold rush to the Rocky Mountain region, the Harkers prospered, selling their fresh beef, poultry and farm produce to the eager miners passing through the supply town, as well as to the citizens.

In addition to his ranching, Harker's experience with Native Americans in the Oklahoma Creek Nation proved invaluable to the Colorado Territory politicians, and he was asked to serve as one of the first Indian agents in the newly formed Colorado Territory. It is most likely that during his time as Indian agent, Harker met another Indian agent of the Colorado region, Judge James Castello, of El Paso County, or that the two met through their mutual involvement in the Republican Party. In any case, the Harkers and Castellos would become close friends.

Meanwhile, the Harkers continued to prosper in their new ranching enterprise, buying several head of cattle. Simon Harker also became active in the community, joining the local Republican Party and later became a member of the Masonic Order. In 1863, a third child, George, was welcomed into the Harker family. With his growing family, Simon Harker felt it was time to a file a claim for his land under the Homestead Act of 1862. This Act allowed for granting land in 160 acre plots. When Harker filed his claim for his acreage, for unknown reasons, his claim was contested. Eventually he received eighty acres under the new Homestead Act, with the remaining eighty acres to be granted once the land was "proved up."

The following year, 1864, heavy snowfall in the high Rocky Mountains melted into the rivers and creeks downstream. The result was a devastating flood that rushed along the Platte River and the confluence of Cherry Creek, near Denver. The roaring water crashed through the Harker land, leveling their pasture and destroying much of their home. The financial loss was too much for Simon Harker. He died of a massive heart attack at the age of thirty-nine. Adeline Warfield Harker, at the age of thirty-one, was now a widow, stranded with three young children ranging in age from one to five.

Adeline proved to be resilient while facing diversity. She managed to repair the home and a few of the buildings on the ranch. In July of 1866, with the money she had saved from selling eggs and vegetables from the ranch, Adeline took advantage of a clause in the 1862 Homestead Act that allowed early purchase of a homestead. She was able to purchase the remaining eighty acres of her homesteaded land for one hundred dollars, two years before the final proof was due. Adeline paid in cash and her land was free and clear of any debt.

Two months later, she married a local businessman, Elliot D. Hornbek, in Denver. In 1870, Adeline gave birth to their son, whom they named Elliot, Jr. The marriage seems not be a happy one, as Hornbek abandoned Adeline and the children in 1875. At this point, Hornbek seems to have disappeared from the historical record. Once again, Adeline faced adversity with true female determination.

Adeline, a single mother, widowed by her first husband and abandoned by her second husband, showed true grit and persevered. She worked hard for the next three years to make a living for herself and her four children, by this time aged from sixteen to five. By early spring of 1878, forty-two year old Adeline

Adeline Hornbek was a single mother who ran a successful ranch at the base of Pikes Peak. *Florrissant Fossil Bed NPS*

had made and saved enough money to move her family to the fertile land of Florissant Valley, very near the shadows of Pikes Peak, thirty-five miles west of Colorado Springs. It was 1876, the year Colorado became the thirty-eighth state and the Centennial State, one hundred years following the Revolutionary War and the Declaration of Independence.

To the north and east of the Florissant Valley, the Rocky Mountains dominated the skyline. To the west, high meadowlands with large expanses of native grasses were so abundant that early fur trappers to the area often camped there. This was the land Adeline chose to rebuild her life.

Adeline may very well have been encouraged to relocate to the area by her long-time friends, Judge James Castello and his wife, Catherine. The Florissant Valley was a region fast becoming an important supply center for travelers and miners to the nearby mountains.

Proximity to available transportation in the area was most

likely an important factor in Adeline's choice of a homestead location, as she knew it would be helpful for shipping her cattle and produce as well as for receiving the needed goods she could not obtain locally.

Adeline Hornbek filed a homestead claim, dated 1878. With this single act, she became one of the earliest ranchers in the Florissant Valley and the first female to do so. The land was located approximately one mile south of the growing settlement of Florissant, which Castello had founded in 1870 with a trading post, with the establishment of a post office in 1872. The area Adeline Hornbek chose to homestead ran along a tributary of the South Platte River, which offered water for its fertile soil. There were large meadows for grazing, and a nearby forest of Ponderosa pine trees. Hornbek hired what turned out to be a master craftsman, who utilized several dozen of the plentiful Ponderosa pine trees, cut and seasoned, to build a fine log home for Adeline and her children. Using cornered V notches, the logs were fitted so tightly that the structure required no nails. The roof was steeply pitched and topped with cedar shingles.

When completed in late 1878, the log house was the first in the valley to have more than one story. The Hornbek home was one and a half stories. The log home contained nearly a dozen glass-paned windows. Three bedrooms for the children were upstairs, and Adeline's bedroom was on the main floor. Also on the main floor, laid out in a T-shaped plan, was a sizable kitchen, complete with a baking nook, a well room and a parlor. Adeline furnished her new home with furniture hauled from Denver, arranged neatly in the log house, and included fine pictures hung on the walls. Handwoven rugs covered the floors. Saturday night dances were held in the parlor, where Adeline played her foot-operated pump organ.

There were several outdoor buildings built of Ponderosa pine, including a large barn which stabled several horses and had an attached wagon shed. A large corral for the livestock was built nearby. Other buildings included a chicken house, a milk house, and a cellar house built into the nearby hillside at the north edge of the property. Adeline Hornbek cultivated three acres of her land for a fine garden. She planted vegetables such as corn, lettuce, tomatoes, herbs and potatoes. Her three teen-aged children were given chores and helped with the hard work of running the homestead. A separate section was designated for raising hay for the animals. A pole fence surrounded the property. Her improvements created an impressive, prosperous ranch.

Colorado historian Kenneth Jessen had this to say regarding Adeline's homestead:

> "On her land she had native grass, water and timber-ideal for ranching. She cultivated two acres for potatoes and vegetables. She cut the hay from the native grass and had a herd of over 100 cows. She also had horses, pigs and poultry. While raising her four children, she found time to work on the Florissant School Board and at a local store."

Adeline prospered on her new ranch in the Florissant Valley. However, it was not without trials and tribulations. For instance, Adeline's son, George Harker, later recalled a terrifying incident with the local Ute Indians, specifically Chief Colorow, in an interview for the *Gazette Telegraph* newspaper, in 1937:

> "That as some [Indians] came near the house, and one started to walk to the house, I got the loaded gun and stood at defense at the door. The wily old Indian chief [Colorow] upon being asked into the house quickly sensed what had almost happened and remarked: 'White boy very white. Heap scared.'"

George Harker was fifteen years old at the time and the alarming event obviously stayed in his memory for years. While the Ute Indians did roam the Florrisant Valley, as they had for hundreds of years, for the most part, they were peaceful.

Adeline's children attended a small log school house in the town of Florrisant. Adeline took a keen interest in her children's schooling, becoming secretary of the school district in 1880.

The Hornbek Ranch is now part of the National Florrissant Fossil Bed site. *Wommack*

Following the death of Adeline's friend, Judge James Castello, his son, Frank, took over his father's business operations, transforming the trading post into a profitable mercantile store.

As was often the case with many homesteaders, a steady income of cash was needed. While Adeline worked to prosper her ranching enterprise, in 1883 she also worked as a clerk at Castello's new Florissant Mercantile, eventually running the store for Frank Castello.

Adeline Hornbek became a prominent member of the growing community of Florissant, serving on the school board and hosting social gatherings in her log cabin home. Along with her community service and social activities, Adeline still found the time to maintain her ranch. Further testament to her ambition, El Paso land records reveal that she increased the value of her property substantially before filing the final homestead papers in 1885.

By this time, Adeline's son George was handling much of heavier chores of the ranch operation. He often worked the family's cattle in the Fremont area several miles to the south, where there was an abundance of open grazing land.

There he met and befriended a fellow rancher, Robert Miller "Bob" Womack. Womack believed there was gold in the area and enjoyed the search more than he enjoyed ranching. In a later interview with C. S. Dudley of the *Gazette Telegraph*, Harker said that he and other ranchers would tell Womack that he "was wasting his time; that nothing would come of it for him." Harker went on to say that Womack would often reply, "Just wait. You'll see. I'll find gold. Just wait and see." As it turned out, Womack was right. He found good float in the creek bed in October of 1890. He filed a claim he named The El Paso, with the gold assayed at two hundred and fifty dollars a ton. In April of 1891, the Cripple Creek Mining District was established.

With a new rush of miners to the area, the stage road that ran between Florissant and Fremont (now Cripple Creek, very near the Hornbek ranch), was crowded with miners and travelers. In fact, the family could watch the travelers from cabin windows and visit with them from the edge of their property. Adeline's youngest son, Elliot Hornbek, Jr., gained employment as a stage coach driver along the stage road. Over eight thousand pounds of ore was carried daily by the stage to Florissant for the connection to the Colorado Midland Railroad, which then carried the ore to Manitou Springs for processing. Elliot Hornbek, Jr., in his interview with the *Gazette Telegraph*, said that it "was usually kept a secret just when the most valuable ore was to be brought down and that, strange as it may seem, I cannot remember that there were any holdups or robberies."

With this new economic boom in the Florrisant Valley, Adeline Hornbek sold her beef to the cattle markets and local suppliers in Florissant and Cripple Creek. The added income greatly enhanced her wealth. Her property, a few years after she filed the homestead, was valued at a little over a thousand dollars. Now, with over two hundred head of cattle, twenty-one horses, and several chickens and cows, her ranch was valued at six thousand dollars.

It proved to be a fine decision that Adeline Hornbek had chosen to relocate for the future of her family. With her children grown and living lives of their own, Adeline finally found time to seek happiness in her personal life. In 1899, at the age of sixty-six, she married for the third time to a man much younger than herself. Her new husband, Frederick Sticksel was a Prussian immigrant who worked on her ranch.

Now semi-retired, the couple traveled often to various sites in both the United States and Europe. Frederick and Adeline Sticksel spent nearly five years together before Adeline was felled by a stroke. At the age of seventy-two, Adeline Warfield Harker Hornbek Sticksel died of paralysis on June 27, 1905. She was buried in the Four Mile Cemetery, a few miles south of her homestead.

Two of her four children, Annie and George Harker, stayed in the Florissant area, while her youngest son, Elliot, eventually became a deputy sheriff in Rio Blanco County. Frank Harker later married and moved to Meeker with his wife, Maddie, and daughter Cora, born on November 6, 1898. In an interview conducted by the National Park Service, Cora Harker Wilson said she remembered her grandmother Adeline as a very large woman with red hair. She remembered her as a strong woman.

Adeline Warfield Harker Hornbek Sticksel showed her unique, independent spirit by claiming land under the Homestead Act, proving up on the claims—not once but twice, and ahead of time. Adeline defied the traditional nineteenth-century gender role, and demonstrated how a single mother in the West could succeed in wise real estate choices and through hard work and good management, improve the land, and become the owner of a prosperous ranch. Adeline lived and worked on her Florissant ranch for twenty-seven years and is still remembered to this day.

Adeline Warfield Harker Hornbek Sticksel defied the odds and is a wonderful example of the women of the American West.

Today, Adeline Warfield Harker Hornbek Sticksel's Homestead has been preserved by the National Park Service.

Purchased in 1973, the buildings were renovated in time for Colorado's bicentennial celebration in 1976. The land was incorporated into the boundaries of the Florissant Fossil Beds National Monument.

The Hornbek Homestead, so named for the claim filed in 1878 and signed by Adeline Hornbek, is located approximately two miles south of Florissant, Colorado, on Teller County Road 1, and just north of the entrance to the Florissant Fossil Beds National Monument.

Five buildings on the original homestead are impeccably preserved, impressive log structures that stand the test of time and are a testament to the female pioneer fortitude. The original pole fence, long since gone, has been replaced by in a rustic reproduction of the original.

The area is free and open to the public. Visitors can walk among the log buildings and learn of Adeline Hornbek and the history of her ranch with interpretive panels. The Hornbek log home remains, as does the root cellar to the north on the hillside, accessible by a trail.

Other buildings include the bunkhouse for the ranch hands, which was rebuilt following a fire. The carriage shed was constructed in 1928 by subsequent owners. The barn now located on the Hornbek homestead was moved to the site during the renovation process. As one walks the homesteaded land once occupied by Adeline Hornbek, a sense of the people who lived in homesteads is greatly appreciated.

The Hornbek Homestead is a fine example of the American West and the women who helped to build it.

# Annie and Kitty Harbison
### Devoted Sisters to Family Ranching

The Homestead Act of 1862 particularly specified that no land would be acquired if levied against creditors for debts owed prior to the issuing of the land title. The final requirement was that the applicant must not have raised arms against the United States government or given aid and comfort to the enemy, which was a significant requirement at the time of enactment due to the ongoing Civil War. These particular provisions in the law would apply to the Harbison family, who applied for land under the Homestead Act in 1896, when Annie and Kitty Harbison filed adjoining homestead claims. Annie and Kitty Harbison's father, Andrew K. Harbison, a native of Pennsylvania, married Eliza Jane Green in January 1855. Three children would be born to this union. The first, Henry or "Harry," was born October 19, 1855. James was born a few years later, but died shortly after birth. When the Civil War tore the country apart in April 1861, thirty-year-old Andrew Harbison volunteered with Company D of the 184th Pennsylvania Regiment, where he served for the entire Civil War. Following the war, Harbison returned to his family in Philadelphia.

Approximately a year later, for reasons perhaps best left to family history, Harbison abandoned his family. Eliza Jane Harbison was pregnant with her third child, Clara Jane, born in early 1867.

On December 4, 1867, Andrew Harbison married Mary E. Quinlan in Rockport, Missouri. Again, for unknown reasons, Harbison had told his new wife that he was a widower. Here, they were joined by Harbison's twelve-year-old son, Harry. After their marriage, the couple moved to Brownsville, Nebraska, where Harbison began his new life. There, the first of three children, Annie Harbison, was born on September 5, 1868. Later, the family moved to Leavenworth, Kansas. Their second child, Kitty, was born in Leavenworth, September 16, 1872. A third child, Robert Andrew, was born July 6, 1876.

Kittie Harbison is shown on her beloved ranch in Grand County. *Kaufman House Museum*

In the summer of 1889, Andrew K. Harbison and his second family relocated again, this time to Denver, Colorado. For the next few years, Harbison operated a successful soap rendering business. During this time, Harbison filed on a homestead claim near Greeley.[1]

After two years in Denver, in 1891, Harry Harbison left Denver at the age of thirty-six to start his own business in Grand County. Harbison's idea was to acquire a homestead claim near Columbine Lake, where he could raise commercial trout and sell to the local miners. Unfortunately, Columbine Lake was a natural spring-fed lake which could not sustain the Rocky Mountain trout.[2] Undaunted, Harry Harbison spent two years digging a ditch, two miles long, from the Colorado River to Columbine Lake.

Andrew K. Harbison left his family in Denver while he ventured over the pass to visit his son and observe his business endeavor. Arriving in Grand Lake July 15, 1896, the elder Harbison liked what he saw. Furthermore, he became enchanted with the surrounding area. Harbison decided to join his son. His decision, no doubt, was in part made easier because he had lost his homestead claim near Greeley three years earlier, due to the economic depression of 1893. Harbison relocated his family yet again. Annie and Kitty, both in their early twenties, arrived on September 11, with Mary and young Robert arriving on November 1.

Annie Harbison had a wonderful garden on her mountain
ranch. *Kaufman House Museum*

The Harbison family immediately began the process
of filing for a homestead claim. Due to the provisions in the
Homestead Act of 1862, Andrew K. Harbison was not eligible
to file for a land claim as it had been less than five years since his
previous homestead claim. Nevertheless, Harbison found a nice
area located approximately two and a half miles north of the town
of Grand Lake. Because Harbison could not file for a homestead,
both of his daughters, Annie and Kitty, filed for the allotted 160
acres on adjoining land in the North Fork area of Grand County.
The claims for both Harbison sisters were granted in late 1896.
Andrew Harbison wrote in his journal of the progress being made
at the family's new home: "Since coming here we have done
considerable work on the girls' homesteads – built a cabin and
moved into it on January 8th."[3]

The cabin Harbison referred to was called the "Big Cabin"

by the family, and built on Annie's quarter-section. Another cabin was later constructed on Kitty's quarter-section, overlapping the two homesteads sections. In this way, the Harbison family were able to "prove-up" both homesteads at the same time. Older brother Harry's ditch provided fresh water for the family's needs, as well as for the land that would eventually be cultivated. In the meantime, Andrew Harbison's Civil War pension (four dollars a month), was the only source of income for the family. To help make ends meet, Annie and Kitty found work in the town of Grand Lake, working at the Kauffman Hotel, as well as taking on laundry and housecleaning for various residents.[4]

At the homestead, the sisters' parents, along with younger brother Robert, began preparation for cultivating the land. While Mary planted a sizable vegetable garden, Andrew and Robert cut trees and plowed portions of both homestead properties. The Harbisons were careful not to disturb the little hillside cemetery, located at the western edge of the Harbison sisters' homestead claims. Local ranchers and citizens of the town of Grand Lake had started the cemetery in 1875.[5] The Harbison family cared for the cemetery as time permitted, watering the many evergreen trees surrounding the graves, and Mary would often clear the burial sites of weeds, and even plant flowers.

With the remaining land cleared, Andrew planted a variety of crops. The added income provided by Annie and Kitty enabled the Harbison family to purchase a few dairy cows. This would be the beginning of the family's successful dairy farm. A large section of the homesteads was then devoted to a hay crop.

As the dairy operation began to prosper, the only one in Grand County, Annie and Kitty divided their work between their jobs in town and the much-needed work at the dairy ranch. During the severe winter of 1898-1899, Annie and younger brother, Robert, were returning from Grand Lake with a wagon load of supplies when they were caught in a blizzard. As Annie and Robert attempted to guide the horses through the storm, the horses began to sink in the fast-falling snow. Dismounting from the wagon, Annie and Robert grabbed the reins of the horses and led them, ever so

The Harbison Ranch in winter. *Kaufman House Museum*

slowly, through the deep snow to the safety of the Harbison barn.

The Harbison family were popular with all of the area ranchers. They welcomed their neighbors to the ranch with kindness and friendship. The open hospitality of the Harbison family became legendary in Grand County.

The "Harbison Girls," as they were known in the Middle Park area, were quite popular. One of the local boys from a neighboring ranch, Henry Schnoor, often stopped for a visit at the Harbison ranch. Schooner soon began courting Kitty. In time, Schnoor asked for Kitty Harbison's hand in marriage. Initially, Kitty accepted the proposal. However, after practical consideration, Kitty backed out of the engagement as kindly as she could. Kitty realized that marriage would mean her family would lose her homestead claim, and that her siblings, Annie and Robert, would have to care for both the ranch and her ailing parents without her help.

Kitty Harbison's notions were soon born out. During a routine trip to her stepson Harry's cabin near Columbine Lake, Mary Harbison's sleigh overturned. Mary was thrown to the frozen

The Harbison sisters weathered mountain storms and economic hardship to keep their ranch located in Grand County. *Kaufman House Museum*

ground. Although injured, Mary managed to unhitch the horse from the sleigh and ride back to the Harbison ranch. Mary's quick thinking probably saved her life. However, Mary's hip injury left her bedridden for several weeks.[6] Following her mother's accident, Kitty knew she had to stay on the family homestead and care for her parents and the ranch they had all worked so hard for.

With due diligence and perseverance, the Harbison ranch prospered. The adjoining homesteads had produced a fine dairy operation, serving neighbors and businesses in the town of Grand Lake. In addition to the inviting home cabins on both homesteads, the Harbison ranch included both a cow barn and horse barn. Along with the dairy cows, chickens and pigs were also raised. By this time, the cabins were adjoined, with one side serving as the living quarters and the other as kitchen and dining area.

The hard work paid off. In 1902, after five years, Annie and Kitty Harbison had "proved up" their homestead claims. The Harbison sisters received title to their land in the form of Homestead Patents #5569 and #5570, both signed by President Theodore Roosevelt.[7]

Annie and Kitty Harbison, however proud of their accomplishment, knew it was also due to the efforts and determination of their parents. The sisters were devoted to their parents, as well as to the family ranch. So much so, that neither Annie nor Kitty ever married.

By this time, the ranch was doing well and both Harbison sisters devoted their full attention to the operations of the dairy ranch. Both Annie and Kitty worked the fields, cutting and stacking the hay. They cared for their sizable dairy herd, feeding and milking the cows and cleaning the barns.

Tragedy struck the Harbison family in January 1906. Annie and Kitty's father, seventy-six-year-old Andrew Harbison, died on January 17, 1906. Following the funeral service, burial took place in the family plot of the local cemetery, located on the Harbison ranch property. Andrew K. Harbison became the first burial one encountered in that plot, as it was located near the entrance. His tombstone read, "Andrew K. Harbison – Aug. 19, 1830 – Jan. 17, 1906. Co. D 184th Reg Pa. Vol."

With the loss of their father, it now fell to Annie and Kitty to care for their aging mother, for by this time their younger brother Robert had married Murnie Hawkins. Sisters Annie and Kitty worked the family ranch. The daily demands of ranch work undoubtedly tested their patience. Yet their endurance proved to be the strength of their character. In an effort to help with the family expenses, Andrew's widow, Mary, applied for her husband's Civil War pension.

Annie and Kitty Harbison were able to expand their dairy herd. With the demand of their products, younger brother Robert delivered milk and ice to neighbors and businesses in Grand Lake. In 1907, a strange set of circumstances occurred that would alter not only the lives of the Harbison sisters, but the future of their homesteaded land. Quite unexpectedly, Henry Schnoor, Kitty's former fiancé, arrived at the Harbison ranch. Following Kitty's rejection to his proposal of marriage, Schnoor had gone on with his life, eventually marrying and moving to a small place on Green Mountain. Two children were born to this union, Beatrice and

153

Mary. During his trip to the Harbison ranch, Henry Schnoor was invited into the cabin where he visited with Kitty and her mother while Annie watched over three-year-old Beatrice and one-year-old Mary. Schnoor explained his situation to the Harbison women. He told them that his wife had left Green Mountain, deserting himself and their two little girls. Knowing he could not take care of two little girls and run his ranch, he became desperate. Schnoor had taken the girls to an orphanage in Denver. However, because little Mary was ill, the orphanage refused to take either child.[8] Schnoor was on his way back to Green Mountain from Denver when he decided to stop at the Harbison ranch. Perhaps due in part to concern for her former fiancé, Kitty discussed the matter with her mother and sister. The three Harbison women were soon in agreement: they would take the Schnoor girls and raise them as their own.

Not long after the Harbison women took in little Beatrice and Mary Schnoor, Mary Harbison received a letter from the government in reply to her Civil War pension application. The letter informed Mrs. Mary Harbison that Mrs. Eliza Jane Green Harbison had also applied for Andrew K. Harbison's Civil War pension. Shock and disbelief must have gone through Mary's mind. Before they were married, nearly forty years ago, Andrew had told Mary that his wife had died. After the shock of such a revelation wore off, an infuriated Mrs. Mary Harbison fired off a response to the government, contesting the other Mrs. Harbison's claim to the Civil War pension. The government's reply was that Mrs. Mary Harbison had to prove that she had the right to her husband's government pension. Mary Harbison set about an exhausting endeavor. Mary sent a parcel of evidence to the government. Along with her December 4, 1867, marriage certificate from Rockport, Missouri, Mary also included letters from her children by Andrew, proving that she had lived the past thirty-nine years as the wife of Andrew K. Harbison. In time, Mrs. Mary Harbison received her husband's Civil War pension.

The money from the government pension helped the Harbison women as they continued the work of their prosperous ranch. As the years went on, the Schnoor girls became a big help on the ranch. However, when Henry Schnoor remarried, Beatrice, then a teenager, chose to live with her father and his new wife. The younger Schnoor daughter, Mary (affectionately called Mamie by the Harbison women), chose to stay at the Harbison ranch, stating, "The Harbisons are my moms."[9] Beatrice Schnoor married at an early age and sadly died a short time later.[10]

Not long after the death of Beatrice, tragedy again struck the Harbison family. Mary Harbison, the matriarch of the Harbison family, died on April 3, 1923. Following the funeral service, Kitty and Annie buried their beloved mother next to her husband of nearly forty years, in the cemetery located on their land. The tombstone read, "Mary E. Harbison – Sept. 15, 1837 – April 3, 1923. At Rest, Rock of Ages."[11]

Annie and Kitty went on with the work of the ranch. Mary "Mamie" Schnoor, now sixteen years of age, was a great help to the two remaining Harbison women. Mamie enjoyed working on the Harbison ranch, which she called home. Mamie's particular duties included gathering hay, and feeding and milking the dairy cows. Robert Harbison, younger brother of Annie and Kitty, continued to deliver the Harbison family's dairy products to neighbors and Grand Lake businesses. His wife, Murnie, did as much as she could to help her sisters-in-law as well. Along with helping with the cooking and cleaning, Murnie also tended to the grave sites of Andrew and Mary Harbison. It was about this time that Robert Harbison built a fence around the cemetery.[12]

One of the Harbison ranch hands, Clyde "Red" Gudgel, took a fancy to Mamie Schnoor. With Annie and Kitty's consent, Gudgel began courting Mamie. When Gudgel proposed marriage, Mamie said yes. Following the wedding, Annie and Kitty threw an extravagant wedding reception at the ranch. The newlyweds continued to live and work at the Harbison ranch.

In 1928, officials with the Rocky Mountain National Park Service offered to purchase a portion of the Harbison land. Their purpose was to build a road into the park. Both Annie and Kitty refused to sell. However, the officials of the Rocky Mountain

National Park Service were persistent. Negotiations went on for nearly eight years. Finally, a Grand County judge and friend of the Harbison sisters intervened on behalf of both parties. Annie and Kitty Harbison agreed to sell the desired portion of their land only after the Rocky Mountain National Park Service officials agreed to construct the road through an area Kitty and Annie had selected.[13]

Not long after the construction of the road into Rocky Mountain National Park was completed, a portion of the historic Trail Ridge Road, the Harbison sisters built tourist cabins on their land and entered the tourist trade, accommodating summer guests at their ranch. Annie and Kitty offered home-cooked meals to their guests. Their Sunday dinners soon became legendary, and citizens from Grand Lake would often take a Sunday drive to the Harbison ranch just for the Harbison Sunday dinners.[14]

The Harbison sisters enjoyed their new tourist trade for the next few years. However, the fall season of 1938 brought an unusually cold snap to the North Fork Valley. By November of that year, both Annie and Kitty had contracted pneumonia. The illness caused a high fever, sending Kitty to her bed. Also stricken with a high fever, Annie persevered to care for her sister. For the first few days Annie managed to cook and clean despite her illness. All the while, Kitty was growing weaker. After five days, Annie could no longer care for her sister or herself. Mamie Schnoor Gudgel rushed to the "Big Cabin" to do what she could for the two women she had always considered her "moms." Robert and Murnie Harbison also came to offer their help. But there was little anyone could do but make the Harbison women as comfortable as possible.

At noon on Wednesday, November 8, 1938, Kitty Harbison died. She was sixty-six years old. Robert Harbison and "Red" Gudgel removed Kitty's body from the "Big Cabin," taking it to Kitty's own "little cabin" where Mamie and Murnie prepared the body for burial.

With Annie's weakening condition, everyone feared the news of her sister's death would be too much for her. Therefore, the family members chose not to tell Annie that Kitty had died. Annie lingered in and out of consciousness for the next five days.

On Sunday morning, November 13th, 1938, at the age of seventy, Annie Harbison died.[15]

The double funeral service was held at the Grand Lake Community House the following day, Monday afternoon, November 14, 1938. Charles Hulac, pastor of the Grand Lake Community Church, presided over the solemn ceremony for the two Harbison sisters, beloved by many in Grand County. Serving as pallbearers were Henry Schnoor, Al Bryant, Andrew Christianson, Robert Johnston, Len Osborn, and Sam Stone. Mrs. Arthur Link sang "Asleep in Jesus," "Crossing the Bar," and "Abide With Me."

Following the funeral service, Annie and Kitty Harbison were buried side by side near their parents in the Harbison family plot of the Grand Lake Cemetery. A single tombstone was placed in honor of the Harbison sisters.[16]

Mary "Mamie" Schnoor Gudgel inherited the Harbison ranch holdings. Mamie and her husband worked the ranch together for the next twenty years. Annie and Kitty's younger brother, Robert, and his wife, Murnie, also remained at the ranch. Robert continued to make his dairy deliveries for several years. Both Robert and Murnie took great pains to care for their relative's burial sites at the cemetery. Robert regularly ran the pump that delivered water to the graves, while Murnie maintained the grave sites. In time, spruce and pine grew high and boughs graciously dipped over the double grave site of Annie and Kitty Harbison.

After twenty years of ranching at the Harbison homestead, Mary "Mamie" Schnoor Gudgel sold her inherited property to the Rocky Mountain National Park. When the Harbison ranch was sold, Robert and his wife, Murnie, were forced to move, but still managed time to care for their loved ones buried in the Grand Lake Cemetery.

Some ten years later, the officials of the Rocky Mountain National Park Service proposed that the Harbison cabins and outbuildings be preserved. However, due to budget constraints, the proposal was denied.[17]

Murnie M. Harbison died on March 22, 1967. She was seventy years old. Her bereaved husband Robert buried her near his parents in the Harbison family plot in the cemetery on his family's former land. Not far from Murnie Harbison's burial site lay the graves of Murnie's brother, Harold Hawkins, and his wife. Robert Andrew Harbison, the last of the Harbison family, died at the age of ninety-five, on April 16, 1971. Harbison was buried next to his wife and near his parents and sisters in the Harbison family plot.

Not long after the death of Harbison, in 1973 a new superintendent at the Rocky Mountain National Park Service, following the Park Service's preservation of land, deemed the remaining Harbison buildings an eyesore to the beauty of the landscape that was the Rocky Mountain National Park. Therefore, the new superintendent ordered the destruction of the cabins that Annie and Kitty Harbison had constructed to "prove-up" their homestead claim in 1896. This horrific destruction of historic property eventually led to the dismal dismissal of the superintendent.[18]

Today, all that remains of the pioneering ranching women Annie and Kitty Harbison is their tombstone in the Grand Lake Cemetery, located on the land the sisters homesteaded more than a century ago.

# Notes

1. Beaton, *Colorado Women: A History*, pg. 91.
2. Lively, *The Harbisons: An Ordinary Family Who Led an Extraordinary Life*. Rocky Mountain National Park archives (hereafter *The Harbisons*)
3. Kauffman House Museum archives.
4. Lively, *The Harbisons*. Also see Beaton, *Colorado Women: A History*, pg. 91 (hereafter *Colorado Women*).
5. Wommack, *From the Grave*, pg. 128.
6. ibid. Also see Beaton, *Colorado Women*, pg. 92.
7. ibid.
8. Lively, *The Harbisons*. Also see Beaton, *Colorado Women*, pg. 93.
9. ibid.
10. Kauffman House Museum archives.
11. Wommack, *From the Grave*, pg. 128.
12. Kauffman House Museum archives.
13. Lively, *The Harbisons*. Also see Beaton, *Colorado Women*, pg. 94.
14. Kauffman House Museum archives.
15. Obituary clipping from an unknown newspaper, Kauffman House Museum archives.
16. Wommack, *From the Grave*, pg. 128.
17. Lively, *The Harbisons*. Also see Beaton, *Colorado Women*, pg. 94.
18. ibid.

DPL

DPL

# THE WESTERN SLOPE

## Annie Rudolph Huffington
**Pioneer Rancher**

## Bartley Marie Scott
**Alpine Meadows Ranch**

## Elizabeth Hutchison
**Routt County Pioneer**

# Annie Rudolph Huffington
**Pioneer Rancher**

Colorado natives, Annie and her twin sister Mary were born in Paonia on December 13, 1905, to David and Daisy Rudolph. Rudolph, a miner by trade, moved his family west to Burley, Idaho, when the twins were just toddlers. There, Rudolph found work in the local mines. However, in 1910 Rudolph relocated his family again, this time to better mining opportunities in the mines of Pitkin County.

In 1913, Annie's father moved the family back to Delta County where Annie had been born eight years earlier. For the next few years Rudolph found work in the local mines and supplemented his income by working for various farmers in the area. In time, Rudolph was able to provide a modest home for his family, five miles west of the town of Delta in the lower Roubideau Valley. By this time, the Rudolph family had grown to seven children.

When Annie was a young teenager, her life as she knew it, fell apart. Her parents divorced. Annie's mother, Daisy, was left to her raise her seven children alone. Daisy Rudolph found work wherever she could to support her children. Annie later recalled those difficult times: "Mom supported us by tending a big onion patch. I think that's why I hate onion patches to this day. You can't imagine what it was like going up and down those rows on your hands and knees weeding."[1]

Daisy Rudolph also worked at her brother's nearby farm, where he raised a variety of vegetables, including potatoes and onions. Annie remembered, "Mary and I got in on picking them up too. So I've got a lot of memories about onions and potatoes."[2]

Annie and her twin sister Mary drove a horse and buggy

163

five miles to attend high school in the town of Delta. In the winter months, the girls would heat rocks in the oven and then place them in coverings under their feet while they drove the buggy to school. Shortly after high school, Annie began seeing Nelson Huffington, who lived on a ranch in the Escalante Canyon, southwest of the town of Delta.

The Huffington family were one of the six original families that immigrated from England and settled in Delta. In 1859, Huffington's grandparents, Sylvester and Sarah Huffington, journeyed west from Illinois to Kansas by wagon train. From Kansas, the couple spent the next two years traveling further west, eventually arriving in the small settlement that would later become the town of Gunnison, Colorado, in early 1862. There, the men were able to secure temporary living quarters for their families and then continued on with their westward travels.

The men crossed Ohio Pass and entered the Uncompahgre River Valley, where they arrived at the Ute Indian trading post situated very near the original Fort Uncompahgre, burned by the Utes in 1846. The men liked what they saw of the fertile valley and decided to make this their home. After stocking up on supplies at the trading post, the men made the long journey back over Ohio Pass to the Gunnison area. Reuniting with their families, the men loaded the family possessions, food, and supplies into their wagons. Then, the six immigrant families set off for the Uncompahgre River Valley. The journey took three grueling months. The Ohio Pass was again crossed, as were a multitude of rivers and creeks. Annie Rudolph Huffington later recounted the trip as told to her by her in-laws: "There were no roads back then. They would go until they came to a draw they couldn't cross and then they had to dismantle everything and carry the wagon and its contents across piece by piece."[3]

Once the immigrant party arrived in the valley, preparations were made for suitable living quarters. This accomplished, the men began the process of establishing a town site, with Sylvester Huffington, along with George Crawford and

Henry Walker, initiating their plans.

Located at the junction of the Uncompahgre and Gunnison rivers, the men named their five-hundred-acre town site Uncompahgre City for the river, which meant "red water" in the Ute language. Isolated as it was, the town grew slowly. Huffington and other businessmen in the new town, in an effort to further promotion, changed the name to Delta.

Meanwhile, with Huffington's successful business dealings, in 1864 he built a two-story home for his family on West 5th Street, which still stands today. In this house Sarah Huffington gave birth to the couple's first child, the first to be born in the town of Delta. Sylvester and Sarah Huffington named their daughter Della, in honor of the town where she was born and which her father had founded.

More children were born to Sylvester and Sarah Huffington, including Oscar, Nelson Huffington's father. In 1898, Oscar Huffington filed for a homestead claim in the Escalante Canyon, southwest of the town of Delta.

In 1925, at the age of nineteen, Annie Rudolph and Nelson Huffington were married. Following the wedding, Nelson and Annie Huffington moved to the Huffington ranch home at Escalante Canyon. Annie later recalled the trip over the rough terrain: "We went out there in a wagon because they didn't have cars going out there then."[4]

Annie quickly settled into her new life on the ranch. Her husband dug a well close to the house so Annie could haul water to their log home. At the well, Annie would wash clothes in a tub with a scrub board. Annie grew her own vegetables in a small garden she planted near the house. Huffington dug a small depression in the bed of the creek where Annie could store her preserved fruits and vegetables. Annie also raised her own chickens and fed and milked the cows. The Huffington ranch house did not have electricity, so Annie cooked the meals on a wood stove and often used the large fireplace as well.

Along with her domestic chores, Annie worked alongside her husband in clearing the land for planting. After the crops were planted, it was Annie's job to operate the spraying machine. Every year Annie drove a team of horses to rake and mow hay which was then sold. If it was a good crop, the hard-working ranching couple would receive as much as five dollars a ton for their hay. Annie worked hard and took pride in her accomplishments. She later said, "I worked with my husband so long that I just knew what to do as good as any man."[5]

Year after year the Huffingtons operated their isolated ranch in the same routine, with an average annual income not exceeding four hundred dollars. When the crop did bring in good money, the couple made the long journey out of the canyon to Delta, where they would stock up on supplies and maybe a luxury item or two. Annie said, "We'd buy enough groceries for a month. People don't believe it today, but back then you could order your groceries from Montgomery Ward. We'd just send off for whatever we needed and they would get it to us the next week."

Despite their meager income, Annie and Nelson Huffington managed to save enough money to buy a few peach trees. Annie cared for the trees herself. She knew they would do well in the climate of the area and the sales of the fruit would eventually improve the Huffingtons' economic condition.

Meanwhile, the Huffingtons were granted a permit to graze five hundred head of cattle on the Uncompahgre Plateau very near their home. Over the next few years the Huffingtons managed to build their livestock enterprise. They applied for and received four additional grants to graze their cattle. The Huffingtons' operations proved to be a great success.

With the growing cattle ranch, Nelson and Annie Huffington were able to hire ranch hands. The couple offered the best wages they could afford during this time of the Great Depression, and with so many men out of work, the hired ranch hands were grateful for the work. Due to the remote location of their ranch, Huffington built a bunkhouse for his hired help. Huffington even managed to build a thirty-two-volt electrical system in 1940.

In addition to her domestic chores, ranching duties, and

caring for her beloved peach trees, Annie also prepared meals twice a day for as many as sixty men. Annie later recalled:

> I had a cooking job most of the time we were married. I cooked for the hands when they worked the cattle, when they pruned, when they thinned fruit and all through the harvest. It seems like all I did was cook and wash dishes. I had people tell me the only reason they came to work [for us] was for the food.

The Huffington's successful cattle enterprise afforded the couple modern conveniences in their remote location. Not long after the birth of the couple's son, Bonsall, electrical service was established in the remote canyon. Huffington purchased a modern refrigerator. Annie recalled, "We just graduated from one thing to the better."[6]

Another modern convenience acquired by the Huffingtons came about by pure happenstance. The tale is best described in Annie's own recollection:

> Nelson found a little bear cub that was so small he put it in his pocket and we made a pet out of it. We would bring it to town in an old Model T and feed him ice cream cones until he got cranky from being full. Finally, it got to the point where he was snapping the heads off the chickens and turkeys. We were thinking of getting rid of the bear when a guy offered us a new Maytag washer for him. Well, he took the bear off to the circus in California, but we heard later on the bear got loose and tore the tops off a lot of cars.[7]

The improved roads and the Huffingtons' automobile enabled Annie to travel to the town of Delta more frequently. With this occasional freedom from her ranching duties, Annie eventually became active in the Delta community.

One of the first organizations Annie joined was the Katherine Rebecca Lodge #65. Annie became a faithful member and later served as secretary, a position she dutifully held for forty-four years. Annie drove the thirty-five miles into Delta twice a month for all those years to attend the meetings. Annie also became a charter member of the Delta County CowBelles, as well as of the National CowBelle organization. A few years later, Annie joined the Ladies Encampment group where she served as scribe for forty-two years.

As the Huffingtons' cattle enterprise increased, the Huffingtons were able to build a cookhouse and bunkhouse at each of the five ranch locations. This allowed the hired hands a sense of comfort in the isolated area, as well as home-cooked meals.

The Huffingtons' beef became a prized commodity in all of Delta County, as well as throughout western Colorado. Annie's peach trees grew to a large orchard, one of the largest peach orchards in the state. For sixty-five years, Annie and Nelson Huffington worked their ranches and prospered in the remote Escalante Canyon.

When Nelson Huffington died in 1987, Annie moved to the town of Delta. Moving to town was a permanent move into the modern world for Annie Huffington. Among the modern conveniences available to Annie were an electric stove and oven, an electric washer and dryer, and a telephone.

Adjusting to living in town, Annie Huffington enjoyed driving her car to the grocery store, something she was never able to do with convenience in Escalante Canyon. She continued to be active with her many causes and organization affiliations. In 1992, at the age of eighty-seven, Annie joined the Ladies Auxiliary Patriarch Militants. Annie enjoyed being a member of the new group, although she remarked in an interview just days before her death, "You have to salute all the time. It's march, march, march [and] salute, salute, salute."[8]

Despite her advanced age, Annie maintained her natural hard-work ethic. She insisted on cutting her own grass with a gas-powered lawn mower, an invention she found amazing. Next to the carefully mowed lawn, she planted a garden. Annie also raised her own chickens and sold the eggs to local restaurants in town. Annie later commented, "I have never bought a town egg in my life."[9]

Annie Huffington adjusted well to life in the "city" after sixty-five years of ranch life in the remote Escalante Canyon. In her last years, Annie did reflect on her ranching life. She enjoyed the life and missed her beloved peach trees. Annie said, "It was a good life and I miss it."[10]

Annie, after all the years of feeding ranch hands, still enjoyed cooking for large groups. Just days before her death, she prepared a holiday dinner for members of her latest group, the Happy Hour Club. It is said her homemade fruit pies were a big hit among the group.

Annie Rudolph Huffington died on Saturday, December 23, 1995. She was ninety years old. The funeral service, held at the Taylor Mortuary in Delta, occurred on Thursday, December 28, 1995, with burial in the Delta Cemetery, next to her husband and ranching partner of sixty-five years.

## Notes

1. The *Delta County Independent*, December 26, 1995.
2. ibid.
3. ibid.
4. ibid.
5. ibid.
6. ibid.
7. ibid.
8. ibid.
9. ibid.
10. ibid.

# *Bartley Marie Scott*
## Alpine Meadows Ranch

B artley Marie Scott, a Colorado native, was born on March 28, 1896, on her family's homestead in the Dallas Creek Valley, near Ridgway, Colorado. The second child of Bartley and Ida Culver Scott, she was blessed with her father's blue eyes and red hair; thus she was named for her father. By the time she was eight years old, Marie, as she was known, could rope cattle from horseback.

Marie's father, Bartley Scott, had journeyed west with his parents from Sand Hill, Missouri, in 1882. First settling in the growing mining town of Ouray, Colorado, Bartley Scott soon filed for a homestead claim. By the spring of 1883, Scott had moved to the lush valley along Dallas Creek, approximately ten miles north of Ouray. There, Scott began preparations to "prove-up" his claim.

Scott would often make trips for supplies about a mile further north to the small ranching community of Ridgway. With Scott's frequent trips to the town, he soon became a popular figure. In 1890, Ida Josephine Culver arrived in Ridgway to accept a teaching position in the town's one-room schoolhouse. Ida Culver was a very practical and perceptive woman. Following her first year as the town's school teacher, Ida managed to purchase a home of her own in Ridgway. With Ridgway being such a small town, it was inevitable that Scott, the bachelor rancher, and Ida, the school mar 'm, would eventually meet. After courting for a year, the two were wed in Ridgway in 1893. While Ida Josephine Culver Scott quit her teaching position of three years to become a rancher's wife, she refused to sell her house in town.

Ida settled quite easily into her new life. A year later, Ida and Bartley Scott welcomed their first child, Lorraine. Both Scott girls, Lorraine and Marie, enjoyed a yearly childhood on the family ranch. Sadly, their innocent years were disrupted with the death of their father.

In 1904, thirty-four-year-old Bartley Scott died, possibly from stomach cancer. Bartley Marie Scott's life changed forever. Her beloved father, who had taught her how to rope and ride, was gone. Yet Marie's strong character and work ethic would be shaped by her mother as she worked alongside her to continue what her father had started.

With hard work and the help of her daughters, Ida Scott was able to continue the small cattle enterprise and, in time, even enlarge it. Ida gave the girls chores which were expected to be done. Marie was charged with clearing the hayfields as well as doing a good share of the cooking and cleaning. All the while, Marie was expected to keep up with her school work. It was a grueling routine for a young adolescent, but Marie relished the challenge. Marie quickly learned the seasonal routine of cattle ranching. She helped during the spring calving, cut the hay in the summer, worked the fall roundups, and participated in the winter feeding.

Marie loved working on the ranch, so much so that she quit school after the eighth grade. Her mother, a former teacher, obviously disappointed at her daughter's decision not to finish her education, realized her daughter's strong will. Ida Scott therefore relented and allowed Marie to continue with her work at the ranch.

During the next three or four years Marie would often take in stray calves. She cared for them herself and in time had a small herd of cattle she could call her own. Then, at the age of sixteen, Marie informed her mother that she intended to buy her own ranch.[1]

Following her mother's example, Marie set out to earn her own independence. With money she had borrowed, Marie purchased her first piece of land at the foot of Dallas Divide, in the Alpine Meadows area of Ouray County, just west of Ridgway.

The Dallas Pleasant Valley Woman's Club. Bartley Marie Scott is shown second from right. *Ouray County Ranch House Museum*

Not surprisingly, Marie did very well for herself. Over the next several years, she bought and sold cattle and improved the quality of her cattle herd. Marie also made substantial improvements on her ranch. In time, various outbuildings, including barns and sheds, were added, as well as additional corrals. The ranch-house was comfortable, yet modest, much as Marie herself was. It was a small framed house, but had a large kitchen, which included a large wood-burning cookstove, as Marie loved to cook. Her home had large windows all around which provided wonderful views of Dallas Divide and the lush green valley surrounding her ranch.[2]

During the years of the Great Depression, Colorado's industrial base, including the cattle industry, suffered economically as did the rest of the country. With almost no market for her cattle, Marie resorted to hunting elk and deer, selling the meat to local markets.[3] The income helped for a time, but Marie was soon forced to find a paying job, the only time she strayed from her beloved ranch. Marie took a job with the U. S. Land Bank, which required quite a bit of travel. Before leaving for a trip to Kansas City, she managed to sell a few head of cattle. Transporting the cattle to the railroad shipping point at Placerville, over the Dallas Divide, Marie received half of the sale price. When the cattle arrived at the Denver stockyards, Marie received the balance of her $7,000 sale. Before Marie left Denver, she placed a call to her mother, letting her know that a wire transfer would be sent to the bank in Ridgway. However, Ida Scott informed her daughter that the bank had recently closed. Now, Marie had thousands of dollars in cash at her disposal in a depressed economy.

Marie completed her Kansas City trip for the U. S. Land Bank and promptly quit her job. She returned to her Colorado ranch and began buying adjacent land. Prices were exceedingly low during the Depression years and Marie was able acquire more than three thousand acres at well below market value. With this purchase, Marie was able to increase her property holdings as far as thirty miles north, to the small town of Norton.

Not long after this land purchase, Marie made a trip to Telluride to purchase cattle. There, she met Robert "Bob" Valiant, a local cattle rancher. Marie, interested in Valiant's Hereford cattle, engaged Valiant in conversations regarding his cattle operation. Over time the couple grew close and eventually married. The marriage did not last long. Thirty-four-year-old Marie had married a much older man and the age difference proved to be too much to overcome. The divorce was final on July 26, 1937.

Following the divorce, not only did Bartley Marie Scott reclaim her maiden name, she bought out all of her ex-husband's cattle interests. Marie had a great sense of humor and later had this to say about her failed marriage: "I traded him off for twelve cats some time ago and have been better off since."[4]

Marie continued her seemingly never-ending quest for land. Much of this was acquired through foreclosures or from defaulted tax situations. Marie's brother-in-law, Lorraine's husband William Harney, later wrote, "If a bucket of dirt was for sale, Marie would buy it."[5]

With her enlarged land holdings and successful cattle enterprise, Marie hired more ranch hands. One of these men was her former husband, Bob Valiant. Despite her feelings about the failed marriage, Marie respected Valiant's knowledge of Hereford cattle. With Valiant's expertise, advice, and guidance, Marie purchased prized Hereford bulls from Texas. Marie fed her cattle with the hay grown on her ranch and added a precise mixture of oats and grains. In time, Marie was able, with careful breeding of Hereford cattle, to "get renowned specimens of the best cattle on the Western Slope."

Marie soon discovered that her Hereford cattle acclimated quite well to the high altitude of the Colorado Rocky Mountain region. The cattle were able to endure the harsh winter conditions and produce healthy calves in the spring.

Bartley Marie Scott proved herself to be equally as hard-working as her ranch hands. By working long days alongside her hired hands and not asking anyone to do tasks she would not do herself, Marie earned the respect of her employees. Marie felt the same about those who were loyal to her. Years later, when her ex-husband fell ill, Marie provided the necessary funds for his health care. Following the death of Robert Valiant, Marie commented, "He wasn't much of a husband, but he was a hell of a good hired hand."[6]

Marie's land grab continued, and the five-foot-tall redhead, weighing barely a hundred pounds, was a force to be reckoned with in a heretofore man's world. Brent Jensen, a young Bureau of Land Management employee, had many dealings with Marie Scott and the two became friends.

By the 1950s, she owned more than 100,000 acres, stretching west from her Alpine Meadows Ranch, west of Ridgway, to the Utah state line. More ranch hands were hired just to tend and repair the nearly three hundred miles of fence.

Cattle ranchers from all over the state came to Marie's ranch to purchase her prized Hereford bulls. About this time Marie joined the Cattlemen's Association and was also accepted into the National Western Stock Show. It was at this venue that Marie showcased her prized Hereford bulls.

Marie was one of the first in the region to diversify into grazing cattle and sheep. Marie hired Charlie Cristelli to herd the

Bartley Marie Scott's ranch can be seen just outside of Ridgway. *Ouray County Ranch House Museum*

sheep, always careful to separate them from the cattle. Cristelli built separate gates on the Scott land for the sheep and tended to the births of the new lambs. Cristelli, one of Marie's most loyal employees, insisted on living in his small trailer, which he could move with the roaming of the sheep herd. He would work for Marie for more than fifty years.

Another loyal employee was Mario Zadra, whom Marie hired when Zadra was just a teenager. As a hired hand, Zadra did a bit of everything on Marie's ranch. He enjoyed the diversity of the many odd jobs Marie assigned him to. Zadra would remain in Marie's employ for nearly all of his adult life. Shortly before his death, Zadra was interviewed by the *Denver Post*. He referred to Bartley Marie Scott as his "second mother."[7] Duane Wilson was another devoted employee. He was foreman of Marie's Alpine Meadows Ranch until the day she died.

Through her many land dealings, Marie became somewhat of an expert at land and water rights. Marie used her expertise in water rights to build one of the largest irrigation systems on the western slope. Marie's water project covered nearly all of her

100,000 acres, west to the Utah state line.[8]

Marie knew the value of water. It was crucial for her land and livestock. Therefore, Marie had an ongoing battle with beavers in the creeks and small rivers that ran through her land. Marie would carry dynamite and blasting caps with her as she rode the range. When she saw beaver dams she would use her arsenal of weapons to destroy the dams.[9]

Not long after the irrigation achievement in Marie's legendary ranching career, she was interviewed for an article which later appeared in the nationally-known publication, *The Farm Quarterly*. At the end of the glowing article, describing her as a "fiery redhead" and extolling all of the Colorado's western slope cattle queen's accomplishments, the article ended with, "Marie Scott never sleeps—Marie Scott ain't human."[10]

Now in her sixties, it was clearly obvious that Marie Scott was indeed human. After years of tending her cattle on horseback, she now rode the range in the comfort of her jeep. Marie remained determined to work her ranch as long as she could. It was her life; it was what she loved more than anything. Marie later said, "Every morning I hit the floor at 4:30. I work 'cause I like to."[11]

Marie had always managed her own account records of her many ranch holdings and livestock sales and purchases. It was an unconventional system at best, but it worked for Marie. However, as Marie grew older and her eyesight grew weaker, she realized she needed someone she could trust to take over the enormous task of managing the accounts of her ranch dealings. Marie respected her loyal employees, but had little regard for most everyone else. Marie had no tolerance for shoddy work or underhanded dealings, something she often called "monkey business." Marie once said, "The more I know of people, the more I like my dog."[12]

Marie turned to her most trusted friend, Mabel "Sally" Lewis. Lewis took on the daunting task of putting Marie's accounting in order. She gathered the many notebooks, papers and files that were scattered all over Marie's house, for her only "office" had been her oak dining room table. As Lewis managed Marie's accounts, one of the first things she did was sell Marie's cherished red Jeeps. Then Lewis acquired a pink Cadillac in which she drove Marie around the ranch. Friends of Marie's, including Howard Talbert and Mario Zadra, were shocked that Marie allowed the sale of her Jeeps. Lewis serve as Marie's general caretaker until the day Marie died. Marie had also appointed Lewis as the executor of her will, which would become a point of contention following Marie's death.

As methodical as Marie was in acquiring her massive land holdings, she was equally methodical in the sale of much of her land. Marie enlisted the advice of her trusted employee, Mario Zadra. Marie and Zadra spent long hours at her dining room table discussing how best to diversify her wealth as her health continued to decline. Marie contacted Brent Jensen, the young employee at the Bureau of Land Management, who had aided Marie in many of her land acquisitions.

With the help of both men, Bartley Marie Scott began liquidating her assets. This enormous land sale was an obvious attempt to avoid the exorbitant estate tax laws in place during the 1970s.[13] Mario Zadra was able to purchase several parcels of Marie's land, at a fair price, as were other close friends of Marie's. After Marie's death, these legal land sales would be questioned by Marie's family as well as other heirs named in her will.

Following this liquidation of assets, Marie's one-time 100,000 acres of ranch land was reduced to just over 25,000 acres. Bartley Marie Scott had spent her entire adult life realizing her lifelong dream: a ranch of her own. She had exceeded everyone's expectations by developing one of the largest ranches on the western slope. Now, her beloved Alpine Meadow Ranch was reduced to a quarter of what she had spent a lifetime building.

After the sale of land, Mario Zadra continued to council Marie. Zadra also strongly advised Marie to make legal arrangements to protect her remaining property.[14] Marie followed his advice and had a will drawn up. It would be another source of contention following her death.

As Marie's heath declined and with her eyesight nearly gone, she reached out to her close friends and asked them to come to her home at what remained of the Alpine Meadows Ranch. One of the first to visit the ailing woman was her foreman, Duane Wilson. Marie informed him during their conversation that she was leaving her ranch house to him. Another devoted employee and advisor, Mario Zadra, visited several times. During their many long conversations over the next several months, Zadra later recalled one of the last things Marie said to him, "This place is going to be yours. Clean it up."

At the time Zadra did not know what Marie meant, but as time went on her meaning would become clear, at least in his mind.

Brent Jensen was another who came to visit Marie at her request. Jensen, the Bureau of Land Management employee who had helped Marie with selling much of her land, had developed a close friendship with Marie over the years. According to Jensen, Marie told him, "I have these heirs and you are one of them."[15] Jensen went on to say, "You could have knocked me over with a feather."

Howard Talbert, another loyal employee for many years, was also summoned for a visit with Marie. Talbert had always displayed a strong work ethic that Marie greatly admired. Talbert visited Marie several times as her health continued to decline. During one of these visits Talbert's wife, Frances, later termed a "business meeting," Marie informed Howard Talbert that he was named in her will and that he would receive a portion of her land, as Frances Talbert later recalled, "She [Marie] was going to leave him some land where he could run his cattle."[16]

Brent Jensen and Mario Zadra were two of the last close friends to see Marie before she died. Jensen later recalled the situation he encountered, saying Marie was "living in a strange situation reminiscent of Howard Hughes." Jensen described how all the furniture in Marie's home was covered with sheets, and during his visit with Marie she was "propped up in a chair in the kitchen, and draped in a sheet." Mario Zadra, on one of his last visits with his friend, was given a blanket that Marie had once placed over her couch. That very same sofa was moved into the kitchen shortly after Jensen and Zadra's last visits. There, with her eyesight nearly gone, and the loss of physical movement, Marie was made as comfortable as possible in her final days.

On November 5, 1979, Bartley Marie Scott died at the age of eighty-three.

Despite her wealth, Bartley Marie Scott, once the largest land owner on the western slope, requested a simple ending to her extraordinary life. It was typical of this otherwise ordinary woman. At the funeral service all of Marie's closest friends and very few of the remaining family members paid their final respects. Marie lay in a simple wooden coffin, dressed in Levi jeans and a red western jacket.[17] Burial followed in the Ridgway Cemetery, not far from Marie's ranch.[18] The burial service was equally simple, adhering to Marie's wishes. Marie's common casket, covered with roses, was placed under a tall pine tree near graves of her parents and other family members.

Following the death of Bartley Marie Scott, the executor of her will, Mabel "Sally" Lewis, revealed the details. There were twelve heirs to the remaining property of the legendary female rancher. One of the heirs, Denise Adams, was not yet twenty-one years old. She later commented, "The 'dirty dozen,' we were called."[19]

Marie's attorney, William Waldeck, received a portion of the land, as did Richard "Dick" Swyhart, a heavy equipment operator who did many jobs for Marie, and Howard Noble, a nearby rancher and county water commissioner. Delbert Frasier, a feed salesman and longtime friend of Marie's, was named in the will, as well as Fred Richardson, who had worked for Marie for years. Charlie Cristelli, the loyal sheepherder, and Brent Jensen, the Bureau of Land Management employee, were also named as heirs, as Marie had promised them. Another heir named in the will was Marie's friend and executor, Mabel "Sally" Lewis.

Marie's few family members were not mentioned in the will, and this caused much consternation. Denise Adams, who received over ten percent of Marie's land, later said, "There were a lot of other bad names [called] and a lot of jealousy."[20]

Three loyal friends and employees to whom Marie had promised land—Howard Talbert, Mario Zadra, and Duane Wilson—were not listed as heirs in the will. Mario Zadra later commented, "Some people were added to the will, I don't know what the scoop was. I didn't want to know."

Howard Talbert's wife, Frances, later recalled, "He [Howard] had worked so hard. He felt so cheated."[21]

While Lewis was charged with executing the division of Marie's land, as stipulated in the will, Duane Wilson continued to live at the Alpine Meadows Ranch, maintaining the property and overseeing the ranch hands.

Meanwhile, Marie's distant family members, as well as several of the heirs, began raising questions about the validity of the will. David G. Wood, Marie's personal banker, later recalled: "The phone was always ringing. There were relatives who were shocked at not getting anything. There were people claiming to be cousins and other people who said she had promised them something." Brent Jensen remembered, "It was like a bunch of chickens fighting over the wheat. People being people, once she was gone, I don't think she had a clue what would happen."[22]

When the twelve heirs received their share of the inheritance, Lewis auctioned off the remainder of Marie's land. When this transaction was completed, Duane Wilson was forced to move off the ranch.

With high interest rates of the 1970s, the estate of Bartley Marie Scott owed the Internal Revenue Service nearly seventy percent of the auction proceeds, approximately seven million dollars. For the next few years, Lewis only paid the interest on the amount owed to the IRS. This had a rippling effect with several of the heirs.

Some of the heirs who did not receive land were bequeathed a monetary amount. The disbursement of these monies were made yearly from Marie's estate, managed by Lewis. These particular heirs realized their yearly inheritance check was less, as the tax interest payments had begun to cut into their share of the inheritance. When several of these heirs questioned Lewis and she failed to take any action, they petitioned the county court to have Lewis removed as executor of Marie's estate. The court agreed to the request and David G. Wood, who had served as Marie's personal banker, became the personal representative for the estate. Wood later recalled, "A lot of people just didn't know what was going on. And a lot of people made it their business to question what was going on."

One of those who "made it their business to question" was Howard Talbert. Howard and Frances Talbert took their case to court, suing the estate of Bartley Marie Scott. David G. Wood, acting as executor of the estate, along with attorneys, represented the interests of the estate.

Curiously, about the time the Talbert's case was coming to trial, Mabel "Sally" Lewis, the former executor of Marie's estate, left the country with her husband. The couple purchased an oceanside villa in Mexico. Several heirs, as well as the Talberts, strongly believed, although never proved, that Lewis left the country with more than her share of the inheritance Marie had left her. Mario Zadra was one of those that questioned Lewis' sudden departure. He remembered the comment Marie had made to him during one of the last visits before she died: "This place is going to be yours. Clean it up." Zadra now believed he knew what Marie meant. He thought it had to do with individuals who were aiding Marie with her business affairs as her health was declining.

The Talberts spent the next five years in and out of the courtroom. Finally, as a settlement seemed possible, the Talberts were given access to the property records and land contracts. It was a mound of confusing paperwork, which the Talberts suspected Lewis created deliberately. During one court session, Frances Talbert, frustrated at trying to make sense of the records, asked the court, "Where did the pink Cadillac go?" The judge asked David G. Wood, executor of Marie's estate, to clarify the question. Wood replied that the pink Cadillac actually belonged to Mr. and Mrs. Lewis. This answer, with no supportive paperwork, eventually led to a final settlement. After taxes, Howard and Frances Talbert received approximately eighty thousand dollars.

The estate of Bartley Marie Scott was again contested in the courts a year later. On December 31, 1986 a case was filed with the Colorado Court of Appeals, Div. II: The Estate of Marie Scott a/k/a Bartley Marie Scott, Deceased, Robert E. Brice and Mt. Sneffles Company, Claimants-Appellants, v. David G. Wood, Personal Representative-Appellee, No. 85CA0739.The charges against Marie's estate read in part:

> On February 17, 1982, pursuant to a contract entered into with claimant Brice, the Estate conveyed a portion of real property which the decedent had owned to Brice who thereafter conveyed the property to Mt. Sneffles. On June 9, 1982, the Estate conveyed the identical property to Mt. Sneffles by quitclaim deed. The property description in each of these deeds is identical. It is undisputed that the description omits land which the parties intended to include, and includes land which they intended to exclude.[23]

David G. Wood, acting on behalf of the estate of Bartley Marie Scott, lost the case filed against the estate and promptly appealed, based on a mistaken land survey. Judges Smith, Kelly and Van Cise filed their written summation of the appeal, which contained the following opinions:

> In 1984 the same mistake in the legal description was carried forward into a deed given by the Estate to a third party conveying land adjoining the land sold to the claimants. This third party, however, caused a survey to be made based on the description contained in its deed and erected a fence on the boundary line as disclosed by the survey. Thus, the claimants and the estate then became aware of the mistaken property description contained in the deed. The claimants thereupon filed their claims against the Estate seeking reformation of the deeds or, alternatively, for the imposition of a constructive trust on the funds paid to the Estate for the sale of the land to the third party. The Estate declined to reform its deed to the third

party, and it rejected the claims of Brice and Mt. Sneffles as barred by the statute of nonclaims,15-12-803(2)(a), C.R.S.[24]

The judges further wrote:

Because the statutory definition of the term 'claim' contains exceptions which do not specifically address disputes concerning title which arise during administration of the estate, and because the decedent here had no title after her death, this dispute is a claim subject to 15-12-803(2), C.R.S., which provides: "All claims against a decedent's estate which arise at or after the death of the decedent, including claims of the state and any subdivision thereof, whether due or to become due, absolute or contingent, liquidated or unliquidated, founded on contract, tort, or other legal basis, are barred against the estate, the personal representative, and the heirs and devisees of the decedent, unless presented as follows: (a) A claim based on a contract with the personal representative, within four months after performance by the personal representative is due; (b) Any other claim, within four months after it arises."

The appellate judges further concluded that:

In this case, both claimants and the estate agree that the mutual mistake in the deeds was not discovered by either of them until the estate conveyed the adjacent land to a third party on July 5, 1984, and the third party erected a boundary fence pursuant to an accurate survey. Claimants presented their claim to the estate on September 11, 1984, well within four months from discovery of the mistake. Thereafter, the estate offered rescission as a remedy. When this offer was refused the estate adopted its present position. We hold that the claim was timely under 15-12-803(2)(b), C.R.S. We hold that the performance due by the personal representative was not the original issuance of the deeds, but rather, it was the duty to reform the deeds, or otherwise correct the error, upon discovery of the mutual mistake. Also, we hold that under 15-12-803(2)(b), C.R.S., the claim asserted by claimants did not arise until July 5, 1984, when the mistake was discovered. Thus, the claim was timely filed under 15-12-803(2), C.R.S. To hold otherwise would cut off plaintiffs' rights even before they were aware of the existence thereof.

Finally, the judges ruled:

We hold that the claim asserting the equitable right to imposition of a constructive trust was likewise timely filed under 15-12-803(2)(b). That claim, which is alternative to the reformation claim, results from the fact that on July 5, 1984, the estate conveyed to a third party a portion of the land which it had originally agreed to convey to claimants and which was erroneously excluded from the original deeds. Claimant's entitlement, if any, to imposition of a constructive trust for its benefit, thus, could not have arisen unless, and until, the estate either received, or was entitled to receive, payment for the land to which claimants assert an equitable right.

Bartley Marie Scott, a remarkable woman in a man's world, single-handedly built the largest ranch on Colorado's Western Slope. However, when her health began to decline, she did her best to protect her assets and take care of her loyal friends. In her declining years, she may have sensed that her financial matters were being compromised, for Marie had made the comment to Mario Zadra, "This place is going to be yours. Clean it up."[25]

During her lifetime, Bartley Marie Scott was respected as a forthright honest woman. In all of her land dealings, Marie had no tolerance for underhanded or scrupulous financial transactions. Marie often used the colorful term, "monkey business" when referring to such actions. The monkey business that occurred with Marie's estate following her death was something she would have never tolerated in life.

For those who did benefit from the death of Bartley Marie Scott, they referred to their inheritance as "Marie's money."

Perhaps Brent Jensen said it best: "Really the payoff for me was having associated with her. For me, that was worth more than the money."

## Notes

1. Sammons, *Riding, Roping, and Roses*, pg. 24.
2. Colorado Women's Hall of Fame 2010 inductee, Bartley Marie Scott.
3. Ridgway Museum archives.
4. Sammons, *Riding, Roping, and Roses*, pg. 24.
5. Ridgway Museum archives.
6. Sammons, *Riding, Roping, and Roses*, pg. 26.
7. The *Denver Post*, August 15, 2010.
8. Colorado Women's Hall of Fame 2010 inductee, Bartley Marie Scott.
9. Sammons, *Riding, Roping, and Roses*, pg. 26.
10. The *Farm Quarterly*, Fall 1960.
11. The *Denver Post*, May 29, 1983.
12. ibid.
13. The *Denver Post*, August 15, 2010.
14. ibid.
15. ibid.
16. ibid.
17. Sammons, *Riding, Roping, and Roses*, pg. 33.
18. The cemetery, located two miles west of Ridgway, is the old Dallas Cemetery, situated on Dallas Divide Road (Colorado Highway 62). Wommack, *From the Grave*, pg. 443.
19. The *Denver Post*, August 15, 2010.
20. ibid.
21. ibid.
22. ibid.
23. Colorado Court of Appeals, Div. II.
24. ibid.
25. The *Denver Post*, August 15, 2010.

# *Elizabeth Hutchison*
## Routt County Pioneer

Elizabeth Doggett Hutchinson was the first woman rancher of Steamboat Springs. As such, she may have been a victim of a land grab.

Not much is known of her early life. She was born in Maysville, Mason County, Kentucky, in 1832.[1] She married at a young age and the couple purchased a small parcel of land near Hannibal, Missouri, which they set about farming. In due course, Elizabeth bore two daughters, Martha and Katherine.

When the Civil War broke out, Elizabeth's husband enlisted in the Confederate Army. Elizabeth continued to farm their land and raise her daughters alone. It is not known when or how her husband died; however, by war's end, Elizabeth was a widow at the age of thirty-three.

Within a year Elizabeth hired a man to help her with the menial labor of the farm. It would prove to be a fortuitous decision.

Frisbie Dewey Hutchinson was born in Canaan, Columbia County, New York, on June 6, 1844. The son of Benjamin Baldwin and Clarissa Dewey Hutchinson, he was named for his mother's first cousin, Navy Admiral George Dewey. Frisbie received his formal education in Canaan, after which the family moved to Michigan, where Benjamin engaged in farming.[2]

As soon as Hutchinson turned eighteen he enlisted in the Seventeenth Michigan Infantry, on July 21, 1862. Hutchinson was a private soldier serving with Company C. He and his fellow soldiers saw action in seventeen battles, including one that earned them the moniker of the "Stonewall Regiment." On May 12, 1864, Frisbie Hutchinson was taken prisoner at Spottsylvania Courthouse

This is believed to be the only known photograph of Elizabeth Hutchinson,
shown with her ex-husband and child. *Legacy Ranch, Steamboat Springs*

in Virginia. He was incarcerated at the Andersonville prison in
Georgia until the close of the war. In April 1865, when the war
ended, Hutchinson had been imprisoned for eleven months.
Following his release, Hutchinson was sent to Camp Chase, Ohio,
for medical attention, as his health had severely deteriorated. He

was mustered out of service on June 10, 1865.[3]

Returning to Michigan, Hutchinson furthered his education. He enrolled in an auctioneer school and eventually learned the trade of stonemason. Apparently neither trade allowed for a decent living, or else Hutchinson grew bored. In any case, by 1866 Hutchinson found himself in the employ of Elizabeth Doggett.

While Hutchinson managed to perform his farm chores, he did suffer from weakness from time to time. During one particular health crisis, Elizabeth nursed Hutchinson back to health, staying by his side through the ordeal. As often is the case, the two grew close, and on October 10, 1867, Elizabeth Doggett married Frisbie Dewey Hutchinson. The bride was thirty-four and the groom was twenty-three. The couple continued with the farm. To help make ends meet, Hutchinson took a variety of jobs, including auctioneer work and selling life insurance for the German Life Insurance Company of Rockford, Illinois, as well as the Home and Phoenix of New York.

In 1881, the Hutchinson family traveled to Colorado where Frisbie's parents had relocated in 1872. The couple stayed with his parents in Montezuma for three months. So encouraged by the improvement of his health, Elizabeth and Frisbie returned home to make plans for a permanent move to Colorado. Three years later, Hutchinson traveled alone to Colorado where he rented a ranch ten miles north of Denver. Here he lived for over a year, learning how farm irrigation worked in an arid state, the management of topsoil crops, and the economics of western farming.

Finally, in 1885, the Hutchinsons sold their farm and made the permanent move to Colorado. A year later, Frisbie Hutchinson preempted a section of land six miles southwest of Yampa, Colorado. He would later file a homestead claim on an additional 130 acres.[4]

It is interesting to note that at this time Elizabeth was living in Steamboat Springs. She began investing in several businesses as well as acquiring land in Routt County. Elizabeth either paid cash for these acquisitions or managed to obtain bank loans. This sudden influx of cash and credit leads one to believe she and Frisbie possibly separated and Elizabeth received a cash settlement. In any case, the two are never again linked together despite both living in the same county.

Elizabeth purchased a very successful coal mine in the Twentymile area of Oak Creek, southwest of Steamboat Springs. Elizabeth's Hutchinson mine provided her with enough income that soon she was independently wealthy. This allowed more investments, which brought more wealth.

In 1890, Elizabeth's older daughter, Martha, along with her husband, Bud Hoskinson, and their three daughters, Meda, Murl, and Mona, moved to Steamboat Springs. Elizabeth must have been thrilled to have family, particularly her granddaughters, with her in Colorado. With financial security and family at her side, Elizabeth filed for divorce in Routt County in 1893. Her divorce was granted on September 20, 1893.[5]

Elizabeth filed a homestead claim in 1898 with the intent of operating a ranch. The land, 130 acres, was located one mile south and west of Steamboat Springs. Within a year she had proved up her claim and received title to the land. While Elizabeth built outbuildings and hired men to plant hay, the Hutchinson Ranch was strictly a working ranch, thus Elizabeth did not live on the property.

After the first successful hay crop, Elizabeth sold her ranch in 1900. So successful were subsequent hay crops that the land became known as "The Haymeadows." Herbert J. Kilburn purchased the property and continued with its hay operation.

Sixty-seven-year-old Elizabeth was not done investing.[6] With her proceeds, she purchased additional parcels of land, including a section of land in the Fairview Addition of Steamboat Springs. On September 15, 1904, Elizabeth filed on 130 acres in Township 1 North, Range 85 West, Section 26, in Routt County.

Shortly after the purchase of additional property, various real estate groups—the powerful Yampa Valley Land and Cattle Company, for one—and landowners began to file lawsuits against Elizabeth. The town of Steamboat Springs was booming and ranch land in Routt County commanded premium prices. Therefore, Elizabeth's land holdings were a desired commodity. While Elizabeth vigorously fought the lawsuits, her finances quickly dwindled. It is most likely that this was the desired effect by those who sued her. Eventually, they got her land.

It was also during this time that Elizabeth began to suffer from ill health. She moved in with her daughter Martha and her family. Unfortunately, her health did not improve. It is possible Elizabeth suffered from the diseases of Alzheimer's or dementia, as she would wander off from Martha's home and be gone for days. Over the years Elizabeth's condition worsened. Eventually, after years of unsuccessful medical attention, Martha was forced to take drastic measures. In 1910, Martha presented her mother's case to a Routt County judge in an effort to have Elizabeth judged insane.

Judge Charles A. Morning agreed to hear the case. The inquest procedure was conducted in the small county courthouse facilities at Hahns Peak, the county seat of Routt County. Because court cases dealing with the insane were extremely rare, the Routt County newspapers covered the procedures on their front pages. An example is the June 24, 1910, issue of the *Yampa Leader*. Under the headline, "Mrs. Hutchinson Insane," the following article appeared:

> Mrs. Elizabeth Hutchinson of Steamboat was taken to Hahn's Peak by Sheriff Campbell yesterday, and an inquisition is being held today to pass upon her sanity. It is said that for some time her mental condition has been going from bad to worse, and it was decided best to place her in an institution where she can have proper medical attention. Mrs. Hutchinson is an old timer in Routt county, and for many years was the owner of the famous Hutchinson coal bank in Twenty-mile park. She is the mother of Mrs. Bud Hoskinson of Steamboat, and at one time, from 1890 until 1892, she resided near Yampa.

After hearing testimony from Elizabeth's daughter, son-in-law, and one granddaughter, Judge Morning agreed to impanel a jury to pass judgment on the mental case of Elizabeth Hutchinson. Apparently due to a recent large fire in the region, the judge was unable to find six men within a few miles of Hahn's Peak to serve as jurors. Therefore, he summoned six women from nearby farms and ranches to serve at the hearing. This caused a sensation, as women had not yet been given the privilege by the state to serve on a court trial. To get around this, Judge Morning claimed a county hardship and temporarily suspended the all-men practice. This sensational trial was being talked about across the state.

The *Telluride Daily Journal* printed the *Associated Press* coverage of the trial on the front page of their paper dated June 24, 1910.

Women Compose Jury Which Says Another Is Insane
By Associated Press, Hahn's Peak, Colo.
Unable to find a sufficient number of men eligible for jury duty, Judge Morning of the county court suspended the custom of men and summoned a jury composed wholly of women. With a true sense of the responsibilities imposed on them, every one of the women of the venire responded, and with the same sense of duty apparently when their deliberations of the evidence proved one of their own sex insane, they returned the verdict of guilty without hesitation. Only six are required on an insanity case jury. After all had qualified, their names were submitted as follows: Maud Keller, Mrs. M. Q. Starr, Marry Creswell, Kate Pulley, Emma McCormick and Mrs. Alice Ryan [sic]. The defendant was Elizabeth Hutchinson. Evidence was given by relatives and other witnesses, and when the case was submitted to the jury the court gave these brief instructions.
"I don't know whether to address you as the jury or a juress, but in either event the evidence is now submitted to you, and fate of the defendant is in your hands. Consider the evidence in an unbiased and impartial manner, and when you are able to agree on your deliberations do not permit the sex of the defendant to prejudice you in rendering a verdict."
The jury was out only a short time, and returned a verdict of

guilty, then left the courtroom to return to their household duties. Since the fire [at] Hahn's Peak, the county seat of Routt county, [sic] has less than thirty inhabitants, and there were not enough eligibles in Judge Morning's entire district to form a venire.

Also on June 24, 1910, the *Routt County Sentinel*, under the headline, "Pioneer Goes to Pueblo," ran a story on the insanity trial:

There is something new every minute at Hahn's Peak. This week Mrs. Elizabeth Hutchinson was tried for lunacy before a jury in the county court. Owing to the scarcity of men Judge Morning was up against it, as the street urchin would say, for jurors, and he did not know how to relieve the dilemma. Finally one of the women at the Peak suggested that he secure a jury composed entirely of women. This caused the popular judge to go through every leaf in the statutes. He could not find where the female sex was barred from jury duty, and he got the sheriff busy at once. Here is the list: Mrs. Marshall Starr, foreman; Miss Maud Keller, Mrs. Mary Crisswell, Mrs. Kate Pulley, Mrs. Emma McCormick, Mrs. Alice M. Reagen. The jury whispered to the judge that Mrs. Hutchinson, according to evidence, was simple minded and that she should be taken care of. The court did the rest and the lady, accompanied by the sheriff and her grand-daughter, Miss Murl Hoskinson, started for the asylum at Pueblo this morning. Mrs. Hutchinson had a splendid home with her daughter, Mrs. Hoskinson, but frequently would wander off and remain away for days. This caused considerable alarm, and it was thought best to place her where she could receive protection and perhaps recover her mind. Several years ago Mrs. Hutchinson owned considerable property, among which was the Hutchinson coal mine in Twenty Mile from which she received a splendid income annually, but through foolish litigation owing to the hallucination that others were trying to beat her out of her possessions, she lost everything. As she has but a short time to live on account of advanced age her many friends in Routt County hope that she will pass the last few days in comfort.

On the morning of June 26, 1910, Elizabeth Hutchinson was admitted to the Colorado State Insane Asylum in Pueblo, Colorado. Elizabeth's admission record lists her occupation as "Housekeeper."[7] Elizabeth would have been given hospital clothing and personal hygiene supplies, and shown to her room.

On June 29, 1910, the *Steamboat Pilot* printed a follow up story on Elizabeth's plight.

Judge Morning Has Jury of Six Women

Mrs. Elizabeth Hutchinson was Thursday adjudged insane before Judge Morning in the county court and will be brought down today. Tomorrow she will be taken to Pueblo, being accompanied by her granddaughter, Miss Murl Hoskinson, who will give her attention on the trip. The trial held before Judge Morning yesterday was unique in the annals of the state, for the jury was composed entirely of women. The following ladies qualified and performed the duties of citizens with credit, showing that women do not shirk any of the responsibilities which go with the ballot: Mrs. Kate Starr, Mrs. Emma McCormick, Mrs. Kate Pulley, Mrs. Mary Creswell, Miss Maud Keller and Mrs. Reagan. It was a novel scene during the important trial with the jury box filled with women to pass upon the sanity of one of their sex, and it sets a new standard and precedent for women throughout the United States, and will be a powerful argument in support of women suffrage.

While this early observation may have had merit in future cases, it did not necessary help Elizabeth. Held at the state's insane asylum, perhaps against her will, she would spend the rest of her life at a drab, cold, and often uncaring facility.

A physician or assistant would have seen her at a prescribed time every day. The female matron oversaw the duties of service personnel on the female ward, such as changing bedding, cleaning and diet of the patients. While Elizabeth would have been able to receive visitors, it is not known if anyone did visit her.

Elizabeth Hutchinson, aged seventy-nine, died alone at the insane asylum in Pueblo on January 2, 1913. She was buried at Pueblo's Roselawn Cemetery.

Today, Elizabeth's Hutchinson Ranch is listed on the Routt County Register of Historic Places. Owned by the City of Steamboat Springs, it is operated by the local Yampatika group. Named for a local Ute tribe, the Yampatika group hosts tours of the ranch as well as open-space management in conjunction with Colorado Parks and Wildlife.[8]

A fine tribute to Elizabeth Hutchinson, the pioneer woman rancher of Steamboat Springs.

## Notes

1. 1880 Census, Ralls County, Missouri. Elizabeth lists her age as forty-eight.
2. Biographical entry found in *Progressive Men of Western Colorado*, A. J. Bowen & Co., 1905.
3. Hutchinson family history written by great-grandniece Rebecca Goodwin, located in the archives of the Tread of Pioneers Museum, Steamboat Springs.
4. ibid.
5. Routt County Court Records and the Colorado Divorce Records.
6. 1900 Census, Routt County, Colorado.
7. Records held in the archives of the Colorado Mental Health Institute, formally the Colorado State Insane Asylum. Sheila Farizio, Medical Records Department.
8. A copy of Elizabeth's original Homestead filing is on display at the ranch site.

# THE ROCK CANYONS

## *Josie Bassett*
**A Pioneer Hellcat**

## *Ann Bassett*
**Colorado's Cattle Queen**

## *Evelyn Fuller Mantle*
**The Legend of Hells Canyon**

Josie Bassett sits with her horse at Cub Creek. *Uintah County Regional History Center*

# Josie Bassett
## A Pioneer Hellcat

*"I drove my first husband, Jim McKnight, out of the house at the point of a gun and told him never to come back. Let's just say that some men are harder to get rid of than others."*

S o said Josephine Bassett McKnight Ranney Williams Wells Morris in a taped interview in 1961. She married five times over the course of her adventurous life. She divorced four of her husbands, running one off at gunpoint, and the fifth husband died of natural causes, according to the coroner and two separate investigations. Yet rumors and even oral history from Josie's own family have persisted to this day that Josie poisoned her fifth husband.

Josephine Bassett, born in 1874, was the oldest child of Amos Herbert and Elizabeth Bassett. She was four years old when her parents and younger brother, Samuel, settled in Brown's Hole, Colorado, an area spanning the borders of Utah, Wyoming and Colorado. Josie later spoke of the journey:

> I just barely can remember it. I was four years old. They had a team of oxen, and wasn't I afraid of those oxen! Oh! But I rode with –them—I rode with Uncle Sam Bassett and his oxen all the way. We landed in Green River City. You see, there was no roads to Brown's Park [Hole] from Rock Springs at the time. We come over the mountains to Green River City to Brown's Park [Hole] with teams and wagons. One team was oxen, two steers. I'll never forget it in the world. I loved those cattle, but when they were unhitched, I was afraid of them. I would run and get upon that wagon and ride with the steers every time,

you know I was terribly scared. [1]

     The Bassett family first stayed with Herb's brother Samuel, an early pioneer in the area, as Elizabeth was in the final trimester of her pregnancy with the couple's third child. Josie described her uncle's cabin as "a funny little old log cabin with two rooms, no floors and no windows." Josie's little sister, Anna, known as Ann, was born in this cabin on May 12, 1878.

     Herb Bassett was a man out of place in the rugged Brown's Park frontier. On the other hand, Elizabeth loved the area and she loved the land. It wasn't long before the couple had a few head of cattle that became the income of the Bassett family. Later, Elizabeth used her own money to purchase a nice herd of Durham cattle. Josie later recalled, "My father didn't know how to brand a cow—neither did she [Elizabeth], but she tried."

     As the ranch began to show a profit, the Bassetts were able to hire ranch hands, including Isom Dart, a former slave, and Madison Matthew (Matt) Rash, both of whom were former employees of the Middlesex Cattle Company, a large cattle company which had expanded their operations into Brown's Park. Other hired ranch hands would later include Jack Fitch, Angus McDougall, and James "Jim" Fielding McKnight.

     The Bassett ranch was soon known as a welcoming place to neighbors and strangers with no questions asked. Herb and Elizabeth Bassett may or may not have known of the outlaw element that frequented the area. Nevertheless, the couple raised their children in the open atmosphere of the West. They were taught at an early age to rope, ride, and shoot, as well as contribute to the operation of the ranch in the form of assigned daily chores. This childhood upbringing would become ingrained with all of the Bassett children, as was their love for Brown's Park, which their mother, Elizabeth, successfully renamed in 1881 from Brown's Hole to Brown's Park.

     Josie had fond memories of her childhood. She often played in the sand near Vermilion Creek with nearby Indian children of her own age. "I was perhaps five or six at the time, and I remember it so well. We didn't speak the same language, but we got along famously. We made little houses out of wet sand and clay, and diverted little rivulets from Vermilion Creek to make play rivers. It sounds like a silly thing, but it made such a strong impression, I can recall it as though it was yesterday. On the other hand, I'm not sure I could remember what I did yesterday."[2]

Josie mistakenly said she was fifteen years old when she first met Butch Cassidy (alias George Cassidy at that time). This was in the spring of 1886 (Josie was twelve years old), and the first reference of the famous outlaw in Brown's Park. Cassidy, fond of horse racing, rode a champion bay mare owned by Charlie Crouse to victory at a horse race held at the nearby Beaver Creek racetrack, which Josie and her younger sister Ann had attended. Josie later said:

> I thought he was the most dashing and handsome man I had ever seen. I was such a young thing, and giddy as most teenagers are, and I looked upon Butch as my knight in shining armor. But he was more interested in his horse than he was in me, and I remember being very put out by that. I went home after being snubbed by him and stamped my foot on the floor in frustration. [3]

Surrounded by mountains, with plenty of water and good grazing in the valley below, Brown's Park seemed a perfect place for a hideout, and Cassidy took advantage. Forming his gang of outlaws, later the notorious Wild Bunch, Cassidy's first hideout became the area around Brown's Park. Among the various outlaws who visited, passed through, or made their home in Brown's Park were Cassidy's close friends Matt Warner and Tom McCarty, as well as Elzy Lay, George "Flat Nose" Curry, and Harry (the Sundance Kid) Longabaugh.

Herb and Elizabeth Bassett welcomed the outlaws, provided shelter for them, offered them temporary work, and did business with them often, supplying them with beef and fresh horses. Josie evidently didn't mind the added company at all: "And let me say they had some cute boys with their outfit. It was a thrill to see Henry Rhudenbaugh [sic] tall, blond & handsome." [4]

During that summer, Cassidy spent a great deal of time around the Bassett Ranch. He spent time with Herb Bassett, reading his newspapers and books. But Josie, years later, had a different recollection of the twenty-year-old Cassidy, describing him as "a big dumb kid who liked to joke." Even so, it was only a matter of time before Josie and Butch Cassidy became lovers. Later, Josie recounted the teen affair of the heart: "After one of Butch's rich uncles died [euphemism for a bank or train robbery,] we put him up, hiding him in the hay loft. He used to say, 'Josie, I'm lonely up here. Come out and keep me company.' He asked me, 'What am I going to do to keep from being bored?' Well, all I can say is, I didn't let him get bored."[5]

The teenage affair ended when Cassidy left the Park and Josie was sent to Craig to finish her high school education. In 1890, at the age of sixteen, Josie's parents sent her to the Catholic finishing school, St. Mary's of the Wasatch, in Salt Lake City, Utah.

Josie thoroughly enjoyed her time and education at St. Mary's. However, Josie's schooling was sadly disrupted in December 1892, when her beloved mother, Elizabeth, suddenly died at the age of thirty-seven. She arose from bed early one morning when she heard a ruckus outside her window. Leaping from bed to investigate, she saw that her favorite milk cow was caught up in a herd of cattle being rounded up by the large cattle barons. Furious, Elizabeth saddled her horse and rode out to claim her cow. With a few choice words, she cut her cow out of the herd and returned it to the Bassett ranch. It proved to be a trying day for Elizabeth and she retired to bed early that night.

Josie later recalled the event: "She went to bed at night all right, and woke up about four o'clock in the morning just deathly sick. Just terribly sick. Father was there and Jim McKnight was there, and - I don't know - some of the cowboys. And they couldn't get a doctor, of course. All they could do - all they thought of was hot applications and that relieved her, of course, but she died."[6]

The *Craig Empire Courier* newspaper reported the death of Elizabeth Bassett in the December 16, 1892, issue of the paper:

A Sad Event
A messenger from Brown's Park arrived Monday bringing the sad intelligence of the death of Mrs. E. Bassett. Her children, Sam, Josie and Anna who have been attending school, immediately started for home.

Josie always believed her mother died of appendicitis, while Ann believed her mother's death was from a miscarriage. The Bassett family grief was deep. The matriarch of the family and anchor, particularly for Josie and Ann, was gone. When Herb encouraged Josie to return to school at St. Mary's, she refused, telling her father she was needed at home. Josie later said, "I was away at St. Mary's when my mother died. I didn't go back, I stayed home then because my father needed me so bad. My father was perfectly lost. I had been two years at St. Mary's to November, two years and a half, purtnear."[7]

This was a particularly difficult time in Josie's life, which accounts for her incomplete statement. Not only was she grieving for the loss of her mother, she also came to the realization that she was pregnant with Jim McKnight's child. She hated to let her father down, but she had no choice.

On March 21, 1893, nineteen-year-old Josephine Bassett and James McKnight were married in Green River City, Utah. The couple returned to Brown's Park, where Josie gave birth to a son they named Crawford, on July 12, 1893. Her father may have been disappointed but eventually welcomed the new family. On the other hand, Josie's Uncle Sam Bassett offered Josie one of his mining claims, the surrounding land, and the cabin, on the condition that she take care of him until his death. Josie agreed, and she and Jim, along with their infant baby boy, moved to Beaver Creek at the southern edge of Brown's Park. The couple built a cabin of their own near Sam's. Josie planted a garden and Jim built a barn and additional buildings on the land.

Although Beaver Creek ran through the McKnight's land, the high creek banks were above the level of their land. According to Bassett biographer Grace McClure, it was Josie who solved the problem of getting the water down to their land. She and Jim "cut an irrigation ditch extending four or five miles across the brush to a point where the creek came out of the hills, grading the ditch in a gentle slope to their land." The surrounding ranchers thought little of the effort, calling it "McKnight's Folly." Josie was confident in her idea, as it stood to reason "that the water would have to flow downhill."[8] Josie was vindicated when she and Jim shouted with glee as the floodgate was opened and the water gently flowed down through the ditch.[9]

Josie loved ranch life. She enjoyed riding on horseback, checking the cattle and observing the land. When she wasn't in the saddle, she cared for her family. This diverse woman also delighted in the domestic duties of a wife and mother. While caring for her son, she also cooked, cleaned and maintained the cabin for her family. She laundered their clothes in a washtub over an open fire in the yard with lye soap she herself had made. She planted apple trees and harvested the vegetables from the garden for the family meals. All the while, she managed her busy time to care for her Uncle Sam. When her sister Ann returned home from school, she hosted the 1896 Thanksgiving dinner party for all the families in Brown's Park. From her memoirs, Ann says guests also included Matt Rash, Isom Dart, Elzy Lay, and Harry Roudenbaugh (Harry Longabough, the Sundance Kid.) In Ann's memoirs she described the event in great detail, including what the women wore. Of Josie's dress, Ann recalled:

Josie's dress for the party was a sage green wool. Many-gored skirt, tight to the knees then flared to the floor to sweep up the dirt. Josie was married, I was not. By the way, Josie played a 'Zither' and rather well. She was accompanied by Sam Bassett on the fiddle and Joe Davenport with a guitar.

This account of Josie by Ann lends another insight to the character, talent and diversity Josie possessed. A hard-working rancher, she could also grace social events with style and glamor. It is also a bit revealing as to the physique of the woman. When Josie wore the green dress "tight to the knees," she was pregnant with her second child.

In the spring of 1896, the McKnights were blessed with a second son, Herbert, named for Josie's father but known as "Chick." By this time, Isom Dart was working with Jim McKnight, following the death of Elizabeth Bassett. Although Dart had his own small cattle herd on Cold Spring Mountain, above the McKnight land, he had arranged a working partnership with McKnight, much as he had with Elizabeth Bassett. The relationship between Dart and the McKnights was a close one. Dart enjoyed spending time with the young McKnight boys and often stayed with them when Jim was busy and Josie traveled by horse and buggy the ten miles to the Bassett ranch to visit with her father, brothers, and sister Ann. As Butch Cassidy had returned to the Park that same year, Josie may have visited with him on these trips to the family ranch. While the McKnights were away, Isom Dart never tired of playing with the little McKnight boys, and he would sing songs to them and play rodeo games with them just as he had with Elizabeth and Herb's children, including Josie.

In February 1898, two tragic events occurred in Brown's Park, and the Bassett ranch specifically, that would be the beginning of the end for the outlaw element in the Park. J. S. Hoy had filed complaints of cattle rustling and murder against John Jack "Judge" Bennett and Patrick Louis "P. L." Johnson.

At the time, Johnson, rumored to have killed a man, was leasing a portion of Hoy's land and Hoy suspected he was the reason a few of his cattle were missing. Bennett had an interesting outlaw background. He possessed a long criminal record, culminating with a charge of "assault with attempt to commit murder," following a December 28, 1887, incident in Lander, Wyoming. Convicted of the charge, he spent five years in the Wyoming State Prison in Laramie. Released on April 26, 1892, he roamed the area of Brown's Park tri-state region, becoming a familiar figure. James Hoy would later write, "Bennett was so handy with a gun that he thought no man or set of men dared to attempt to arrest him, and he had threatened to kill nearly every man in the valley. One man he had disliked in particular, and said he intended to 'shoot off an arm and a leg to see how he could move around.'"

Josie Bassett McKnight later said, "Johnson was a fool. He got in with Bennett, and Bennett used the Valentine Hoy place as a hangout."[10]

In April 1897, Bennett was in Baggs, Wyoming, where he was involved in a kangaroo court of sorts at the Bull Dog Saloon. Participants included Butch Cassidy and other members of the Wild Bunch.

The Hoy complaint alleged that on February 17, 1898, at the ranch of Valentine Hoy (near Pine Mountain along Red Creek, just over the state line in Wyoming), P. L. Johnson had shot and killed sixteen-year-old Willie Strang. It was an innocent action by the young boy that brought the ire of Johnson and the death of Strang. Strang had accidentally or playfully spilled water on Johnson's shirt. Johnson's reaction startled Strang and he ran away from the scene. Johnson followed him to the barn, raised his pistol and fired. The bullet hit the young boy in the back, and Willie Strang died a few hours later.

Johnson, along with Bennett, immediately left the Hoy ranch, on a pair of Hoy horses, heading south for Powder Springs, an area northeast of Brown's Park, on the state line of Colorado and Wyoming. Forty-six-year-old Charlie Crouse formed a posse and tracked the men as far as they could. Meanwhile, Valentine Hoy and William Pidgeon, a witness to the shooting of young Strang, buried the boy on the Hoy land.

Thirty-six-year-old Routt County Sheriff Charles Willis Neiman received the warrants a week later and left Steamboat Springs, near the county seat of Hahns Peak, on February 25th, with the warrants in hand. Although he knew Hoy's ranch was just over the state line in Wyoming, he had no idea that the outlaws had gone to Powder Springs. This had always been a difficult situation for the sheriff's department regarding jurisdiction, and the very reason outlaws chose Brown's Park as a hideout.

Meanwhile, at Powder Springs, Bennett and Johnson met up with two dangerous escaped convicts, David Lant from the Utah State Penitentiary, and Harry Tracy, who had murdered three guards, from the Oregon State Penitentiary. The newly formed group formed a plan. Bennett would stay behind, purchasing supplies, and would join the other three at Lodore Canyon, the eastern edge of Brown's Park.

Sheriff Neiman arrived in Craig, where he enlisted the assistance of Routt County deputy sheriff Ethan Allen Farnham. The men spent the night at the Vaughn ranch and left the following morning for Brown's Park and the Bassett ranch, where they hoped to obtain information and raise a posse. Arriving that evening at the Bassett ranch, they were greeted by sixty-three-year old Herb Bassett, two of his sons, thirteen-year-old George and seventeen-year-old Elbert "Eb," and twenty-year-old John Strang, the older brother of the murdered Willie Strang.

Following supper, Sheriff Neiman persuaded John Strang to ride out in the cover of darkness to recruit a posse. His intention was to ride off in the morning in pursuit of the men he had seen that day, as he had reason to believe they were the men he held warrants for. Shortly after midnight, Strang returned with a group of men, including Valentine Hoy, William Pidgeon, E. B. "Longhorn" Thompson, Boyd Vaughn and twenty-nine-year-old Jim McKnight.

The following morning, Monday, February 28, these four men—along with John Strang and Eb Bassett—left the Bassett ranch with the sheriff and his deputy. At the base of Douglas Mountain, the men discovered an abandoned campsite with camp gear, bedding and five horses remaining at the site. Obviously aware they were being followed, the hunted men left on foot for the rugged rocky terrain of Douglas Mountain. The sheriff and his men knew it would be an ambush if they were to follow them over the rocks with no trail to follow. Therefore, Sheriff Neiman made the decision to wait them out.

The next morning, March 1, 1898, a group of the posse discovered fresh footprints in the snow leading to Lodore Canyon. The posse split up. Thompson and Strang stayed at the campsite with the posse's horses, while young Bassett and Vaughn were sent to a prominent rock point where they had a commanding view of the valley below, watching in the event that the outlaws might double back. Neiman, Farnham, Hoy, Pidgeon and McKnight then set off on foot up the side of Douglas Mountain. About mid-afternoon, Neiman knew his decision was the correct one, as the posse found a smoldering fire.

As Neiman was standing near the fire, Valentine Hoy started up the rocks toward a split rock. Neiman told Hoy not to get too far ahead of the posse just as Hoy stepped on a small rock. At that instant, two rifle shots rang out in the rock canyon, and Valentine Hoy fell, half sitting and half kneeling against the rocks. Jim McKnight was following Hoy up the rock cliff and saw one of the outlaws, later recognized as Harry Tracy. McKnight fired a shot toward the outlaw, who immediately ducked back for cover. For over an hour, the posse hid in cover of rocks and cedar, as the outlaws above clearly had the advantage. As for the outlaws, the only escape they had was the rushing cold waters of the Green River. As evening approached, Neiman's posse, leaving Hoy's body behind, one at a time slid back down the mountain and to the camp where Thompson and Strang were holding the horses. The group of men, with heavy hearts and no choice, left on horseback for the Bassett ranch, leading Hoy's horse.

On their solemn journey, the group headed to pick up Bassett and Vaughn, when they were met by Vaughn riding toward them. He told the sheriff that he and Bassett had observed a lone rider who stopped and fired three shots in the air as he headed out of the mountain range. Waiting a few minutes, he fired again. Believing this was a signal to the outlaws, Vaughn and Bassett rode down to the valley below and in a friendly, leisurely way approached the man. Bassett recognized the man as John Jack "Judge" Bennett, who was involved in the aftermath of the death of Willie Strang. Vaughn let the sheriff know of the scheme he and Bassett had quickly concocted. In a friendly gesture, Bassett invited the "stranger" to the Bassett ranch for the night. Bennett, accepting the invitation, left with Bassett; as Vaughn explained he would soon follow.

Josie later talked about Eb's experience with Bennett:

> Well, my brother Eb was just a big boy then, about seventeen, and he was scared to death of Bennett. Bennett was kind and pleasant to Eb and Eb was to him, and they went home to Bassett's. My father had the post office and he sold tobacco and little things like that. So Bennett said, "We're all out of tobacco," and that made Eb more scared than ever. He thought, "We! Who are 'we'? Wonder who the other people are."[11]

Meanwhile, Neiman and the rest of the posse rode hard to reach the Bassett ranch ahead of Bassett and Bennett. When Bassett and Bennett finally arrived at the ranch, Eb Bassett corralled the horses while Bennett approached the ranch house.

Inside the Bassett home, Josie Bassett McKnight watched the arrival of her younger brother through the kitchen window. She and her two young sons had been staying at the ranch for safety after McKnight joined the posse. Josie was baking a large batch of cookies when Bennett walked in. He checked his gun at the door, which was customary, and Josie invited him have a seat at the table and offered him some of her warm cookies.

As Bennett was enjoying the cookies, deputy sheriff Ethan Farnham walked in. Farnham addressed the man, asking if his name was John Bennett. Bennett replied in the affirmative. Farnham then ordered the man on his feet. As Bennett stood, Farnham showed him the arrest warrant for cattle stealing and told him to put his hands up. Over sixty years later, Josie Bassett McKnight recalled the incident:

> I had quit baking cookies to listen to what was going on. I was

so scared. I could hardly speak, I was so scared. I thought, "Now if he's got a six-shooter he'll kill Farnham," but he had set his gun down at the back door when he came in. So he held his hands up high and Farnham arrested him, put the handcuffs on him and he didn't make much fuss about it. He swore and made a lot of threats about what he would do when he got loose. He was an impudent-looking man.[12]

Farnham took his prisoner to Herb Bassett's post office at Lodore, not far from the Bassett ranch, which also served as a temporary jail when needed. Farnham handcuffed Bennett to a cot and guarded him. Bennett's verbal assaults against Farnham only increased. In Josie's later interviews, she said, "He carried on like a gray wolf. You never heard such terrible yells and screams and swearing. We could hear him from the kitchen, hearing him carrying on that way."

The following day, March 2, 1898, near the noon hour, seven masked men entered the temporary jail and leveled a shotgun at Farnham and took his keys, while others moved toward Bennett. They threw a gunny sack over Bennett's head, removed the handcuffs from the cot and placed them on his wrists. While one of the men guarded Farnham, the masked men then took Bennett out of his jail cell and to the adjacent Bassett ranch. Bennett was placed on a buckboard and a noose was placed around his neck, the knot properly placed behind his right ear. The free end of the rope was then thrown over one of the pine gateposts. The masked men, in a swift motion, then drove the buckboard out from under Bennett. However, the drop was too short to break Bennett's neck and he swung in the air for nearly four minutes before his body finally slumped in the cold mountain air.

Years later, Josie said, "I cooked dinner for the men who lynched Jack Bennett. At the time I didn't know what they'd done. After dinner I went outdoors to hang some dish towels on the clothesline, and there he was, swinging from the corral gate."

According to Brown's Park historian John Rolfe Burroughs, who interviewed Josie about a year before her death, she named three of the masked men as Harry Hindle, Lilton Lyons and Jim Warren. When asked who the others were, Josie "pled forgetfulness with a twinkle in her eye."[13] Following dinner, the men again donned their masks and returned to where Farnham was being held. They then released him and rode away from the Bassett ranch. Farnham left his temporary prison and found Bennett hanging from the Bassett ranch gatepost. He cut down the body and dragged it up the draw above the ranch house. He then wrapped the body in a blanket, dug a shallow grave and placed the body of John "Jack" Bennett in the grave. After he covered the grave, Farnham placed rocks over it, in an effort to deter the coyotes. Years later, Crawford McKnight, the older son of Josie and Jim McKnight, was interviewed by John Rolfe Burroughs. He said he and his younger brother didn't believe that there really was a body in that spot above their grandfather's ranch. Crawford said he was about fourteen when he and younger brother, Chick, filled with curiosity, decided to find out for themselves if the legendary lynching story was true. They took a pick and shovel from their grandfather's ranch and walked up the draw behind the house to the grave site.

> Chick and I dug down two or three feet. I was swinging the pick and when it hit what seemed to be a hollow place, and when I raised the pick there was a skull on the point. Believe me, we scraped that skull back in the hole and covered it up in a hurry. We must have been a trifle pale around the gills when we went back to the house, because Granddad said, "Well boys, did you find anything?" We allowed as how we had, and were satisfied that the hanging really had taken place.

Sheriff Neiman and his deputy sheriff, Ethan Farnham, continued their search for the escaped convicts. The murder of Valentine Hoy had brought a new round of willing posse members, including Isom Dart and again, Joe Davenport and Jim McKnight.

At a point of five or six miles south of Powder Springs,

and near one of the Davenport sheep ranches, Farnham, using field glasses, spotted the three fugitives sitting on a hill. Farnham and his posse rode toward them. As the men saw the horseman approaching, they rose from their seated position. When the posse were within range, Farnham yelled to the men to halt. The three men ran off in the opposite direction. As the posse quickened their pace after the men, Farnham again ordered the men to stop. Johnson obeyed the order, turning toward the posse with his hands in the air. Lant and Tracy ran toward a hollow where they disappeared from sight. Joe Davenport recalled the capture of the escaped convicts in an interview in the March 1 issue of the *Rock Springs Rocket*:

> We then incautiously surrounded Tracy and Lant when they might have dropped all five of us. We did not realize what a desperado we had to deal with. They took refuge in a depression in the snow. I alighted from my horse, crawling among the greasewood until I saw Tracy's head sticking up. I didn't shoot. Lant, realizing that he was trapped, started to rise in order to surrender. But the dare-devil Tracy was gamey. He pointed his weapon at Lant and shouted, "Get down there, you blankety-blank-blank." Lant then dropped back as Tracy shouted at us, "We'll tell you fellows we're quitting. But we want protection. We don't want to be strung up." After we guaranteed them safety, Lant appeared first with hands aloft. His feet broke through the snow as he approached, and he fell. Pete Swanson, thinking it was a ruse, shot at Lant, but missed him. Tracy then reluctantly appeared, but with his gun in his belt. Knowing the man was desperate, Farnham took a quick shot at him on the spur of the moment, but also missed. It surprised the fearless outlaw, and he could not restrain his anger, but shouted, "You're a fine bunch of cowards, firing at a man with his hands in the air." We still didn't know we had such a noted criminal as Tracy until someone recognized him later. "Gents," he said, "give me a cup of coffee, a fresh horse, and twenty-five-yards head start, and I won't bother you no more."

Of course Farnham declined the request, handcuffed the men, and the posse set out for the Rock Springs-Brown's Park road. In an ironic twist of fate in this entire outlaw episode, the posse encountered J. S. Hoy and Willis Rouf on horseback. Following the riders was twelve-year-old Felix Meyers driving a buckboard containing a wooden coffin with the remains of Valentine Hoy. The group were en route to Rock Springs, where they would ship the body by train to the family home in Fremont, Nebraska. However, Deputy Sheriff Farnham, while sympathetic to Hoy's situation, insisted that Hoy, as the police magistrate for Brown's Park, return with the posse to oversee the trial of Johnson, Lant and Tracy. Understandingly, J. S. Hoy was quite upset at the ironic turn of events. Again, Joe Davenport related the angry exchange:

Which one of you men killed my brother? "Well one of us here did it," Tracy replied defiantly. We continued on down Irish and Bull Canyons to Bassett's ranch. As we approached the house, Farnham sent me ahead to tell the remainder of the posse waiting there that we had our men, and to keep cool and not get excited."[14]

The hearing was held in the large living room of the Bassett home, with Justice of the Peace for the Precinct of Lodore, Routt County, J. S. Hoy presiding. The room was filled with witnesses and bystanders, including Herb and Eb Bassett, and Jim and Josie McKnight. Hoy, in remarkable composure given he was presiding over a legal matter which resulted in the death of his brother, held the hearing from the head of the Bassett family dining table. The accused, Lant and Tracy, were stoic during the proceedings, although Tracy displayed an air of contempt from time to time. Following the hearing, J. S. Hoy issued the following ruling, dated March 5, 1898:

On the above date, P. L. Johnson, David Lant and Harry Tracy were brought before me by the Sheriff of Routt County charged with the killing of Valentine S. Hoy on the afternoon of March 1, 1898. I examined the three prisoners, the testimony of P. L Johnson being in writing. The other two testified, but their testimony was not reduced to writing. I also examined Sheriff Charles Neiman, E. A. Farnham, and James McKnight. To me, the evidence taken and the circumstances surrounding the killing of Valentine S. Hoy was sufficient to bind the prisoners over to the district court without bail, and they were accordingly remanded to the custody of the Sheriff to be confined in the county jail until the decision so rendered by due course of law, except in the case of P. L. Johnson, who was turned over to the custody of Deputy United States Marshal Charles Laney, who claimed Johnson on a writ of requisition from the Governor of Wyoming. Mittimus remanding Lant and Tracy to the county jail contains the names of the four principal witnesses in the prosecution, to wit: Charles Neiman, E. A. Farnham, James McKnight, and J. S. Hoy.[15]

Following what essentially became the end of the outlaw element in Brown's Park, life returned to ranching for the folks in the Park. For Josie, that meant caring for her family back at Beaver Creek. Although both Josie and Jim were hard-working and ambitious, each had a dominant personality, which caused friction in the marriage. While Josie was content, Jim was not. He began to spend more and more time away from home. He often crossed the Green River, frequenting the Brown's Park "Men's Club," a saloon operated by Charlie Crouse. Josie could not understand her husband's actions. In her mind, she expected her husband to enjoy the warm family home she worked so hard to provide. Josie later said, "I disagreed with him [McKnight] because he was on the wrong track, I thought. I didn't like that whiskey business. I couldn't stand it."

The troubled marriage escalated to domestic violence in the spring of 1900. Following the death of Josie's beloved Uncle Sam Bassett the previous year, the Beaver Creek land became Josie's through inheritance. Jim wanted to sell the land, move to

Vernal, Utah, and open a saloon. Josie refused. The couple fought constantly and whispers of physical violence drifted down to the community of Brown's Park. In March 1900, Herb Bassett took his daughter to Hahns Peak, the county seat of Routt County, to file a restraining order against James "Jim" McKnight. Divorce proceedings soon followed. McKnight was furious. He not only rounded up their cattle and moved them off the land, he also took their children away from Beaver Creek and Josie. Of course, he had no legal right and Josie would find the legal means to retaliate. In a taped interview, Crawford McKnight later recalled the unbelievable actions of Jim McKnight:

> My dad kinda kidnapped me and my brother, took us to Salt Lake and then up to Smithfield and turned us over to old Aunt Jodie Heath. I don't know if she was dad's aunt really but she was a fine old woman. I liked her a lot. Well mother wanted us kids brought home naturally, and she had papers made out and they deputized a little guy in Rock Springs to come out to serve papers and a warrant for his arrest and a subpoena to appear in court.[16]

The April 14, 1900, issue of the *Empire Courier*, a Craig newspaper, ran a long article reporting more bloodshed in Brown's Park. This time, it involved Jim and Josie McKnight.

> Shooting at Brown's Park
> James McKnight Probably Fatally Wound by Deputy Sheriff W. H. Harris
> James McKnight, of Brown's Park, was shot and probably fatally by Deputy Sheriff W. H. Harris, also of Brown's Park, on Wednesday evening, April 4, about 9 o'clock at the Edwards ranch on Beaver Creek. Mrs. McKnight had obtained a summons and an order from the county court restraining McKnight from disposing of his property, and a bond for $2500 for his appearance, were placed in the hands of Sheriff Farnham to serve on McKnight at Brown's Park. The Sheriff

arrived at Bassett' on the 31st of March, a day in advance of Bassett and Mrs. McKnight. The Sheriff found that McKnight had already disposed of his property and left for Utah...Not knowing whether or not McKnight would ever return, Sheriff Farnham appointed W. H. Harris, formally of Rock Springs, to serve the paper should McKnight return, and left for Craig.

Legend has it that Harris nailed the restraining notice on the Bassett gatepost, the very one that John "Judge" Bennett had been hanged by the mob two years ago.

The *Empire Courier* continued their coverage:

On April the 4th Mrs. McKnight sent word to her husband that she was very sick and wished to see him and "fix up matters." About dark he made his appearance. Those present at the ranch were: Miss Blanche Tilton, Miss Ann Bassett, Carl Blair, Larry Curtain, Geo. Bassett, Eva Hoy, [Mrs.] Valentine Hoy, and Mrs. James McKnight. Mrs. McKnight was in bed and the women were giving her medicine and applying numerous mustard plasters. A little later, [Sheriff] Harris happened along and went into the house. McKnight said, "How do you do, Harris?" and the latter replied, "How do you do, Jim?" Miss Tilton then invited both men to stay the night. Harris turned his horse in the corral and McKnight said he guessed he would go home, which is just across the line in Utah, and started for the door. Harris said, "Jim, I have a letter here for you to read" and handed him the summons which Jim read and threw on the table and remarked "that is only a matter of form." He then started for the door and Harris asked him if he could give bonds for those papers. He said "yes!" and started for the door again and Harris said he would put him under arrest until morning. McKnight did not answer, but opened the door and went out. Harris followed and called to him three times to stop but [McKnight] paid no attention to the command and Harris shot twice, one ball taking effect in the left side near the spine and glanced upward. Jim fell and called on Harris to shoot him in the head and finish the job. All rushed out of the house and the excitement was at a high pitch. Miss Ann Bassett, sister of Mrs. McKnight, being very demonstrative about the catastrophe which had befell her brother-in-law.

Another Bassett legend passed on over time is that Josie was the one who shot Jim McKnight. Although she wasn't even present at the scene of the shooting, Josie later responded to the accusation, "If I had shot him, I wouldn't have missed."

Whether or not Josie was really "sick" is obvious conjecture. However, what we do know is that she sent the letter to her estranged husband in an obvious ruse to get him across the state line into Colorado so that Sheriff Harris, who just so happened to be in the neighborhood, could serve McKnight with the divorce papers.

The newspaper article ended with a strange twist of fate, one that would not only effect the McKnights and the Bassett family, but all of Brown's Park as well:

Tom Hicks, new to the area, rode to Vernal, a distance of forty-five miles, in four hours and a half, and wired McKnight's relatives at Salt Lake and his brother, Frank McKnight, arrived Friday night and is looking after him. [Jim] McKnight signed the papers on the 7th and Harris came to Craig, arriving last Monday, and delivered them to Sheriff Farnham and returned to Brown's Park on Tuesday. [17]

Obviously covering a shooting in Brown's Park was news; however, the depth of the coverage regarding the domestic situation between Jim and Josie McKnight speaks to the sensationalism of the era, as divorce was quite rare. This point is proven in the June 2, 1900, issue of the *Empire Courier*:

There was quite a delegation of Brown's Park citizens here this week. They left Thursday for Hahns Peak to attend the county court next Monday when the divorce case of Mrs. James McKnight against her husband will be tried before Judge Voice. Those who will appear in the case are A. H. Bassett, father of Mrs. McKnight, Miss Anna Bassett, George Bassett, Carl Blair, Joe Davenport and Mrs. E. B. Thompson.

A second article in the same issue of the paper reported further details:

Lew Ranney arrived here last Sunday from Brown's Park. He accompanied James McKnight who was on his way to Hahns Peak to attend county court. Mr. McKnight has about fully recovered from the wound he received in April at the hands of Deputy Sheriff Harris. His injuries were not as serious as at first anticipated and, although three efforts were made with Xrays the bullet was not located and he still carries it as a reminder of his unpleasant experience.

The June 16, 1900, issue of the *Empire Courier* reported the outcome of the legal proceedings:

Mrs. Josie McKnight secured a divorce from James McKnight in the county court at Hahns Peak last week on the grounds of cruelty. Elaborate preparations had been made for a bitter legal fight on both sides, but Mr. and Mrs. McKnight, after meeting at Hahns Peak, decided between themselves to settle the question of allimony [sic] costs and custody of their two children out of court so as to avoid airing their troubles before the public. Mrs. McKnight left for Salt Lake last Tuesday for the children, armed with a letter from Jim to his sister, with whom they have been living, to turn them over to her. Mrs. McKnight will make her home in Craig with Mr. and Mrs. McLacklan for a short time. Mr. McKnight will embark in the sheep business in Utah. When they bade each other goodby [sic] at Craig no animosity existed between them and they parted with best wishes for each other.

In the few meetings Jim and Josie had after the divorce, they were cordial with one another, but it could hardly be described as friendly. Josie later described her ex-husband: "He was undoubtedly Scotch. It was hardly in his favor. He wasn't a bad man—he was just a Scotchman, that's all."[18]

Josie and the boys returned to the ranch on Beaver Creek, where she did her best to return to a normal life for herself and her children. Isom Dart came around from time to time to check on Josie and the boys. However, that very summer, murder rocked the lives of Josie, her sister Ann and all of Brown's Park to their very core.

In July 1900, Madison Matthew (Matt) Rash, the fiancé of Josie's sister Ann, was murdered at his cabin on Cold Spring Mountain. Josie immediately took the boys and headed for the family ranch. She did her best to console her younger sister. Then, just three months later, Isom Dart was shot in cold blood near his cabin on the same mountain. The *Craig Courier* reported the murder:

> Another tragedy occurred in Brown's Park Thursday morning of last week, Isom Dart, a negro, falling victim to an assassin's bullet. The murder occurred on the Cold Springs ranch. Dart and George Bassett were walking together from the cabin to the corral and when about twenty steps from the cabin door, a shot was fired from the direction of the corral and Isom fell dead. Young Bassett ran back to the cabin, in which were Sam Bassett and Lew Brown, who saw Dart fall when he was shot. The young men were afraid to venture out after the killing and remained in the cabin for four hours. Finally they left the cabin and started for the Matt Rash Ranch. The murderer had stood behind a tree 120 yards from where Dart fell. His tracks where he stood were quite plain and it was evident that the murderer had his horse tied a short distance behind him. The horse was shod and his trail was easy to follow. Sam Bassett and Billy Bragg followed the trail eight miles and when they quit it was perfectly plain.

When the news of Isom Dart's murder was known, several heavily-armed citizens, including Josie Bassett McKnight, traveled on horseback to Cold Spring Mountain. The group found Isom Dart's body, approximately halfway between the cabin and the corral. At the base of a large Ponderosa pine tree near the edge of the corral, two .30-.30 bullet shells were found. The men were shocked at the discovery. Only one man in the area was known to carry a .30 -.30 lever action rifle. That man was the stranger, James Hicks, the very man who had helped Jim McKnight when he was shot the previous spring.

After the group buried Isom Dart, just west of his cabin in a nice aspen grove, they went to the Routt County sheriff with the evidence. It would later be proven that Hicks was indeed Tom Horn, but there was never any proof to charge him with the murders of Dart and Rash.

The Bassett children had known Isom Dart nearly their entire lives. Josie said of her long-time friend, "[He was] *just a good, honest old colored man who never hurt anybody.*"

Now that Josie had her sons back with her, she needed to make a living for them. The circumstances were different now, she was a single mother in a man's world. Confused and reeling with emotion following the divorce, and deaths of Matt Rash and Isom Dart, she turned to her father for advice. She would take his advice, but always regretted her decision, as is clear in the following portion from her taped interview:

My father thought that the [pause] He said - that was wrong of my father - he said, "Now a woman with two little children to send to school has no business living alone on the ranch." I had 680 cattle, and I could have managed that outfit just as well, far better than I could living in town, because I wasn't used to that town business, and I don't like it and never did. George Bassett could have helped me and would, and that's why I should have stayed. But I sold out on father's advice and went to Craig and went into the hotel business, something I didn't know a thing about. But I made out all right. I made a living and lived very decent.[19]

Josie and the boys moved to Craig, where she leased the Elmo Hotel. Rooms for the guests and boarders were on the second floor, as well as separate living quarters for Josie, Crawford and Chick. She enrolled the boys in school and renewed old friendships with many folks she had known in Craig over the years, including Charles A. Ranney, who was the high school principal when she attended school in Craig. Ranney, a member of one of Craig's leading families (Ranney Street having been named for the family), was Grand Master of the Masonic Lodge, and owned the town drugstore.

Ranney became interested in Josie and the two began to court when Josie could find the time away from her hotel. He took her on long buggy rides and the two fished in the rivers, an activity Josie truly enjoyed. When Ranney proposed marriage, Josie, a divorced woman in an era when divorce was frowned upon, readily agreed. After all, a respectable man of means would support her and the boys, and she would finally get out of the hotel business that she so detested.

In April 1902, twenty-six-year old Josie Bassett married thirty-three-year old Charles Ranney. The April 26, 1902, issue of the *Craig Courier* reported the event:

> C. A. Ranney and Mrs. Josie McKnight were united in marriage Thursday afternoon by Rev. H. E. Anderson. The wedding occurred at the Tucker residence which Mr. Ranney recently purchased and refitted in anticipation of this happy event. The marriage was strictly a home affair, only relatives of the young people being in attendance.

Josie rid herself of the hotel, moved into the splendid home with her sons, and settled into a life of bliss. It was not to be. Crawford and Chick hated their new stepfather. Ranney, a strict disciplinarian, took a hard stance with the boys from the beginning. Crawford, who had his grandfather Bassett's mild, gentle nature, never understood Ranney's cruel actions. Chick, on the other hand, while engaging and outgoing, possessed the same strong-minded will and ambition as his grandmother Elizabeth Bassett and his Aunt Ann Bassett. Chick was constantly scolded, whipped and demoralized by his stepfather. At the age of eight, the strong-willed boy saddled a horse and left for Brown's Park. As the sun went down and the coyotes began to howl, Chick returned home. The event was not lost on Josie. She wrote to her sister Ann, who had recently married Hiram "Hi" Bernard, asking her if she would take in her youngest son. Ann and Hi Bernard agreed. From then on Chick lived in Brown's Park with Aunt Ann and Uncle Hi and stayed with his mother in Craig during the school term.

Ann and Hi both grew very fond of the boy. They understood his wild nature and were patient with him. Hi Bernard had his own manner of discipline, tempered with individual attention and understanding. Bernard treated Chick as a man and expected the same in return. Bernard introduced Chick, at the age of ten, to the cattle experience, and Chick was a quick learner. Bernard took Chick to a spot on the Green River where cows often got stuck in the slimy mud. He helped Chick pull the animals free, and let him rescue the calves from the cows that could not be saved. He then gave the dogies to Chick to raise and care for. A mutual respect formed between the two and for the first time, young Chick respected authority. The Bernards bought Chick clothes, boots and a saddle. Hi and Chick would often ride horses over to Craig or even north into Rock Springs, Wyoming. The two grew very close, so much so that when Hi Bernard drew up his will after his divorce from Ann, he left everything to Herbert "Chick" McKnight.

As for the mild-mannered Crawford McKnight, who remained with his mother and stepfather, he would later comment on living with Charles A. Ranney:

He was not malicious but he was hell on discipline. He was a school teacher and we kids had to stay in line. Like the Army, you ask? Hell, it was worse than the Army. In the Army there's a certain slack but there wasn't any slack around him! If he said "Bounce!" you better bounce. He's been a strict old bachelor too long. I minded my mother because she made me want to mind her, but he was cold to everybody, with not a very definite sense of humor.[20]

When a new drugstore opened in Craig, Ranney was under pressure from the competition and his disposition at home only got worse. Ranney eventually sold his drugstore and bought a ranch on Fortification Creek. As pleased as Josie must have been at returning to ranch life, their domestic life did not improve. The couple began fighting and hurling verbal assaults at one another. Josie had finally had enough. After nearly four years of marriage, in early July 1906 Josie packed her bags and she and Crawford left the Charles Ranney home for the last time. Josie was always vague about this period in her life, but she did state in her taped interviews, "I would have stayed with Mr. Ranney - he was a fine man - if he hadn't been so hard on the children."

It is quite possible that Josie found another reason to leave Ranney: another man. For in July 1906, as soon as her divorce was final, she married Charles Williams, another druggist, in Baggs, Wyoming. Crawford McKnight later described his second stepfather as "a railroad man and a prizefighter who was also a pharmacist." He also said they later lived in Brown's Park and that he was a good man, and that Williams was a "city man who didn't like the country." When they moved back to Baggs, Josie ran the Vernon Hotel. Josie's sister Ann told her dear friend Esther Campbell that Williams was a "sports promoter." An issue of the *Craig Courier* dated October 16, 1905, ran the following notice: "Charles Williams, Snake River's favorite 'pug' will go to Craig and Hayden to fight a match with someone who has been sending challenges from that country."

After just six months of marriage, Josie Bassett McKnight Ranney Williams, filed for divorce in November 1906. She listed the cause as "desertion." Then, throwing caution to the wind, despite her Catholic childhood upbringing, six months later she married Emerson "Nig" Wells and the two moved back to Brown's Park.

Years later and well into her eighties, with decades of

emotional reflection, Josie commented on this period of her life:

> I wanted to do something, to get away off somewhere. I wanted
> to be in the hills - I don't know what I wanted. I didn't want to
> be in town. I knew I had to [be] at school time. And every year
> as long as the boys went to school I went with them. I went and
> located right there so I knew where they were every night. They
> finished school in Craig, and then they finished high school in
> Baggs. And then they were ready to go to Rawlins, the both
> of them. Then Crawford went to Mary University in Rock
> Springs and Chick "outlawed" on me and went home, back
> to Brown's Park, and went to work with cattle. He wouldn't go
> to the university, said, "I'm not interested and I'm not going
> to stay." Then he went home to my father. Then Crawford
> finished in the university and both went back to Brown's Park.

When the newlyweds returned to Brown's Park, they rented
the old Davenport ranch, which was then owned by the bank.
Wells, once a range foreman, now began his own cattle ranch.
Josie was happy to be back in her homeland and back, once again,
to ranching, her true love. Wells was a likable fellow. Crawford
McKnight said he was "a helluva nice guy." Yet Wells was also
an alcoholic. As time went on, it began to affect his health. Josie
insisted he see a doctor who confirmed the drinking as the problem
to Wells health condition.

Wells refused to stop drinking. He would often come home
in a drunken delirious stupor. Josie, raised by her temperance
father, did not like liquor, yet tolerated her husband's drinking
until it got out of hand and affected his health. Josie decided to
take matters into her own hands. She saw an advertisement for
the "Keeley Cure," which boasted "A positive and permanent
cure for liquor and drug addictions." Josie purchased the product,
a concoction of caffeine and tartar emetic, which is also a heart
depressant, that produced vomiting when ingested. Josie would put
the concoction in her husband's coffee, but it did not stop Wells
from drinking.

In 1912, Josie and Emerson made plans to attend the Christmas holidays at Linwood, Utah, located on the Utah-Wyoming border. The couple left early to reach Linwood, as a snowstorm was forecast. Josie later recalled the trip: "We arrived at Linwood after driving from Brown's Park in a buckboard in one of the coldest blizzards of the year. We didn't plan on staying as long as we did, but the snow was so deep and the wind blowing so cold."

Josie had been reluctant to even make the trip, given her husband's condition and knowing that there would be lively celebrations and much drinking. However, the snowstorm continued and the couple were forced to stay at Minnie Crouse Ronholdt's boarding house. This was an uncomfortable situation for Josie, as she and Minnie, the daughter of Charley Crouse, never got along while growing up in Brown's Park. Josie recounted the tragic events of New Year's Eve 1913:

He [Wells] was a good man, a good farmer and as good a man as ever lived, and he got on those whiskey drunks and went like foolish people. I didn't want to go, but the Rifes came - Guy Rife and his new wife and another Rife boy and his wife - and they wanted to go to Linwood. I didn't want to go. I thought, now if we go there they'll all get drunk. Wyoming was a regular honky-tonk and those men proceeded to go that honky-tonk and get drunk. Well there was a dance and I stayed at the hotel with Mrs. Rife - we had rooms at the hotel [Minnie Crouse Ronholdt's boarding house.] Mrs. Rife's husband, Orrin Rife, he didn't drink at all, but he couldn't get those fellows to the room to save him. Mrs. Guy Rife wanted me to go with her to the saloon to get the men. I said. "I didn't take them there and I never went to a saloon ever, and I'm not going." I knew an old Mexican. He worked in Brown's Park - forget his name, old Joe something, an old man. He came over and told me, "I hate to tell you, but Wells is terribly drunk. They're running a game and I stole his watch away from him and I brought it to you." Well, I didn't know what to do. I couldn't get him away from there. We danced the first night. I went to the dance and tried to stand it all I could. I couldn't do anything else. I went with Minnie and a whole crowd of women and went to the dance. That was New Year's Eve and they danced all night 'till sunup. I didn't. I went home and went to bed. The next night they danced again. I went for a little while, and went back and went to bed. The next morning there was a man from Kansas City - a horse buyer, I forget his name. He was a very nice man, and he came to me and said, "I think your husband is ready to quit drinking." He said "He's down in the living room." I went and he was there. I said, "Wells, I brought you a cup of coffee. Do you think you can drink it?" He said, "I'll try. I feel like hell this morning." I said, "As soon as it comes sunup time, we'll start for home." We had a team that wasn't very safe, kind of a tricky outfit. But I thought, I can drive anything to get out of here. So he drank a little of the coffee and he didn't drink any more. I helped him get his shoes on and helped him get his sweater on. Then I got a basin of warm water for him to wash his face and I said, "Now, if you can eat some breakfast, I'll bring it over here. I think you're too shaky to go up that hillside with ice on it, back to the other hotel." He said, "I won't want any breakfast, I feel like hell." He kept saying that to me and I said, "I'm awfully sorry, but I can't help. You did it yourself." He kept acting like he was sick to his stomach, and I said, "Are you going to throw that whiskey up? I wish you would." So I got a slop bucket and set it there by him - and I saw that something was wrong. The horse buyer said to me, "If I was in your place I'd give him a drink of whiskey. He needs it." And I said, "I think he needs anything but a drink of whiskey, but if you think that's all right, I will get it." I gave Wells a drink, then combed his hair and put the bottle back. Well, he kept turning, kind of twisting around like he was in misery somehow, I don't know what. But I knew he was wrong. And finally he just straightened right back and died. He threw up a little kind of foam, right from his lungs of course. Well, I laid him down and I didn't know what to do. I was stranded. I was just - I might as well have been drunk. There I was, clear up in Linwood thirty miles from home.[21]

Charley Olmey, a cowboy from Brown's Park, was also at the New Year's celebration in Linwood. He offered to take Josie's buckboard and horses to the nearby town of Green River, Wyoming, to buy a casket and return to Linwood. Meanwhile, several women prepared the body of Emerson Wells and laid his body outside of the hotel in the freezing January air. The local authorities visited with Josie, examined the body and the room where the death occurred. However, there was no one in the small town to perform an autopsy or sign a death certificate. When Olmey returned the following day with a pine coffin, Josie was allowed to take the body of her husband back to Brown's Park. Josie related the solemn event:

> We put the body in a homemade pine box put together by M. N. Larsen, and loaded it in the back of the wagon, and drove back to Brown's Park in freezing weather. We took him back there, and then the next day I took him down and buried him by Uncle Sam, down in that cemetery. It was on the - he died on the third day of the month of January and was buried on the seventh. And the whole country was there. There were lots of people in Brown's Park then, lots of people.[22]

Suspicion and rumors were whispered almost from the moment Well's body was laid in the casket. How was it possible that a relatively young man could die so suddenly for no reason except for the previous three-day drunken stupor? These rumors were fueled by none other than Minnie Crouse Ronholdt, no friend of Josie Bassett McKnight Ranney Williams Wells. Perhaps out of spite from childhood days; the reason is hard to discern, for Minnie Crouse Ronholdt spread the gossip that Josie had actually poisoned her husband. She spread reports that she had overheard the couple fighting and that she had personally witnessed Josie refusing a woman to take a glass of milk to Wells. There were many who did not believe Ronholdt's wild accusations against Josie, pointing to the fact that Josie had been questioned and cleared by the Linwood authorities.

Undaunted, and evidently on a personal quest of some sort against Josie, Ronholdt, so sure of Josie's guilt in the poisoning of her husband, took her accusation further. She wrote an article for the *Green River Star* newspaper which hinted at the poisoning theory, writing: "It is the opinion of those who saw Wells just before he died that he swallowed poison, perhaps strychnine, as his actions were similar to the actions of men who had been known to die of the effects of an overdose of that drug."[23]

However, the newspaper refused to publish the accusatory article. As the rumors grew, other stories filtered throughout the Park, to ridiculous dimensions. It was said that Well's grave was dug up and there was no body in the coffin. Some even said it was the Vernal, Utah, sheriff who dug up the grave. No matter that the grave site was located in Colorado, therefore he would have been out of his jurisdiction. Nevertheless, this story was told and retold with the wild tale that Josie must have dumped his body somewhere along the road between Linwood, Utah, and Brown's Park, Colorado.

Obviously, none of the rumors were true. Despite the writings of a handful of authors to the contrary, Josie was never suspected of any wrongdoing by the authorities regarding the death of Emerson Wells. Even so, Minnie Crouse Ronholdt Rasmussen, who later remarried, always maintained her position that Josie killed her fourth husband. Well into her nineties Rasmussen gave a taped interview which can be found at the Vernal Public Library, Vernal, Utah.

Josie, a widow at the age of thirty-nine, began planning her future. She didn't have the money to buy the Davenport ranch where she and Wells lived and looked into homesteading a place of her own. Meanwhile, she continued to operate the ranch with Ben Morris, the ranch hand previously hired by Wells.

Because Wells had hired Morris, a thirty-four-year-old Oklahoma cowboy, Josie trusted him. He was good-looking, had a great sense of humor and was dependable around the ranch. It wasn't long before the working relationship between the two became intimate. Yet Morris was not at all as trustworthy as Josie thought. In the summer of 1913, Josie's oldest son, Crawford, rode over from Craig for a visit with his mother. While there, he observed a couple dozen sheep in a corral with a nose brand belonging to Henry Nebb, whom Crawford had once worked for. Crawford, years later, remarked on the character of Nebb, "He was a nice fellow and an honest one. If he owed you a nickel you'd get it." Crawford confronted his mother about the sheep. When she said she knew nothing about them, he told her that they were stolen sheep. Again, Josie denied any involvement.

In a disgusted rage, Crawford McKnight stormed out of the house and rode directly to the home of Henry Nebb. He told Nebb that he had found his sheep at his mother's ranch. Nebb told Crawford that he had suspected that his missing animals were at his mother's ranch. Not wanting to cause trouble with Crawford's mother, who Nebb believed was innocent, he did tell Crawford that something needed to be done. Crawford offered to drive the sheep to Nebb's ranch. And he did.

Crawford and his younger brother Chick then confronted Morris about the stolen sheep. A surly and abusive Morris countered and told the McKnight boys it was none of their business. Enraged by the confrontation by the boys, a fight ensued. Morris was a large man and when he swung at one of the boys, the other reacted. It took both of them to subdue Morris. Chick hit Morris with the butt of his gun. Morris fell to the ground, unconscious. Josie looked on, helpless to stop the fight. When it was over, she had a few words for her sons, and they had a few words for her regarding the thief she had taken up with. This incident separated mother and sons for several years.

When the lease was up on the Davenport ranch in the fall of 1913, Josie and Ben Morris pulled up stakes and headed for a homestead Josie had filed on in Utah. It was a portion of Ute land that the government had recently opened for settlement. When Josie first saw it, the beauty of the region, the lush green meadows

Josie is pictured at her cabin on Cub Creek. *Uintah County Regional History Center*

and quiet solitude, she must have sensed that this land, this place, would be where she would live the rest of her life. For the spot she chose was a vast open meadow at one end and the base of Blue Mountain, almost like a rock fortress, at the other end. The 160 acres that Josie chose was filled with flowing springs, which meant water for planting, open space for grazing livestock and—perhaps most important to Josie—the land was miles away from any of the other new settlers who would come to the area.

Herding fifty head of cattle and fifty sheep, they crossed over Blue Mountain and settled on the homestead along Cub Creek, approximately fifteen miles east of Vernal, Utah, not far from the Green River and a few miles southwest of the Mormon town of Jensen, Utah. Not long after settling on their new place, Josie Bassett McKnight Ranney Wells married Ben Morris, on November 24, 1913, in Jensen, Utah.

In the spring of 1914, Josie and Ben cleared brush, built a corral for the cattle and built coops for chickens. The sheep grazed in the open meadow. Josie planted a large vegetable garden as well as saplings of apple, apricot, and plum trees, the beginnings of what Josie hoped would be a fine orchard. Josie and Ben built two small but adequate cabins. The cabins, built side by side and facing the ridge of Blue Mountain, were for the Morris couple and for Josie's father, Herb Bassett, when he came to visit.

Not long after the cabins were built, the Morrises received their first visitor. Josie's sister Ann arrived for a much-needed vacation after being acquitted for the second time of cattle rustling in Brown's Park. When Herb Bassett finally came to visit his daughter, he stayed at the cabin Josie and Ben had built for him and helped build a small cabin for Ann on her new property. The ever-flighty Ann soon became bored and left the ranch for extensive trips. Josie later said, "Ann could never be satisfied if it were too long a ride to town."[25]

After two years of marriage, Josie began to grow weary of Ben Morris. The well-mannered, easy-going Josie became impatient with her husband's crude behavior. When Josie caught Morris mistreating a horse, she had finally had enough. Morris had used a spade bit on a feisty horse, which was known to control the animal. Furious, Josie rushed to the horse, whose injured mouth was ripped and dripping with blood. Enraged, Josie ran to the cabin and returned with a frying pan, waving it at Morris to get off her property. An astonished Morris immediately left. At a store in Jensen, he was asked what happened. He replied, "She gave me fifteen minutes to get off her property, and I only used five of them."

Josie eventually went to Jensen and filed for divorce. Hiram "Hi" Bernard, Josie's former brother-in-law, later said, "Josie Bassett McKnight is a jolly good natured woman, she works like a steam shovel and then she hunts up some unworthy bums and gives away the proceeds of her labor. Her hobby is husbands, she has had five or six good men and discards them one after the other without a backward glance."[26]

For the next forty years, Josie lived alone at Cub Creek. However, it was not without its share tragedy, controversy and shady activity.

In November 1925, Josie was deeply saddened when her younger brother, Elbert "Eb" Bassett, committed suicide in Brown's Park. The *Craig Courier* ran the following headline in the November 19, 1925, issue of the paper: "Lodore Rancher Suicides Eben [sic] Bassett of Brown's Park Took Poison at home of Frank Lawrence on Big Gulch early Thursday Morning Was one of Pioneer Cattlemen of Northwestern Colorado Was to have appeared in Court today to answer charge of killing cow."

Eb had been involved in a few underhanded dealings and was heavily in debt. In an effort to save the Bassett family ranch, Eb had deeded it to his brother, George. When Eb was investigated for fraud, a judge ruled that deeding the ranch to George was an effort to hide assets and Eb lost the family ranch. Josie believed Eb was remorseful for losing the ranch and "just grew tired of living." Crawford, however, later said that he was in love with a woman "he could never have."

Josie went to Brown's Park, where she and George held a small service for Eb and buried him in the Bassett family cemetery. Eb willed the few assets he had left, particularly cattle, to his older sisters, Josie and Ann. As Ann was in California with her husband, Frank Willis, it was left to Josie to round up what was left of Eb's cattle. She arrived in Zenobia Basin in Brown's Park on a chilly November day. As she gathered the cattle for the long trip back to Cub Creek, a few local ranchers watched and checked that none of the animals had their brands. She realized Eb's reputation in the Park was not a good one. Years later, George Bassett's daughter, Edna, remarked about the bond between the two brothers:

> As far back as my knowledge goes, Eb did many things, terrible things, that were extremely hurtful and expensive, Dad seemed to take it all stoically, trying to smooth things over, make amends. They were friends, they worked together some, saw a good deal of each other, and I know Dad was fond of Eb, making it that much harder for him to bear Eb's transgressions.[27]

Dispirited, Josie drove the cattle to her Cub Creek ranch. In time, Josie built a new cabin with the help of her grandson Frank. She installed large windows and used concrete for the floors. The fireplace was the only warmth for the cold winter months. The kitchen was adequate for Josie's needs, although she still hauled fresh water from the spring.

To supplement her income, she began making her own brandy and whiskey. The era of Prohibition had been the law of the land for years, and considering times were tough and she had a fine fruit orchard, Josie decided to take advantage of the situation. She erected a still, supplied by her brother-in-law, Frank Willis. She was particularly proud of her apricot brandy, even sampling a bit for herself from time to time. When warned by family and friends that revenue agents were looking for her still, she destroyed it. However, during the years of the Great Depression she supplied food, particularly rustled beef, to others in the area. It was a particularly depressed economy in this remote area of Utah. Many suspected Josie's generosity came from illegal means, but no one said anything.

Then in January 1936, a local rancher and bitter adversary, James "Jim" Robinson, accused Josie of rustling his cattle, butchering them, and then selling the beef to local families. Josie was arrested and charged with cattle rustling, just as her sister Ann would be. Josie's bail was paid by local ranchers, including her one-time lover, Ed Lewis, and Josie immediately hired an attorney. Wallace Calder was also the president of the local branch of the Mormon Church. After hearing Josie's story, he was convinced of her innocence and that Robinson framed her.

When the trial began the following month, sixty-two-year-old Josie arrived dressed in a fine dress, looking very much like a common gray-haired grandmother.

Years later, Josie, perhaps with a chuckle and a wink in her eye, spoke about the trial:

> I put on a frilly dress, wore sensible shoes, and had my hair done in a domestic style on the top of my head. I looked like a

petite little grandmother as I stood before the judge. I said to the judge and the jury 'Your Honor, do you seriously believe that a little old lady could kill and butcher out even one beef cow by herself?' [28]

In 1948, *Life* magazine ran an article on Josie. Ann and her husband Frank were visiting at the time of the interview. Ann must have been jealous that her sister was about to get national attention for her lady life as a rancher, but she never let on. The *Life* magazine editor even mentioned that the story could possibly become a Hollywood movie. Now the sibling rivalry that had always existed between the sisters simmered in Ann. Frank and Ann drove Josie to Vernal for the interview. There was a stark contrast between the sisters, as Ann was dressed in high fashion and Josie wore overalls, a felt hat and tennis shoes. Josie had been told, and Ann had not, that the photo shoots would include Josie on horseback, photos of her with a shotgun, and photos of her shooting. Obviously, it was Josie and not Ann who dressed for the part. When the article was published with the title of "Queen of the Rustlers," Ann was enraged.

Josie would later get the last laugh with her sister's rivalry, when in 1967, Hollywood did make a film loosely based on Josie's life. It was titled "The Ballad of Josie," with Doris Day in the starring role. It was nothing close to Josie's life, but made for good box office receipts.

Meanwhile, the added attention from the *Life* magazine article garnered Josie much publicity. Teachers brought their students out to her ranch, where Josie would captivate her young audience with stories and show them around her working ranch. In Maybell, Colorado, southeast of Brown's Park, a women's group often hosted Josie, touting her as one of Colorado's pioneer women. In 1953, in keeping with the pioneer theme, Jay Searle, president of Vernal's roping club, enticed Josie, with a swank rodeo outfit and a brand new saddle, to be the rodeo queen in the annual rodeo. At the age of seventy-nine, Josie sat astride a fine pinto and galloped around the arena waving her hat at the crowd as they stood and cheered. Josie even participated in a horse race and finished in third place. Josie was showing no signs of slowing down.

The 1950s were good and bad years for Josie.

At the close of the 1950s, Josie felt her health was suffering. A neighbor took her to the hospital where she was diagnosed with a bleeding ulcer. While in the hospital, she fell out of bed and broke her collarbone. After some time recuperating in the hospital, a stubborn Josie insisted on going home to Cub Creek. She resumed her work on the ranch, although her right hand plagued her a bit.

For years, newspaper reporters and curious writers had often made their way to Cub Creek to interview Josie. Many were interested in her life and her time at Brown's Park, particularly after the sensational book, *The Story of Butch Cassidy*, by Charles Kelly, was published in 1938. She usually shooed them off her land. Josie later said of Kelly, "When Kelly dies and goes to hell, the Devil will shun his company for lying about the dead."

However, when G. E. Untermann, curator of the Vernal museum, came to visit, Josie agreed to meet with him. He had known her brother, George, and spent considerable time with him. She talked freely of her life at Browns Park, and her life at Cub Creek. At the age of eighty-five, Josie's mind was still very sharp. When Untermann introduced her to Murl Messersmith of Dinosaur, Utah, she agreed to a series of taped interviews. Messersmith even took her to Brown's Park, where she guided him to the various sites, such as the old Bassett ranch, the cabin where she had lived during her marriage with Jim McKnight, the first schoolhouse at Vermilion Creek, the site of her Uncle Sam's cabin, and the various graves that dotted the area, including the Bassett family cemetery.

On May 28, 1964, during one of these walks, Josie suddenly fell to the floor and suffered a fatal heart attack. Josephine Bassett McKnight Ranney Williams Wells Morris was dead at the age of ninety-four.

Following the funeral service in Vernal, Utah, the Vernal Mortuary provided a funeral car for the transportation of Josie's body to Brown's Park for burial. As the funeral procession approached the site of the Bassett family cemetery on the land where Josie grew up, they were greeted by a large crowd of Brown's Park citizens as well as several friends from Rock Springs, Wyoming, who were there to pay their respects to their friend and the pioneer legend. Burial services were conducted by J. Arben Jolley. Pallbearers were grandsons of Josie's, as well as husbands of her granddaughters, including Nelson Eaton, Jim Lube, and his son, Jim Lube, Jr., Robert Smuin, Larry Wanner, and George McKnight. After a brief ceremony, Josephine Bassett McKnight Ranney Williams Wells Morris was buried within the iron fencing of the family cemetery, next to her mother Elizabeth, and near her sister, Ann.

Josephine Bassett McKnight Ranney Williams Wells Morris once reflected on the philosophy of life, saying, "You have to keep in action to keep from getting old. I don't intend to let myself get old."

# Notes

1. Josie Bassett taped interviews by Murl Messersmith, July 6, 1961. Dinosaur National Monument, Jensen, Utah (hereafter Josie Bassett taped interviews)
2. ibid.
3. ibid.
4. ibid.
5. ibid.
6. ibid.
7. ibid.
8. McClure, *The Bassett Women*, pg. 49.
9. That historic ditch that Josie Bassett McKnight built in 1893 provided water for the lower lands until the construction of Highway 40, west from Maybell stretching into Utah.
10. Josie Bassett taped interviews. Josie incorrectly uses Valentine Hoy when it was Jesse S. Hoy's ranch.
11. ibid.
12. ibid.
13. Burroughs, *Where the Old West Stayed Young*, pg. 165.
14. Joe Davenport interview, *Rock Springs Rocket*, March 1, 1929.
15. J. S. Hoy manuscript, Denver Public Library.
16. McClure, *The Bassett Women*, pg. 68.
17. Tom Hicks was the alias used by the killer for hire, Tom Horn.
18. Josie Bassett taped interviews.
19. ibid.
20. McClure, *The Bassett Women*, pg. 109.
21. Josie Bassett taped interviews.
22. ibid.
23. Minnie Crouse Ronholdt Rasmussen always maintained her position that Josie killed her fourth husband. Well into her nineties Rasmussen gave a taped interview which can be found at the Vernal Public Library, Vernal, Utah.
24. Josie Bassett taped interviews.
25. McClure, *The Bassett Women*, pg.124.
26. Hiram "Hi" Bernard's remark regarding his former sister-

in-law is found in *Confidentially Told*, the 1917 unpublished manuscript by Frank Willis.

27. McClure, *The Bassett Women*, pg. 142.
28. ibid.

# Ann Bassett
## Colorado's Cattle Queen

L egend, lore, mystery, romance and even murder: these are only a few of the many controversies surrounding the life of "Queen Ann," the legend of Brown's Park. She became one of the most noted frontier women in Colorado, and gained a reputation as one of the toughest in the West.

What a woman Ann must have been! She was small in stature, with dark hair, pretty features, and high-spirited in personality. By the age of eight, she could ride a horse, handle a gun, and curse as well as any man on the Bassett ranch.

Anna Marie Bassett was the younger sister of Josie Bassett. She was born to Amos Herbert Bassett and Mary Eliza ("Elizabeth") Chamberlain Miller Bassett on May 12, 1878. Anna was the first white child born not only in Brown's Hole, but all of northwestern Colorado. Elizabeth could not nurse baby Anna, so local ranchers came to the aid of the Bassett family, finding an Indian woman who agreed to serve as a wet nurse. Elizabeth was so grateful to the Ute Indians, she spent as much time with them as she could, engaging in long conversations. Finally, the Bassetts acquired a milk cow for baby Anna. The milk cow was not only a blessing to the Bassett family, but the beginning of their eventual cattle herd. The army pension Herb received monthly was of great assistance to the struggling family as they built their new life in the West. Herb, with the assistance of friendly neighbors, built a five-room, single-story log home for his family. However, during the construction of the home, the children, Samuel, Josie and baby Ann, broke out with measles. Elizabeth set up comfortable bedding under the cottonwood trees, where they could rest in the fresh air. True to her pioneer spirit and character, she kept one eye on the

Ann Bassett fought the large cattle barons of Brown's Park and won. *DPL*

children while helping her husband hew the logs for the cabin.

The land on which Herb built his home was open on the south end and sheltered by the hills on the other three sides. A gentle flowing stream of cold mountain water wandered its way through the homestead. Across the valley was the site of Lodore Canyon. Herb planted a vegetable garden and Elizabeth, with a strong determination to succeed in this western land, began buying Durham cattle. Ann later described the home decor:

> There was a big cook stove, innumerable iron pots and brass kettles, feather beds, several "spool" beds. All these shipped from Grandfather's Virginia plantation and hauled to the ranch in wagons. Most important was the large cook stove—built to last not to lift. There were a few choice pieces of china for which we had no use for. He [Herb Bassett] became resolutely set against hauling any more "boughten" house furnishings. Birch grew in profusion along all the streams. Rawhide was plentiful. Father solved our problems by making small tables and chairs using birch for the frames, and rawhide strips for seats and backs. Cushions were made of buckskin filled with milkweed floss. The curtain problem was made for mother to solve. She traded Indian Mary ten pounds of sugar for a bale of fringed buckskins. Father fashioned curtain rings from the leg bones of deer, and thus we made drapes for the windows. The home contained good books such as Shakespeare's complete works, Shelley, Keats, Dickens, Byron, Longfellow, and many other works of poems, literature, and travel. My parents had brought books from their eastern home. Others were given us by Judge Conway. Bassett's ranch was a place for people to congregate, relax and read.[1]

Within a year, Herb's health had improved dramatically. Elizabeth's cattle herd was growing as well. In 1879, Herb and "Buffalo" Jack Rife built a cabin in Zenobia Basin, so named by Elizabeth. Again, Ann related the details of her father's cabin: "Father cut logs, dragged them to the site by saddle horse, and hewed timbers for the door facings and floors for a three-room cabin which still stands intact." The cabin was in a grassy meadow at the base of Douglas Mountain, several miles south of the ranch, where Herb intended to move the cattle for the summer months.

Before the herd was moved, the cattle were branded. The Bassett brand was the Zee Bar Kay. Z-K was branded on the left side of the animals, while the left ear was split and the right ear was cropped.

While Herb did his fair share in the family cattle enterprise, it was Elizabeth who operated the ranch. She worked with the cattle, kept an eye out for any roaming animals, participated in the branding, and learned to use a rifle and shotgun. She rode the fence line daily and surveyed her land on horseback. Herb strung four-stranded barbed wire around his property, the first rancher to do so in Brown's Hole. Later, Herb, with the help of Tom Davenport, was the first to grow grain in the area and used cradles and scythes to harvest the grain for feeding the animals.

In addition to the cattle, Herb and Elizabeth began raising thoroughbred horses. This was a great desire of Elizabeth's, the granddaughter of a noted breeder of fine horses in Virginia. Elizabeth soon gained a local reputation as a respectable breeder of her thoroughbreds. Esther Campbell bought one of the Bassett's horses. Esther and Ann became close friends. Esther later described the day young Ann Bassett first saw Campbell's buckskin horse, recognizing it as one from her mother's stock:

> They owned the original mare, the "Tippecanoe" mare, and raised many good colts from her. Her father [Herb] bought the mare from some people traveling through the country from Tennessee. She was high-lifted and they had a wire tied around her tongue to control her. Her tongue was almost cut in two. Mr. Bassett felt sorry for her and bought her. Her colts were always full of life and willing to travel. Ann had a team of buckskins for a buggy wagon. She drove them from Douglas to Craig from sunup to sundown, and they would be pulling at the bits when they trotted up the last hill to Craig.[2]

Herb and Elizabeth both believed in raising their children to help on the family ranch. At a very early age, the Bassett boys, Samuel, Elbert and George (both Elbert and George were born in Brown's Hole, on June 21 of 1880 and March 29 of 1884, respectively), all learned to rope and ride and were given their chores on the ranch.

The strong-willed Elizabeth insisted her two daughters, Josie and Ann, learn the same ranching skills. She raised her daughters to be strong and independent in the rugged, isolated area of Brown's Hole. Ann later described the chores that went with a working ranch:

> We had to work. Horses, cattle, or sheep, as the case might be, required constant care. The farming, raising and "putting up" hay was a part-time job. Our system of living depended on individual productive industry for its well-being. Staple groceries and clothing had to be hauled from Rock Springs, Wyoming, by wagons over rough roads, a hundred miles away. It required about ten days to complete the round trip. This was done spring and fall. All farming was done the first few years. There were only a few plows in the country. These plows, as were other farming equipment, were used or loaned all around the area where needed. Grain was threshed by driving horses over the bundles placed on the ground in clean swept corrals, and cleaned of chaff by a homemade fanning mill.

Both girls were accomplished horsewomen at a very young age. Being a sophisticated southern woman, Elizabeth rode sidesaddle and always in a dress. Both Josie and Ann preferred riding their horses as their father and brothers did, and wearing pants. Ann greatly admired the accomplishments and character of her mother. She later wrote, "Mother was a natural executive as well as an excellent horsewoman." She also commented on her mother's riding habits: "Her outfit consisted of a beautifully fitted 'habit' of rich, dark blue material, long-skirted and draped with grace. For trimming, there were a number of gleaming brass buttons. She was a blonde. Mounted on her thoroughbred horse, 'Calky,' she was a picture to remember."

In time, the Brown's Hole early era of the mountain men

and explorers gave way to the Brown's Park era of settlers and cattle ranchers; the early pioneers of Brown's Park formed a tight-knit caring community. Due to the isolation, rugged area and harsh conditions, it was human nature as well as a necessity. When the only doctor in the area, John D. Parsons, who had delivered Ann, died in 1881, Elizabeth served the Brown's Park area as the community doctor. Ann recounted one of the many occasions where her mother's services were required:

> One young man of our neighborhood was riding near a barbed-wire fence and his horse ran into the wire, which cut the flesh of the cowpuncher's leg to the bone. It was a deep, bad cut. Mother was called as usual. She put five stitches into the flesh, with sewing or sack needles as used on horses and cattle, with common table salt as an antiseptic, and herbs gathered by the Indians to stop the flow of blood.

While Elizabeth lent her medical skills for the good of the community, Herb established the first public school district in northwest Colorado. Four students attended the first school term in 1881, held in the dugout home of Henry and Jennie Jaynes. The students included the two Jaynes children and the older Basset children, Josie and Sam. Ann and her younger brothers would later attend the same school, improved by the construction of a fine log building. Education of his children was a priority to Herb Bassett. The earliest public record of the Bassett children's educational development appeared in an early Craig newspaper, the *Colorado Pantograph*, printed in the November, 1892, issue: "The Misses Bassett and Mr. Matt Rash arrived in the city Monday from Brown's Park. The young ladies are here for the purpose of attending school, and are stopping at the home of Mr. Joe Carroll."

As the Bassett cattle ranch began to show a profit, improvements were made on the property. Barns were built, as well as a corral for the horses. A bunkhouse for hired help was erected. Herb piped the spring to bring the water closer to the to the log

The Bassett family ranch in Brown's Park. *Museum of Northwest Colorado*

home and to provide irrigation for the garden. He established hay fields, becoming the first man in the Park to do so, providing winter forage for the cattle and horses. Herb and Elizabeth Bassett were well-known in Brown's Park for their hospitality to guests and generosity and kindness to their hired hands. With Elizabeth's outgoing nature and Herb's ability to entertain with music and intelligent conversation, the Bassett ranch became the social hub of Brown's Park. The Bassetts had made good friends in the Hole, including Judge Conway, the Jarvies and Charlie and Mary Crouse.

The Middlesex Cattle Company also moved into the area. The company, financed by Boston interests, located their operation just north and west of Brown's Park. The local manager, John Clay, intended to build a large cattle empire. Among the several cattle brands they registered, one brand, known as the "Vee Dee Connected" or "Flying Vee Dee," commonly known as "VD cattle," soon became known throughout Brown's Park. Clay threatened to "buy all the 'little fellows' out or drive them out of the country."[3] Gun had moved his cattle north of Brown's Hole, near the headwaters of Beaver Creek in the fall of 1879. In Ann's memoirs, she recounted the incident:

Jack's cattle, supplemented by the herds of the settlers
in Brown's Park, were the only users of the range until
the Middlesex outfit, who controlled the greater part of
southwestern Wyoming, began to move their herds southward,
and they came like a flood, devouring and consuming
everything in their path. When they reached Beaver Basin,
Jack Gun saw that it was useless for him to stand alone with his
small herd against the thousands and thousands of cattle being
pushed onward and southward.

When the Middlesex Cattle Company began their
encroachment into Brown's Park, the ranchers held firm, with only
two ranchers selling out to the corporate cattle company.

Young Ann once found a sickly stray calf that carried the
Middlesex brand. The manager of the Middlesex Cattle Company,
which owned the calf, gave the animal to little Ann. Ann brought
the animal home, and her tender care and complete attention
saved the calf's life. Later, a roving Middlesex cowboy spotted the
calf and returned it to the Middlesex herd. Eight-year-old Ann
confronted the manager of the Middlesex Company with great
determination, demanding her given cow be returned to her.
Retrieving her animal, she took it back to the Bassett ranch, and
immediately persuaded one of the ranch wranglers to alter the
brand on the cow. It was her first experience at a rumored career
of cattle rustling that would remain throughout her life, and may
have been the driving force that later gained her fame as she fought
against the large cattle companies.

All over the tri-state area of Colorado, Utah and Wyoming,
the large corporate cattle ranches were ruthless and did everything
legal, and even illegal, to acquire good ranch land in Brown's Park.
Several ranchers reported stolen cattle, including the Bassett ranch.
Herb strung barbed wire fencing around his land, the first in the
Park to do so. Elizabeth finally had enough of the large cattle
companies threatening her and the other ranchers of Brown's Park.
With her charm and keen business sense, she was able to hire Isom
Dart, a former slave, and Madison Matthew (Matt) Rash, both of

whom were former employees of the Middlesex Cattle Company; and Jack Fitch, a friend of Dart's. Other hired ranch hands included Angus McDougal and James (Jim) McKnight. While Matt Rash worked for the Bassett ranch, he had acquired his own piece of land some two miles west of the Bassett ranch, along a nice flowing creek, later named Matt Creek, where he built a cabin and grazed his own small herd of cattle. Nevertheless, he worked very well with Elizabeth and the two soon became good friends, so much so that Elizabeth gifted him with a fine sorrel mare with four white stockings and a white star on her forehead. The mare would become his favorite saddle horse.

As the children grew older they were each taught to ride horses. Ann explained: "Learning to ride in early childhood was a necessity. For training in balance, bucking contests were improvised. Our hay corral was the arena. From this training we developed what proved to be quite a game."[4]

In 1882, a stranger by the name of Hambleton, along with two friends, came to the Bassett ranch looking for one of their hired men, Jack Rolla. Jennie Jaynes, who had been hired as cook for the ranch hands, greeted the visitors and directed the men to the barn and corrals where they could find Rolla. The strangers approached the corrals, finding Rolla with his back to them, and shot him in cold blood. Several ranch hands, along with Herb and Elizabeth, quickly ran to the scene and drew their guns on the strangers. Mrs. Jaynes gathered the Bassett children into the safe shelter of a nearby building. Ann later recounted the horrible murder:

> He [Jack Rolla] was a pleasant-mannered young fellow from Texas who came to the Bassett ranch in 1882. A good hand with horses, he was hired to break bronco on the ranch. It was in the late fall of that year that three strange men arrived about noon, and were asked to eat dinner with the family. While Mrs. Jaynes, who cooked for us at the time, was preparing the meal, one of the strangers asked her if Jack worked there. Mrs. Jaynes replied, "Yes, that is Jack saddling a horse at the corral."

One of them pulled a gun and shot Rolla as he was reaching for a bridle. He ran behind the barn, where he fell, mortally wounded. The one who had done the shooting said his name was Hambleton and that Rolla had shot and killed his brother in Abilene, Kansas. Hambleton had trailed Jack Rolla for two years to kill him. Rolla confirmed Hambleton's statement in part, explaining that a man of that name had married his sister. Mother spiritedly informed Hambleton that it was not the custom of the northwest to shoot an unarmed man in the back. By the determined threat of her leveled Winchester, she lined the trio up against the bunkhouse wall, and directed the wounded Rolla to kill his assassin, or all three men, if he wanted to. Rolla was too weak to hold a gun and he died a few hours later. While mother and Mrs. Jaynes were administering to the dying cowboy, father and Perry were guarding the prisoners. Harry Hindle went to notify the settlers of the park, and to get Charles Allen, Justice of the Peace, to the scene of the crime. Night came and father began to think with deepening apprehension. A lynching could be in the making. He advised the captives to go to the barn and feed their horses, and he warned them to ride directly to the county seat, over a hundred miles away, and surrender themselves to the law. When neighbors arrived at the Bassett ranch, the murderer and his companions had escaped. Naturally, they failed to do as father had instructed, and were never heard of again. The method subscribed to by my father in the matter of advice to the shooters would have been in direct conflict with the opinion of mother and Mrs. Jaynes. Therefore, he did not commit himself and tell the true story for some time afterwards.

On December 11, 1892, just as the Christmas season was being celebrated in the Bassett household, tragedy occurred in the family. The ambitious and always energetic Elizabeth suddenly fell ill and took to her bed. Within days, Elizabeth died suddenly at the age of thirty-seven. Her untimely death was attributed to either appendicitis or a miscarriage. She was the first to be buried in the private cemetery on the Bassett ranch.[5]

While it was Elizabeth Bassett who began the war against the large cattle companies, it would be her daughter, Ann, who would carry on her legacy and finally finish it. Her sister, Josephine, would later write, "Ann was a visionary and up in the air a good part of the time."

Both Ann and her older sister, Josie, loved life in Brown's Park. The attractive Bassett girls were well-skilled with horses and roping, and could shoot nearly as well as any of the hired hands on the Bassett ranch. The Bassett girls, as sisters often do, had their share of conflict with each other. As the oldest Bassett daughter, Josie was expected to look out for her younger siblings. Ann resented the constant scoldings from her older sister and often went to her parents in tears. Of course, Josie would be scolded, to the delight of Ann.

Ann inherited her mother's wild temper. During the range war between her mother and the Hoys, Ann would throw rocks at any of the Hoys who happened to pass by the school yard. Following their elementary schooling, Herb sent each of his children to Craig to finish their education.

In the spring of 1886, twelve-year-old Josie and her eight-year-old sister Ann attended one of Charlie Crouse's local horse races. Crouse was known throughout the Park for his prized horses as well as his occasional cattle rustling. Outlaw and part-time Brown's Park resident near Diamond Mountain, Matt Warner, whose real name was Willard Erastus Christiansen, later wrote, "Charley Crause [sic] , that good-hearted old cattle rustler from Brown's Park."[6]

One of Crouse's hired hands, exceptional with horses, was a man known as George Cassidy (George Leroy Parker.) This particular horse race was greatly attended as Crouse's sorrel gelding was to race against Ken Hatch's award-winning black mare from Ashley Valley. George Cassidy rode Crouse's sorrel to a roaring finish.

So caught up in the moment, both Bassett girls became enamored with the handsome blond man who won the horse race.

The girls found any and every excuse they could to visit the Crouse ranch just to be near the dashing cowboy. While this became great entertainment during the hot summer of 1886, their efforts often gained them no more than a smile or nod from Cassidy. As summer turned to fall, both girls were back in school and their summer crush was soon a fading memory. According to Ann:

> I never saw Butch Cassidy dance or get drunk, or carry a gun in sight. I am not presuming to say he was not an outlaw later. But what I do say is I had seen him many times before and after he was called an outlaw and he was at all times a well-mannered fellow. Cassidy continued to work for Charlie Crouse for a year then went away.[7]

Cassidy would indeed leave the area for months on end but would eventually wander back to Brown's Park.

After completing her local education in Craig, Herb sent Ann to St. Mary's of the Wasatch in Salt Lake City, Utah. This was the same school Josie was attending when Elizabeth died. While Josie enjoyed her experience at the school, Ann hated it. At the end of the first term, the nuns asked Ann's father to find another school for his daughter. Ann wrote in her memoirs that she attended "Miss" Potter's School for Girls in Boston, Massachusetts. Josie later told her family that "this was just another of Ann's exaggerations." It is difficult to know the truth, as Ann was prone to "exaggerations," as her sister stated, but it must also be remembered that Ann and Josie had a long history of sibling rivalry. However, Mrs. Potter's School for Girls, located in Everett, a suburb of Boston, advertised in several local and national publications, such as the *Critic*, which ran several ads in their 1894 issues, the time period Ann says she attended the school. The fact remains that Ann was indeed away from Brown's Park attending a school in the East from 1893 to 1895. In any case, Ann wrote of an experience at the school:

Then came a more drastic change in my life—I was sent to the select 'Miss Potter's School for Girls' in the exclusive suburbs of Boston. I departed from home with confidence, anticipating a further enjoyable experience. I found myself in a place so strange it might as well have been located in a foreign land. Not only strange, but at times unbearably disagreeable. Endless months dragged past in a restricted social atmosphere of quaint gentility and—baked beans. My imagination could never have pictured such a situation. I was stifled. My inner turbulence lacked even the relief of proper exercise.

With her schooling complete, Ann longed to return to her western home in Brown's Park. She later said the experience left "a deep impression." When she finally did return in 1895, she brought with her all the latest fashions in clothing and even a new look: Ann was wearing makeup. Ann was a very attractive woman. According to John Rolfe Boroughs, Brown's Park early historian:

> Arriving at maturity, she stood five feet three inches tall, weighed a hundred and fifteen pounds, possessed an "hour glass" figure without the assistance of corsets, which loathing them, she seldom wore, and had large, deceptively mild gray eyes and naturally wavy auburn hair. As spirited as she was high-strung, and highly intelligent, suiting her own convenience or caprice Ann could play the role of cultured young gentlewoman full to over-flowing with gentility plus the innate Bassett charm; or she could be perfect little hell-cat capable of throwing and breaking things, in command of a vocabulary that would cause a livery-stable hanger-on to blush for shame.[8]

Following the death of her mother, Ann, now a young woman, took over the family ranch with one goal: to protect her family's interest and maintain the ranch. Known for her iron-willed attitude, Ann was headstrong and quite demanding. She was not arrogant or superior. Quite the contrary. She got along very well with the hired hands. She rolled her own cigarettes from a pouch of Bull Durham tobacco, in the days when women didn't smoke, and drank her whiskey straight. Older sister Josie strongly disapproved of Ann's unconventional behavior. It only made Ann more obstinate.

At the age of nineteen, Ann had begun a romantic relationship with thirty-two-year-old Matt Rash, a handsome, sandy-haired cowboy and one of her mother's most loyal ranch hands, as well as the former trail boss for the Middlesex outfit (Elizabeth's nemesis). Soon, the two were engaged to be married.

Rash became the first president of the newly-formed Brown's Park Cattle Association and helped to establish a dividing line separating the Brown's Park cattle from those of Ora Haley and his Two Bar Ranch and Cattle Company. Haley, a wealthy cattle rancher from the Yampa River Valley area, had intentions of moving his large herd onto the fertile grazing land of Brown's Park. The registered brand Haley used featured two slanted bars— / / —located on the animal's left hip.

The line Rash and the Brown's Park Cattle Association drew was halfway between the Snake River and Vermilion Creek, a north-south demarcation that managers of the Two Bar Ranch agreed to, for a while. Ann wrote of the new cattle association and Rash's leadership:

Representing our cattle association, he [Rash] interviewed Hi Bernard in the matter of establishing a boundary line between Snake River and Brown's Park. This resulted in an agreement between Bernard and Rash that the hills known as the "Divide," a range of limestone about halfway between Snake River and Vermilion Creek, extending north and south from the Escalante Hills to Douglas Mountain, was to be the western boundary for the Two Bar, and the eastern boundary for the Brown's Park cattle. The arrangement was acceptable to all concerned. There were no fences, so it was necessary to ride Boone Trail and Douglas Mesa to check the drift of the cattle... the Brown's Park cattlemen "pitched" a temporary camp on the Divide, and carried on this line riding during the winter of 1898-1899.

Nevertheless, Ann was concerned by the obvious intrusion by the Two Bar outfit into Brown's Park. She began riding along the eastern edge of the Divide, always carrying a rifle. She would shoot any Two Bar animal wandering over the Divide.

Haley hired perhaps the best-known cattleman in the southern Wyoming basin, thirty-nine year old Hiram H. "Hi" Bernard, to run his newest cattle operation. Bernard began working with cattle in his home state of Texas at the age twelve, in an effort to help his family. He herded cattle along the Chisholm Trail on a few cattle drives and then settled in Wyoming, managing various cattle operations prior to being hired by Haley. Bernard was proud of the fact that none of the ranches he managed ever went out of business under his control.

Ora Haley, who made just as much money in short-term speculations in the cattle market as he did by owning large cattle companies, trusted Bernard's judgment in both men and cattle, so much so that he gave him a company checkbook to buy cattle and, more importantly, land. According to Brown's Park historian John Rolfe Burroughs, "Hi Bernard made Ora Haley a million dollars in northwestern Colorado that he might just as well have made for himself."

Bernard, acting on Haley's behalf, purchased the B. F. Majors-Sainsbury ranch on the lower Snake River, just east of the Park. Ann recounted the incident that would heavily impact the ranchers of Brown's Park:

Hi Bernard, manager for the Haley Two Bar cattle outfit, with ranches near Craig, Colorado, bought the Ben Majors and Sainsbury Ranches on the lower Snake River, thirty miles from Brown's Park. Soon after the transfers of the ranches, several thousand head of Two Bar cattle were driven into Routt County and turned on summer range. The intent of Haley to occupy all of the summer and winter range of the county was clearly demonstrated. There were hundreds of miles of range outside of the Park, yet we with our small herds, isolated in the west end of the natural drift, and with less snow and plenty of feed were again in danger of becoming overrun by the big herds of cattle owned by non-residents[9]

And then Haley set in motion a series of events aimed at a takeover of the small ranches,gain control of the rich grazing land in the Park. Bernard assigned a few of his hired hands to ride the line, keeping an eye on any rustlers. Haley had also joined with four other large cattle companies in Routt County to form the Snake River Stock Growers Association. These men established their own "cattleman's committee," similar to the Wyoming Stock Growers Association based in Cheyenne. The large cattle barons considered anyone who contested their control of the open range a menace, or worse, a rustler. The committee was soon enlarged to include five more Routt County ranchers.

During a secret meeting, the cattle ranchers each agreed to pay one hundred dollars a month to Charley Ayer, who would hire a private stock inspector, ostensibly to procure evidence of rustling in the Brown's Park area. Hi Bernard, as ranch foreman for Ora Haley, attended the secret meeting and later recounted: "John Cobel [sic] offered a solution to the problem that would wipe out range menace permanently [sic]. He would contact a man from the Pinkerton Detective Agency. A man who could be relied on to do the job no questions asked."

In fact, the man hired was none other than Tom Horn, a known killer for hire in Wyoming. Among the men who agreed to hiring Horn were John Coble of Wyoming; Tim Kinney, the former owner of the Circle K ranch, where Matt Rash once worked; and Ora Haley. A hired killer was an abhorrent thought to most folks, but apparently not to the large cattle ranch owners in the tri-state area.

Hi Bernard did his job well for Haley and the Two Bar. He swore out several complaints against ranchers in the Park, accusing them of rustling Two Bar cattle.[10]

The smaller ranch owners of Brown's Park were not intimidated by such actions. To the contrary, anger brewed, especially within Ann Bassett. She was not one to be bullied, and soon found herself in the middle of Colorado's largest range war. Struggling to hold onto her family's ranch, Ann refused to sell and dug in for a fight, while several of the larger cattle companies tried to drive her out. She was described as "a bold young woman that all the cowboys liked and respected." The fighting over land became personal when Ann's fiancé, Matt Rash, was shot dead at his cabin. The former employee of the large Middlesex Cattle Company was obstinately believed by the "cattleman's committee" to be a cattle rustler.

In April 1900, a stranger arrived in Brown's Park, giving his name as James Hicks and his occupation as a horse buyer. He made his rounds, calling on various ranch owners in an unassuming manner, including Matt Rash's cabin. Rash hired Hicks as a ranch hand.

A. G. Wallihan, owner of the stage station at Lay, Colorado, southeast of Brown's Park, met Hicks. Lay said, "I didn't like him. My wife had lived all her life on the frontier, and she was not afraid of God, man, or devil, but she said, 'That man Hicks is a bad man.'"

Ann Bassett, with her female intuition, mistrusted Hicks from the start and soon came to the conclusion that he was not who he said he was. Ann later wrote:

> Representing himself [Hicks] as a ranchman from New Mexico in search of a location for a small cattle set-up, he put up as a guest at the home ranch of Matt Rash, where every courtesy was extended. When the spring roundup started, it soon became evident that he was not a cowpuncher, and he was given a job as roundup cook. The roundup was in full swing when I came home from school and joined the work as usual. His bragging of having been a great Indian fighter, and his descriptive account of slaughters he had accomplished single-handed, [was] extremely obnoxious to me. "Hicks" seemed to recognize the "Indian sign" as unfavorable to his best interests, and he immediately removed his carcass from the roundup. That was the one and only time I ever saw Tom Horn, alias James Hicks.

Ann was prone to exaggeration in her many writings and this is a prime example. Hicks, alias Tom Horn, arrived in Brown's Park in 1900. Ann says she attended the roundup when she returned from school. In fact, Ann returned to the Park after her schooling in 1895, five years before Horn arrived in Brown's Park. In any case, Hicks did leave the area for a week or two. During this time, in early June, dubious unsigned notices appeared on cabin doors of the Park's more notorious cattle procurers, advising them to leave the Park within thirty days or else. The warnings were the subject of local gossip but were largely ignored. Matt and Ann discussed the note they had each received. Ann expressed her concern to her fiancé—that she believed it was a threat from Hicks, Rash's former employee. Ann later wrote of what was happening at the time with extreme indignation:

> Up to that time nothing had seriously blocked the flood of Two Bar cattle. All obstacles had been successfully removed. Facing failure of the plan, the old Johnson County, Wyoming order for "Extermination" of the obstacle, was put into practice. There was hired secretly one who would strike, kill, and leave no sign. One who would not hesitate to shoot down friend or foe, man, woman or child for pay. In Tom Horn was found this killer, a murderer, lusting for blood money.[11]

On the morning of July 7, Matt rode over to the Bassett ranch to see Ann. After a pleasant afternoon with his fiancée, Matt Rash rode off to his cabin on Cold Spring Mountain. It would be the last time Ann ever saw Matt Rash alive. Three days later, July 10, 1900, George Rife and fourteen-year-old Felix Myers rode over to visit with Matt Rash. As they approached the cabin, an awful smell filled the air. Rash's favorite horse, the gift from Elizabeth Bassett more than ten years ago, lay dead near the cabin. A dreadful fear overcame the two as they cautiously approached the cabin. Felix Myers opened the door. Inside, he found Matt Rash, dead on the floor. The stench was nearly overpowering and flies were everywhere. Myers ran out of the cabin screaming for Rife, who determined the badly-decomposed Matt Rash had at least two bullets to his body and had been dead for two or three days. The two rode off to find deputy sheriff Charley Sparks, who rode to the scene of the murder and held an inquest. Sparks and a few other men dug a grave and buried the body of Madison Matthew Rash. The body was so badly decomposed from the July heat that the men covered their mouths and noses with cloths dipped in carbolic acid so as not to breath in the stench.

It is interesting to note that A. G. Wallihan, owner of the stage station at Lay, Colorado, some sixty miles southeast of Brown's Park, spotted the man known in the area as "Hicks." It was near sundown on July 8, 1900. Wallihan related, "I saw a man on a buckskin horse ride to the top of the ridge and stop and look back. Then he came right down to the crossing, and up the other side. He stopped when he got on top, and looked back again. I recognized him as 'Mr. Hicks.' A day or two after that, I heard that Matt Rash has been killed."

Ann, devastated over the death of her fiancé, knew her suspicions of the stranger, Hicks, were correct. Three days after the murder, Ann paid a visit to deputy sheriff Charley Sparks, explaining her belief that Hicks was the murderer.

Two months later, the new sheriff of Routt County, Joe Jones, stopped by the Bassett ranch. He was in the Park to serve a bench warrant on one of the citizens in the area. Ann invited the sheriff into the home and to join them for lunch, requesting that he remove his sidearm. Jones complied, laying the gun on the seat next to him. As the group sat down at the table, Jones recognized the man sitting across from him as the man he was after. Ann, with a coffeepot in her left hand, went around the table offering coffee to her guests. When she made her way to the sheriff, while filling his cup, she very carefully lifted his gun from the seat next to him. Setting down the coffeepot, she raised the gun toward Sheriff Jones, while telling the man the sheriff was after to leave. The man did so, mounting his horse and taking the sheriff's horse with him. Ann held the gun on the sheriff for a full thirty minutes, allowing for the man to make his getaway. She then returned the gun to the sheriff and asked him to leave her house. Sheriff Jones left on foot to track his horse. In the end, he found his horse and eventually apprehended the outlaw.

Not long after this episode, Ann launched her own personal vendetta against Ora Haley, whom she strongly believed was behind the hiring of the man who murdered her fiancé. Ann later wrote, "We would spot a little bunch of Two Bar cattle down by the river. We forced them into the water. Those that made it to the other side, wandered off into the badlands. In any event, they were lost to the Two Bar, who didn't round up west of the Green."

And then shock and disbelief rocked the community to its very core when shots rang out again on Cold Spring Mountain. After the murder of Matt Rash, many single ranchers in the Park sought safety in numbers. Isom Dart was one of those men. With his sizable heard of cattle, he joined in partnership with John Dempshire, sharing a cabin on Cold Spring Mountain. In early October, a few men stopped by to pay a visit. The group included Alec Seger, Griff Yarnell and the two of the Bassett boys, Sam and George.

Early on the morning of October 3, 1900, the men and fourteen-year-old George Bassett left the cabin, heading toward the corral. Suddenly, two gunshots rang out in the solitude of the mountain morning. Both of the shots hit Isom Dart, killing him instantly. The remaining men frantically raced back to the safety of the cabin. The men laid low in the cabin until nightfall, when they made their way out and down the mountain.

After the burial of Isom Dart, an inquest was held regarding the murder. It was discovered that just the week previous, on September 26, 1900, Hicks filed a complaint at the county courthouse at Hahn's Peak, claiming that Isom Dart had altered the brand on a horse that belonged to Jim McKnight. The complaint was signed "Tom Horn."

Ann Bassett's long held belief that Hicks was really Tom Horn proved to be true. In an indignant tone, Ann later wrote:

I believed "Hicks" or Horn, (as he proved to be later) was guilty of killing both Matt Rash and Isom Dart. And said plenty but got no support from neighbors and friends. A letter written by Hicks and mailed to Matt Rash approximately the same day Rash was killed absolved Hicks of guilt. In this situation it did not change sound reasoning. A man could not be in two places many miles apart, on the same day in those slow times when distance meant days. The letter caused greater confusion among the people. All trying to solve a murder mystery and getting nowhere.

Ann told of an unnerving incident at the ranch shortly after the murders:

Three months after the murder of Mat [sic] Rash and Isom Dart a man came creeping up to the house on the Bassett ranch...I sat at a table in the living room playing solitaire. Four young boys, Carl Blair, Gail [sic] Downing and my brothers George and Eb Bassett, were lunching in the adjoining kitchen. Suddenly the night was shattered by blasts of gunfire. Two bullets came splintering through the door, embedding themselves in the opposite wall, less than six inches from where I had been seated. There could not be the slightest doubt for whom those bullets were intended. I dropped to the floor and rolled under the table. The boys doused the lamp and jumped to a side window, to shoot out into the night in the direction the gunfire had come. We remained in the darkened house and speculated on why our shepherd dog had not given the alarm of a night prowler's approach; he did not bark all during the night, which was most unusual. That faithful old watch dog never barked again, he had been strangled to death by the spiteful marauder. Fearful of being clipped by shots from ambush, we stayed in the house under cover until eleven o'clock the next day, when two ranchmen, Pete Lowe and Harry Hindle, drove up to the corral in a wagon.[12]

Ann was full of rage and resentment over the murders of

her fiancé and dear friend at the hands of a cold-blooded killer hired by Ora Haley. Defiant and hellbent on revenge, she launched a personal vendetta against Haley and his Two Bar Ranch empire that would last nearly a decade. "Throwing caution to the winds, I pushed cattle off the range. I had to work alone. My neighbors did not support me in this, my challenge to Haley, and defiance of law and order. No other stockmen were responsible for what I did. I turned the heat against myself by an open declaration of war."[13]

During one of Ann's illegal episodes, a young teenager, Leath Avvon Chew, was a witness. She later described the incident and her first meeting of Ann Bassett:

On a sunny day in June, I decided to shirk my share of the care of the fat baby Ralph, and go explore a trail that took off from Pot Creek , down a piece. I called Smarty, the little brown mare, slipped on a bridle, and mounted her bareback. I was soon single-footing down a "brand new" trail. The trail led down a gentle incline to a river about one-half mile away, whose banks were thickly lined with cottonwood trees. This I knew was the Green River. Across the river, in the low hills to the east, a dust began to rise. The cause of this was at first hidden. As I watched, a small herd of cattle came into sight and rushed for the river. They were followed by four riders, swinging bullwhips or lariats, whooping and yelling. The cattle rushed into the swift water of the river without slacking pace. They were soon in swimming water. Many were carried downstream a considerable distance before gaining the opposite shore. Greetings were called across river. I impulsively decided to cross. Riding upstream about two hundred yards, I signaled that I was coming over. The game little mare took off into swimming water and I, holding the bridle rein and tuft of the mane in one hand, kept the other hand free for emergencies, floating clear of Smarty's submerged back...We were almost even with those waiting on shore with lassos ready. As the horse touched bottom, I was instantly astride her slippery back. "Crazy stunt" was the greeting. "What's your name?" I felt the attractive young woman was unpleasantly abrupt...I retorted, "Smarty kin swim and so kin I." Then I said somewhat belligerently, "I am Leath Chew." The woman said, "You are Mark's sister. I am Ann Bassett." I had heard of Ann Bassett,. but I did not know then that she was attempting to put into action a plan to destroy all Ora Haley's Two Bar cattle...Haley had been credited with trying to get possession of the range in Brown's Park where the Bassetts lived. His method, we were told, was to put two or three hundred head over the divide into Boone Draw, about half way to the Bassett ranch...It was Ann's custom to collect these Two Bar animals and drive them into the Green River.[14]

Ann and Leath Avvon Chew became lifelong friends. Together, the two soon wreaked havoc against the Two Bar cattle outfit. Years later, Avvon Chew Hughel wrote of the many exploits the two women were involved in an effort to exact revenge against Ora Haley:

For hours on end we did nothing but "jerk" Two Bar steers. Riding full-tilt, we dropped the loops of our lariats over their rumps, flipping them in the air...when they came down, sometimes they broke their necks and sometimes they didn't. Tiring of this, we'd spot a little bunch of Two Bar cattle down by the river. We forced them into the swift current. Maybe they made it across to the opposite bank, but more often they were swept into the mill-race of Lodore Canyon and drowned. Those that did make it to the far side, wandered off into the badlands. In either event they were lost to the Two Bar. We were especially active during 1902 and 1903, and we cost Ora Haley hundreds of cattle.

Yet Ann took a very bold and calculated step to win her war against Ora Haley. She courted and eventually married Haley's foreman, Hi Bernard. Ann explained her reasoning and planned execution to sabotage Haley's empire:

Up to the time of Bernard's buying the Snake River ranches for the Two-Bar, no cattle belonging to that outfit had crossed the divide into Brown's Park. They had not fully stocked the range, and found winter feed near the ranches at Lay Creek. Hi Bernard, whose ability to judge cattle and ranges was perhaps unsurpassed, saw the benefit to be derived by complete control of the entire open range between the Utah line on the west, Wyoming on the north, and east to Hahn's Peak; comprising an area of hundreds of square miles of cow range.

For the sake of her ranch as well as relieving her nemesis of his top hand, Ann changed her mind regarding her first thoughts of Hi Bernard. Ann sent a note to Bernard requesting a meeting at her home on Douglas Mountain. Bernard later recounted his thoughts when he received the note from Ann:

> I was not in the mood to put my neck in another loop [for Haley.] Responsibilities kept me around Snake River, and for no reason at all there was a tinge of sentiment in the direction of Brown's Park. I hadn't forgotten that meeting on Douglas Mesa. We are men after all, and when a girl's being savage, she also can be very attractive. At that time I was thinking seriously of throwing my Colorado job overboard, and trying my luck in Oregon. Then I received a message delivered by Tom Armstrong, who was building fence for me west of Snake River. The message was a note from Ann Bassett, asking me to meet her at the Douglas ranch. The message both confused and pleased me. I didn't know what to expect, but I rounded up my courage and sloped out to keep the appointment.[15]

Ann, dressed in her most flattering dress, greeted Bernard with all the dainty charm she could muster. During the course of the evening Ann purposed a business relationship between the two whereby Bernard could move his own cattle herd to Douglas Mountain with free use of the ranch land in return for helping Ann and her brothers improve the Bassett cattle ranch.

According to Frank Willis, Bernard had a counter proposal. Willis included Bernard's reaction to Ann's suggestion in his unpublished memoirs:

> She outlined the program in a very business-like way and said, "You are a cow man, and if you are interested just think the matter over and advise me of your decision at a future date." As simple as that. By that time cattle and range was the last thing on my mind. When we were called to dinner I had turned to ashes, and I did sure need a bracer of strong coffee to pick me up, for I had a counter offer to make and it needed a lot of backbone that I was unable to locate just then. So far the most important part of the contract had been overlooked. I did not intend to let that slip away from me. It was not Brown's Park and a jumble of sand hills I was after. It was a wife. I braced myself and boldly said so. It seemed the most natural thing in the world for a man to fall in love with a striking young woman and want to marry her. She was not a youngster, but was well along toward her thirties. She was a capable woman with a mind of her own, and she meant a lot more to me than a toehold on a piece of country. The woods were full of men, and I was flattered to be chosen as her partner. It was strictly cattle with Ann, and she didn't pretend otherwise.

Ann and Hi Bernard were married in Craig, Colorado, on April 13, 1904. The bride was twenty-six years old and the groom, forty-six years old. It was the first marriage for each of them. Gossip floated among the residents of Brown's Park. How could the woman engaged to Matt Rash who was murdered by a hired killer paid by cattle barons, including Ora Haley, marry his ranch foreman? Ann was a complex woman and had her reasons, but she wasn't often prone to explanation to anyone.

Ora Haley was not a man likely to gossip. A few days after the couple returned to the Park, Haley sent a telegram, the nineteenth-century version of a "pink slip:" Hi Bernard was fired from the Two Bar cattle ranch. Neither Ann or Hi were surprised, and Ann was probably thrilled at another victory against the hated Ora Haley.

The Bernards immediately filed for a homestead claim on the east side of Ann's land on Douglas Mountain. He also secured the water rights in the area. With this acquisition, the Bernard-Bassett land encompassed some twelve hundred acres where they wintered their joint herds of cattle. The marriage of convenience on the part of Ann was exactly what she wanted. With Bernard's expertise in ranch management, the Bassett ranch also improved financially. Ann's sister, Josie, was pleased with the marriage, and sent her son, Herbert "Chick" McKnight to the ranch every summer. Ann and Hi both grew very fond of the boy. Hi Bernard would later write his will leaving everything to Chick.

The couple often took pleasant horse rides together, Bernard on his favorite horse, Old Business, and Ann on her favorite horse, Major, a fine bay gelding, the gift of an early Park pioneer, Joe Reef. It was during one their many rides together that Bernard spotted a man on horseback riding up and down the opposite side of Vermilion Creek, searching for a place to cross in the icy waters of January. Bernard rode as close as he could to holler at the man and offer help if possible. The man turned out to be Jack Chew, the father of Ann's dear friend, Avvon Chew. Bernard learned Chew was going after the local doctor, as his wife, Mary, had given birth to their eleventh child, which had died, and Mary was suffering due to the difficult birth. Bernard instructed Chew to return to his home, as the rushing creek would subside by morning, and he and Ann would cross the creek in the morning and do what they could to help the Chew family in their desperate situation. At daybreak the following morning, the Bernards saddled their strongest horses and forged the icy creek. Hi Bernard recounted the harrowing experience:

> We arranged to have several good ropers - among them George and Eb Bassett - stationed on the bank. If a horse failed to swim, or became entangled in the debris and ice, it would be possible for these men to lasso the rider and drag him to safety

before he went over the falls. When we were set to take the plunge into the ice-jammed water, I stepped my horse in, and he swam high and easy. Then the cowboys shoved the pack horse into the icy water. By dodging the ice, and swimming strong, he made the landing. Ann came last. Her horse reared, and refused to take the plunge. He was a spirited animal; and when she raked him with her spurs, he made a long jump and went under, struggling frantically downstream. Finally, gaining balance and treading ice, he swam low to my horse on the right bank. The horses were cold and scared. We lit out on a keen run, and kept the pace for a mile. With cold air fanning out our wet clothing, we soon were covered with sheets of ice. I roped the pack horse and built a fire in a cedar gulch to warm up a little. We put on our dry things and rode up the mountain. The shock of seeing Ann's horse under water so near the falls almost floored me. That was the first time I realized that I had a bad heart. I damned near died, and thought I wouldn't be able to hold out until we reached the Chew dugout fourteen miles away. I believe the thing that kept me alive that day was Ann riding in the lead with her head thrown back in defiance of all obstacles, determined to reach a sick mother in time to be of help. Arriving at the Chew camp about four o'clock in the afternoon, we found Mrs. Chew very weak and having chills as she tried feebly to feed her hungry brood. I immediately gathered wood, and soon had a roaring fire. We heated rocks to warm the bed, and gave her a hot whisky toddy. When Mrs. Chew was made comfortable, Ann pitched in and put the dugout in order. She prepared supper for the children, and put them to bed. Then she took the only blanket we had to roll up in, and put it over her saddle horse.[16]

During the river crossing, Bernard was scared to death. As he watched his wife disappear under the icy water, he suffered from a slight heart attack, yet he persevered and never did tell Ann. "One wouldn't tell Ann that kind of thing. She would consider such an acknowledgment as a mark of weakness. According to her way of thinking, a full-grown man is not supposed to get sick. She takes life on the bounce, and expects a man to do likewise."

The marriage worked well for a time. However, the age difference and the fact that Ann was not emotionally invested, as Hi was, soon took a toll on the marriage. The two began spending time apart from one another. During the winter of 1909-1910, Hi left the Park for several months on a business trip to Denver. Ann elected to stay behind. Interestingly enough, this was also the first winter she stayed at the Douglas Mountain ranch, rather than winter at the lower elevation of the family ranch. A handful of unemployed ranch hands, including a young cowpuncher by the name of Tom Yarberry, ventured over to Douglas Mountain and eventually to Ann and Hi's ranch. Ann took them in for the winter as well as a woman, Mrs. Hurd, and a man known as J. K. Klinger. This gesture on Ann's part was purely second nature. She had grown up in a home where her parents often took in friends as well as strangers. It was a Brown's Park neighborly custom started by Elizabeth Bassett all those years ago.

When Bernard returned to Brown's Park in the spring of 1910, he was furious that so many strangers were now living in his home. Pitching a tent, he chose to stay outside of the home and whatever Ann had going on. One night, the loud noise from inside the log cabin was too much for Bernard. He fired his rifle into the air. That fired shot put an end to the marriage. The once agreeable couple again agreed, perhaps for the last time, on a divorce.

Ann seemed to have no regrets over the failed marriage. Perhaps, given the age difference and the clash of personalities, she expected it would not last. Or, quite possibly, she had achieved her goal in stealing away Ora Haley's ranch manager.

Nevertheless, Ann continued her vindictive actions against the large cattle barons, particularly Ora Haley. Ann denied access to her water on Douglas Mountain to any Two Bar rancher and their cattle. The Two Bar had suffered financially after Haley fired Hi Bernard. Perhaps Ann thought she was finally gaining an upper hand on her nemesis. When Haley hired forty-year-old William

"Bill" Patton as manager of the Two Bar, Ann's war against Haley took a decided change in direction.

On March 15, 1911, a weather-beaten prospector who introduced himself simply as "Mr. Nelson" showed up at Ann's Douglas Mountain ranch. Ann, as was her neighborly custom, let the man sleep in the barn. The following morning Nelson left the ranch, presumably to prospect in the hills near the area. In reality, this "Mr. Nelson" was a stock detective in the employ of the Two Bar ranch, hired by Bill Patton. The objective was to finally put an end to Ann's vindictive acts against the Two Bar. Nelson was to find evidence of cattle rustling by Ann and whoever else he could.

Three days later, Nelson rode to the Two Bar ranch and reported to Patton that although he had not witnessed the butchering, there were three quarters of a fresh beef hanging in the meat house on Ann's property. He also reported seeing a pair of women's shoes with blood spots, on the back porch of Ann's home. The two men headed back to Douglas Mountain, making camp for the night a mile from the ranch. The next morning, they set out to retrieve what evidence they could. Allegedly, as it would later become a point of contention at trial, the following morning the men found the hide of a recently butchered heifer. Patton hid the hide among the brush. Then the men left to notify Sheriff Ledford, and swore out a complaint of cattle theft against Anna M. Bassett and Tom Yarberry, who acted as ranch foreman after Hi Bernard left the ranch.

Ann, of course, was outraged at the accusation. Being accused of cattle theft was something that not only Ann, but her fellow ranchers, deeply resented. This was a serious charge. It was common knowledge throughout the Park of her vendetta against Ora Haley and the Two Bar cattle ranch. While many of the smaller ranch owners agreed with her, none of them participated in her cause. Yet as time went on, nearly all of those ranchers agreed that Haley and his strong-arm tactics were hurting their own cattle operations.

A hearing was held before Justice Z. Z. Carpenter on March 31, 1911. Following this hearing, Ann learned the esteemed attorney, A. M. Gooding of Steamboat Springs, was in Craig, Colorado representing another party in a cattle rustling case. She made the trip to Craig and met with Gooding. After hearing Ann's version of the charge against her, the attorney did not want to take the case. However, perhaps in an effort to save himself from turning down the genteel lady sitting across from him, he set an enormous fee of one thousand dollars, in advance, believing she would turn him down and seek other council. The charismatic Ann didn't bat an eye as she leaned down and pulled out a roll of cash from her stocking. She then peeled off ten one hundred dollar bills and, with a smile, handed them to the attorney.

The preliminary hearing in the case of *The People versus Ann Bassett and Thomas Yarberry* was held in the District Courthouse in Craig, Colorado. The account in the *Craig Empire* newspaper, dated April 1, 1911, set up the events and all the sensational aspects that would hold the attention of Brown's Park and Craig citizens for months to come:

> Interest naturally centered in Mrs. Bernard, who is really a remarkable personage. Raised in the wilds of Northwestern Colorado, trained from childhood to ride and shoot, she has a splendid education which has been improved by extensive travel. She is said to be as much as at home at a swell social function as while taking her regular "watch" with the other cowpunchers on the roundup. As she appeared in court Thursday, stylishly attired, she looked the part of "Queen Ann" with her wealth of brown hair and stately carriage.

With the *Craig Empire* first using the moniker of "Queen Ann," it soon became the standard in newspapers across the country covering the sensational trial. It would become a "badge of honor" to Ann and a term used by historians to this day. Ann's longtime friend Esther Campbell later wrote, "The name 'Queen Ann' fit her to a T. She didn't want to be anyone else."

The trial began in August 1911 and lasted less than a week, resulting in a hung jury. The citizens of Craig cheered as Ann left the court proceedings. She had won this round and gained many supporters. Historian John Rolfe Brurroughs wrote, "Spiritually as well as physically, she was as tough as rawhide and as resilient as rubber. And yet when she so desired she could be the personification of fragile femininity."

On the other hand, hatred for Ora Haley only grew more intense for many citizens throughout northwestern Colorado. As Ann's second trial began in August 1913, community sentiment swelled in Ann's favor. With the trial again held in Craig, the courtroom was filled with Ann's many supporters who considered the trial as a showdown between the small ranch owners and the large cattle barons. When the prosecuting attorney called Ora Haley to the stand, the trial took a decided turn. On cross examination, defense attorney Saunders asked Haley how many cattle he had in the county. With this direct question, Haley inadvertently admitted to lying to the county assessor. For the first time in Haley's career he had been humiliated in a public setting.

The case of cattle rustling against Ann Bassett Bernard was given to the jury, who after eight hours of deliberation returned a verdict of not guilty. The *Craig Courier* put out a special edition of their paper, the only time in its history to do so. The *Denver Post*, who had a reporter in Craig, filed their story the following day: "Businesses Close, Bands Blare—Town of Craig Goes Wild With Joy."

After a decade, Ann's vendetta against Ora Haley ironically came to an end in a court of law instigated by Ora Haley himself! Ann's popularity only grew with her exoneration by a jury of her peers, while Ora Haley's popularity diminished and his one-time cattle empire suffered dramatically. Back in Brown's Park, Ann rekindled a longtime friendship with Francis "Frank" Willis. The two had known each other for years through his friendship with Hi Bernard. Willis, an engineering surveyor, first came to the area in 1900 to work on the mountain road over Rabbit Ears Pass, south of Steamboat Springs in Routt County. Following the completion of the road, Willis remained in the area, finding work punching cows for the Two Circle Bar. In 1904, he went to work for the

Two Bar cattle operation, under the management of Bill Patton. This was during the time that Patton was learning of the warring factions between Ann Bassett and Ora Haley. Patton offered Willis five hundred dollars to quit the Two Bar job and go to work at the Bassett ranch in an effort to gather evidence of cattle rustling. Willis not only refused the offer, but quit the Two Bar.

Willis had an easy-going personality, something very much needed to handle Ann's flighty nature. He liked to sing and play the banjo, and Ann loved his stories of roaming the range herding cattle. It proved to be a perfect match when thirty-seven-year-old Frank Willis married the forty-two-year-old Ann Bassett Bernard in 1923. Not long after the wedding, the couple went to California where Willis worked in the oil fields for the Richfield Oil company and Ann ran the Cooper Hotel in Huntington Beach. In 1928, Josie's son Chick McKnight and his wife, Edith, moved to Huntington Beach.

It was here in California that Ann received the news in 1925 that her younger brother, Elbert "Eb" Bassett had committed suicide in Brown's Park. Ann was quite saddened by the news and stunned to learn that the cause may have been over losing the family ranch over financial debt. She was never informed and had no idea that her brother was in trouble or that the Bassett family ranch was at risk.

Following their brief stint at sheep ranching, the couple moved to Arizona, where they lived in the Walapai Valley near Kingman, Arizona.

In 1931, the couple purchased a cattle ranch and built a home at Hackberry, Arizona. Chick and Edith McKnight joined them and the two couples worked as partners in the ranch operations. In time it was a fairly successful ranch, with twelve hundred head of cattle. About eighteen months later, McKnight was involved in a terrible automobile accident. With his neck broken in three places, he was out of commission for the next two years. As this was the height of the Great Depression, and with the Willis's ranch struggling financially, McKnight's absence forced Frank and Ann Willis to sell out in 1937.

The couple returned to Colorado, where Frank obtained employment with the Bureau of Mines. This job required travel, and Frank and Ann moved around the states of Colorado and Wyoming. As time permitted between jobs, the Willises traveled to Josie's place on Cub Creek and occasionally visited at Brown's Park.

Ann was heartsick over both the death of her brother Eb and the loss of the family ranch. However, in discussions with her brother George, who retained some of the outlining acreage, she learned that other original Bassett acres were now considered public domain. Ann filed a request to buy the land for its historic value. She received title to nearly thirty-nine acres of land in 1944. The land included the old log cabin where Eb's girlfriend, Mattie Edwards, still lived, as well as the flowing spring and the orchard Ann's parents had planted.

Frank and Ann built a cabin of their own next to the old cabin where Mattie was living. Ann was polite and sympathetic with Mattie at first. After a few months, the woman began to irritate Ann, and she asked Mattie to move out of the cabin. A few weeks went by and Ann asked again. After a few months of Mattie's extended loitering, Ann had had enough. One day when Mattie had made a trip to Craig, Ann burned down the cabin. She was nice enough, however, to place Mattie's meager possessions outside of the cabin before she lit the match.

Ann's happiest times had always been at her beloved Brown's Park, and now she could enjoy her time there, carefree with her husband, Frank. As she grew older, the winters were harder to bear. She and Frank spent the winter months in the small southwestern town of Leeds, Utah. Although the couple were in their retirement years, they enjoyed prospecting for low-grade silver ore at the old abandoned Silver Reef mine near Leeds. Over the years, they not only found great enjoyment in their hobby, but made enough money to supplement their income.

Happy, relaxed and enjoying her golden years, Ann resumed another passion, writing. In her youth she had always kept a diary and enjoyed writing long letters to family and friends.

She became incensed at the many inaccuracies written regarding the history of Brown's Park. The citizens were often portrayed as rustlers and thieves. Her own family reputation was sullied in many publications. Several of her writings survive in published forums such as the Colorado Historical Society's *Colorado History Magazine*, and as portions of her unpublished memoirs, titled *Scars and Two Bars*. Excerpts of this manuscript were published in the *Moffat Mirror* newspaper in the 1943.

In the spring of 1953, Frank and Ann were at their cabin in Brown's Park when Ann suffered a severe heart attack. She was airlifted by helicopter to the hospital in Craig. Frank, worried sick over his beloved wife, never left the hospital. He notified Ann's favorite grandniece, Betty, who notified her father, Crawford McKnight. McKnight brought his mother Josie, to Craig from her cabin on Cub Creek. When Josie entered the hospital room where Ann lay near death, she wept. Josie sat by Ann's bed and held her hand for hours.

Ann, true to her obstinate nature, was anything but a patient patient. She yelled expletives at the nurses and threw things across the room. Finally, she compelled Frank and Betty to obtain a vehicle that could transport her to her home in Leeds, Utah. This they did as Ann told Betty, "I shall not spend one more night in this filthy hole."

By April 1953, Ann was recuperating at her home in Leeds where she wrote a letter to Esther Campbell, an old friend:

The truth is I am very much out of the running right now. About two months ago I was hit by a rather serious heart condition which has set down a lot. If I do the slightest bit of arm exercise I go into a tail spin for sure. Then it's reach for the nitro-glycerine pill and slip it quickly under the tongue to get action. Dr. ordered me to quit work for awhile–or else–ten minutes or less can wind up the tick in an old body. It does not bother me any, its very painful so I do the heavy sitting around and Frank does the work, not much to do.

Ann knew her health was declining. She wrote out her will, leaving her Brown's Park land to her husband, Frank Willis and her brother Sam's son, Emerson Bassett, with the stipulation that the land be passed down to future Bassetts and never be sold. She also requested that she be cremated, and that her remains be spread across her beloved birthplace of Brown's Park.[17]

On May 8, 1956, Ann Bassett Bernard Willis died in Leeds, Utah, just before her seventy-ninth birthday. The *Craig Empire Courier* printed Ann's obituary in the May 16, 1956, issue:

> Mrs. Ann Bassett Willis, who was a former Moffat County resident and who helped make Brown's Park History, died at her home in Leeds, Utah, [last] Wednesday evening, three days before her 79th birthday. Mrs. Willis had suffered from a heart ailment for several years. After a severe heart attack in September, 1953, she became a patient at the Craig Memorial Hospital for about three weeks after having spent the summer at her old home in Brown's Park. She never fully regained her strength. Mrs. Willis requested cremation, her ashes will be placed in the Bassett cemetery on the old home Bassett ranch in Brown's Park and be allowed to blow to the four winds. Her round-up days are over. Her heart has ever been in Brown's Park. She will be returned to its hills and valleys of which she herself has said "the only thing I ever selfishly loved."[18]

When Ann's ashes were sent to Frank Willis following cremation in Salt Lake City, he could not bring himself to scatter the ashes over "her beloved birthplace of Brown's Park." According to Grace McClure in her biography, *The Bassett Women*, Ann's cremated ashes included "yellowish" clumps among the fine ashes. Frank felt he could not honor Ann's wishes, as the ashes were not entirely ashes, as it was believed Ann was cremated with her diamond ring, which made clumps of the ashes.

Whether this was the reason or the bereaved husband just could not part with his wife's remains, Ann's clumped ashes remained in the trunk of Frank's car until his death.

Years later, following the funeral of Frank Willis, Josie and her grandchildren, all adults by this time, finally buried the remains of Ann Bassett Bernard Willis in the family cemetery.[19] Fearing looting or vandalism, Josie did not want a marker for her sister's grave site. Ann was finally resting peacefully in her beloved Brown's Park, "the only thing [she] ever selfishly loved."

Shortly before her death in 1956, she answered a reporter's question with this statement: "I've done everything they said I did and a helluva lot more."

# Notes

1. Willis, Ann Bassett. "Queen Ann of Brown's Park." *Colorado Magazine*, Denver Public Library, Volume XXIX January 1952 (hereafter "Queen Ann.") All quotes by Ann, unless otherwise noted, are attributed to this work.
2. Esther Campbell's quote regarding the Bassett mare can be found in her letters archived at the Bureau of Land Management, Vernal, Utah. An account of the event is also included on page 23 of Grace McClure's excellent work, *The Bassett Women*.
3. Athearn, *An Isolated Empire*.
4. Willis, Ann Bassett. "Queen Ann of Brown's Park," Volume XXIX April, 1952.
5. Wommack, *From the Grave*. The Bassett family cemetery is the final resting place for several of the Bassett family.
6. Warner, *Last of the Bandit Riders...Revisited*, pg.113.
7. Willis, Ann Bassett. "Queen Ann of Brown's Park," Volume XXIX October, 1952.
8. Burroughs, *Where the Old West Stayed Young*, pg. 221.
9. Willis, Ann Bassett. "Queen Ann of Brown's Park," Volume XXIX January, 1952.
10. Willis, Frank. Unpublished manuscript entitled *Confidentially Told*.
11. Willis, Ann Bassett. "Queen Ann of Brown's Park," Volume XXIX January ,1953.
12. ibid.
13. ibid.
14. Hughel, Avvon Chew. *The Chew Bunch in Brown's Park*.
15. Willis, Frank. Unpublished manuscript entitled *Confidentially Told*.
16. ibid.
17. McClure, *The Bassett Women*, pg. 170.
18. Wommack, *Ann Bassett, Colorado's Cattle Queen*.
19. Wommack, *From the Grave*.

Evelyn Mantle at her ranch with visitors. The baby is her only daughter, Queeda. *Uintah County Regional History Center*

# Evelyn Fuller Mantle
### The Legend of Hells Canyon

When nineteen-year-old Evelyn Fuller agreed to marry Charley Mantle, the native of New York knew her life was about to change forever. Evelyn pledged the words, "In sickness and in health, till death do us part," having no idea how that commitment would affect the rest of her life.

Evelyn Fuller was born February 18, 1907, to Evan and Julia Fuller, in Cicero, New York. Two years later, January 14, 1909, her little brother William Franklin was born. When Evelyn's mother contracted tuberculosis, the Fuller family sold everything and moved west for Julia's health.

In 1914, Evan Fuller filed a homestead claim near the top of Blue Mountain, a two-thousand-foot-high dominant landmark that shadows the Yampa River at the very edge of the Colorado and Utah border. Queeda Mantle Walker, Evelyn's daughter, later described the area:

> Blue Mountain begins on the west at the Utah state line and runs east to within a few miles of the town of Elk Springs. A large land mass, the mountain stretches some twenty miles east to west and ten miles north to south. In appearance, the mountaintop looks like great rolling hills of grassland and sagebrush. There is little water and what there is is very precious.[1]

For the first few years, the Fuller family lived in a one-room dugout. There were a few ranchers in the area, but their spreads were miles away from the Fuller place. One day in 1921, a friendly neighbor crossed Turner Creek and made his way to the Fuller homestead. He was Charley Mantle, a twenty-eight-year-old World War I veteran, who was attempting to build a horse training camp. Charley Mantle was born in Vernal, Utah, August 8, 1893, the first child born to John and Mary Ann Jolly Mantle. Tragedy struck the Mantle family in the summer of 1906. Charley's father, John, died following a horrific wagon accident. Later that summer, thirteen-year-old Charley's mother died in childbirth. Charley's baby sister survived, but now the six Mantle children were orphans. The four younger children were taken in by generous families in Vernal and nearby Jenkins, Utah. Charley and his brother Lewellen, known as Wellen, went to live with their father's brothers. Charley found employment with a local rancher where he gained experience with horses and soon became a top hand. When America entered World War I, Charley Mantle was drafted. He was sent to Fort Hood in Texas where he received his basic training with the United States Cavalry. Following training, Mantle was assigned to Fort D. A. Russell at Cheyenne, Wyoming, where he was charged with the care of the cavalry horses and taught horsemanship to the new soldiers. This became his one and only assignment, for not long after his arrival in Wyoming, the war ended.

When Mantle was discharged from the service, he returned for a short time to Vernal, Utah. He had no plans to stay, as he was ready to find a place of his own. After several horseback rides east of Vernal and then south and into Colorado, Mantle finally found exactly what he was looking for. It was a beautiful area on the north side of Blue Mountain, about ten miles upstream of the confluence of the Yampa and Green rivers, and where the majestic Yampa River flowed eastward.[2] As Mantle rode his horse over the area, carefully inspecting the natural attributes, he came across a small cabin, isolated in one of the many rock canyons. Mantle called at the cabin and introduced himself to the owner, William "Billy" Hall. During their conversation, Mantle learned that while Hall had applied for the homestead, he had never "proved up" the claim.[3] Mantle offered to buy Hall's land and Hall agreed. However, it would be two years before Mantle was able to realize his dream.

Finally, in 1923, Mantle had saved the money and paid cash for Hall's property. He moved into the vacated isolated cabin and proudly began making improvements to his new home. He later learned the area was known by locals as "Hells Canyon," a moniker he would come to believe as the years went on. Years later, his only daughter, Queeda Mantle Walker, described the area her father so loved:

> The steep side of Blue Mountain leveled out into flat sage and covered benches of good pasture land. One-thousand-foot cliffs dropped straight and sheer into the gorge carved out by the Bear [Yampa] River. Along the river were fertile green parks, alluring little side canyons, and a land well protected from the elements. Here flourished vegetation he [Mantle] had seen nowhere else in the surrounding country. There was plenty of perfect winter shelter for cattle, too. There were no roads, however, and the only way to get into the country was to ride a horse over Blue Mountain and down the dangerous rocky trails off the mountain into the uncharted canyons.[4]

Charley Mantle managed to make the rounds to the area ranchers, introducing himself and offering his services as a horse trainer. It was during one of these trips that Mantle arrived at the Fuller homestead. Although Evelyn was just fourteen, she was attracted to the handsome cowboy astride his horse. When Evelyn learned that Mantle had set up a corral for breaking and training horses for the local ranchers, she would ride her horse to the corral as often as she could. Evelyn would watch the handsome cowboy for hours, but the busy cowboy paid little attention.

In time, the two began a cordial relationship. On occasion, Mantle even let Evelyn accompany him on horseback as he took the horses out of the corral for training. Then, one day, during the summer of 1923, Charley Mantle showed up at the Fuller place unannounced. He asked to speak to Evelyn and invited her to a dance at a nearby community center. With Evelyn's parents' permission, she agreed to the invitation. By all accounts, the two had a grand time and when the next dancing event was announced, again Mantle escorted Evelyn. It was a glorious summer for Evelyn, but when it ended, she returned to Hayden for her final year of school. At the age of seventeen, Evelyn Fuller, valedictorian of her class, graduated from high school in 1924.

Returning to her home on Blue Mountain, Evelyn and Charley resumed their dates at the local dances. On another occasion, Mantle invited several friends, including Evelyn, for a weekend of fun and adventure. There was plenty of fishing off the banks of the Yampa River, where Evelyn caught the biggest fish of the day, an eighty-pound whitefish. The next day, Mantle guided the group on a horseback trip through the canyons. As horses made their way along rock cliffs and down sage-covered hills, someone spotted a cave below. Dismounting from their horses, the group climbed down a rock wall to the site. As they neared the cave, they were stunned to see small stone structures. It was obvious this had once been the home of Native Americans. Queeda Mantle Walker later described her mother's experience:

> As the quiet group approached, they saw that they were storage bins, expertly built with flat, narrow sandstone slabs. They were round, about two feet deep and sealed on the outside by a reddish dirt which had been made into a thick plaster and patted into place with human hands, leaving prints of fingers and whole hands. Lining one of the bins was a woven basket. Within another they found a piece of soft leather which they guessed was tanned buckskin.[5]

Evelyn was the first to enter the large cave. Inside, the group found evidence of a fire pit. There were several ancient artifacts such as pottery, flint arrowheads, and stone implements. The remote area and the extreme dry air in the cave had preserved these Native American relics for perhaps centuries. It was an experience Evelyn would forever remember and later share for all to see.

As time went on, Evelyn's parents began to voice objections

to their daughter seeing the much-older cowboy, Charley Mantle. Evelyn's pleading did not persuade her parents, nor did Mantle's many visits with the Fullers. During a community dance, Mantle professed his love for Evelyn and asked her to marry him. With great reluctance, Evelyn's father agreed to the marriage.

Elated, the couple left the following week for Vernal, Utah. There, Charley Mantle and Evelyn Fuller were married before a justice of the peace, on August 12, 1926. Mantle's good friends, Thede and Pearl McCarl, served as witnesses to the happy union.[6]

During their trip back to the Mantle Ranch, the newlyweds stopped for the night at the home of Evelyn's parents on Blue Mountain. The following morning at daybreak the couple left for the ranch and Evelyn's new home. Queeda Mantle Walker later described her mother's experience:

> When Evelyn went with Charley to spend her life with him in this rugged area there was no road, no electricity, no running water, no telephone. There was no doctor or grocery store, nor any living soul to depend on but yourself. Their only communication with the outside world was attained by a horseback ride of more than forty miles up the steep rough north side of Blue Mountain, then over the top of the mountain and down the south side. It was a hard life, particularly for Evelyn, who had none of the modern conveniences of the day and yet it was a life that supplied its own special compensations.[7]

Mantle, with the help of friends, had made many improvements on his land. Additional corrals had been built and an irrigation system provided fresh river water to the garden. Against a hill were steps that led to a cellar to store food. And, there was a brand-new cabin that Mantle and his friends had just finished. It wasn't large, but it had two windows and was clean and neat.

It was not long before Evelyn, who was accustomed to her father's farm, realized the hard work of ranching in such a remote area. Mantle-Walker later related:

> My mother, Evelyn Fuller Mantle, was a loving, caring hard
> working woman, who never complained, though she would
> often have been justified in doing so. Mother recognized early
> on that she was going to have to take care of most of the things
> around the ranch that needed doing and if she lacked the skills
> and knowledge at the outset, she trained herself and in the
> process became one of the most accomplished people I have
> ever known.[8]

Evelyn learned to milk cows and care for the horses, alongside her husband. She learned how to plant, cultivate and cut and store the hay that fed their livestock. After a few months alone at their new home, the couple rode their horses out of Hells Canyon and over to the Chew ranch, just over the state line into Utah. Rial Chew and Charley Mantle had enjoyed a close friendship for years. When the Mantle couple arrived, Rial eagerly introduced Evelyn to his mother. The two women became fast friends and stayed behind at the ranch while Chew and Mantle rode out to gather wild horses.

The women enjoyed the female companionship. Mrs. Chew passed on several tips such as a good diet and healthy nutrition, and instructed Evelyn on how to preserve and store fresh vegetables and fruit. She taught Evelyn how to kill, clean, and cook meat. Evelyn learned not to waste food. Animal fat was turned into lard for further cooking. Side pork was used to flavor beans and other dishes, and chicken pieces were added to soups and gravy. Evelyn was taught the proper method of salting butchered meat for preservation and storage. Mrs. Chew also taught her young protégé how to bake, even sharing with her the techniques of baking powder and yeast for biscuits, cakes, and cookies. When the Mantles prepared to ride back to their ranch, Chew and his mother gave them a parting gift. Inside three of the four burlap sacks were two hens, and in the fourth was a hen and a rooster. Although Charley was not pleased, for Evelyn it was the beginning of a new passion, all her own.

In time, children were born. In the summer of 1927, Evelyn was pregnant with their first child. It was a long hot summer in the canyon, but Evelyn did her best to help with the ranch. By the time it came to branding the new cattle, Evelyn couldn't stand the smell. The heat was also a strain on her condition and she simply could not find the strength to help her husband. Fortunately, Charley's brother Wellen and his wife, Lorraine, arrived for a visit. It was the first meeting of the two sisters-in-law, and they soon developed a close kinship. Following a festive family celebration, which also included Evelyn's parents, with a fine meal fixed by Evelyn and Lorraine, the Mantles prepared for their trip to Vernal. There they would stay with their friends, Thede and Pearl McCarl, until the baby was born.

It was a difficult journey out of the canyon for Evelyn, in the eighth month of her pregnancy. Despite the large saddle Mrs. Chew had lent Evelyn, she was extremely uncomfortable during the long ride. After a two-week stay at the McCarl home, Evelyn went into labor and was rushed to the hospital. In the early morning of October 13, 1927, their first son, Charles Evan Mantle, was born. After a few days' rest in the hospital, Mantle took his young family back to the ranch. It was a slow horseback ride, as both parents were very careful with the new baby. Mantle's friends wasted no time in stopping by to see the new baby. Soon, they began calling the baby boy "Potch," and the nickname stuck.

If life in the canyon wasn't already difficult, the added care of a baby brought about more chores. Just the diapers alone added to the laundry, which was now done daily. Heated water was poured into the washtub outside of the cabin and the laundry was scrubbed thoroughly on the washboard until Evelyn's fingers nearly bled. With the constant care of little Potch, Evelyn still had to find the time to milk the cow, care for the chickens, and cook and clean.

With determination and hard work, the Mantles managed their isolation through the winter. That February, Evelyn turned twenty-one. Her daughter later wrote:

Evelyn would be twenty-one on her birthday. She had a new baby, lived in a wild country with no roads. She had no car, lived in a dirt-floor dirt-roof cabin with no electricity or running water. She did her wash in a tub with a scrub board, and was married to a man she adored who saw nothing wrong with all that.[9]

That summer, one of the cats had kittens. Queeda Mantle Walker related, "The kittens were a great help to the family because they kept Potch occupied and everyone could get their work done."[10] Not long after the kittens were walking, a bobcat began roaming around near the cabin. One by one the bobcat caught, killed, and ate all of the kittens. Evelyn decided to rid the area of the bobcat once and for all, for she knew her beloved chickens would be next. Grabbing a shotgun, she waited patiently for the bobcat to appear. As the sun was setting, casting shadows on the canyon walls, the bobcat appeared. As calmly as she could, Evelyn raised her gun, aimed, and fired. Her shot was accurate and the bobcat fell to the ground.

Shortly after the Thanksgiving holiday, Evelyn realized she was again pregnant. Evelyn spent the summer miserable with the heat and her condition. In mid-August, Charley prepared the horses to take Evelyn to Jensen, Utah. His sister, Nancy, had arrived and would stay at the ranch to care for Potch. Again, it was a difficult ride out of the canyon. Arriving at Jensen, they were met by Thede McCarl, who took Evelyn to the hospital at Vernal in his automobile. The doctor examined Evelyn and said the baby would come any day now. Thomas Patrick Mantle was born on August 27, 1929. The birth was extremely hard on Evelyn. After a two-week stay in the hospital, the doctor released her with instructions that she was to limit her time on her feet for two weeks. Evelyn and baby Pat, as he came to be called, spent the next three weeks at the home of Thede and Pearl McCarl. Toward the end of September, Thede McCarl drove Evelyn and baby Pat to the edge of Blue Mountain in Colorado, where Mantle met them with fresh horses for the ride down the canyon and back to the ranch.

The Mantle Ranch is located deep in Hell's Canyon. *Uintah County Regional History Center*

The following summer, Mantle's brother Wellen and his wife, Lorraine, arrived for an extended visit. The couple spent the summer at the ranch and Evelyn thoroughly enjoyed the female companionship, as well as Lorraine's help with the boys and the household chores. The two women grew very close that summer and Evelyn was quite lonely when they left.

The summer of 1932 was extremely dry. Mantle felt sure that the area was suffering a drought, and spent all of his time preparing the animals and conserving what little hay he was able to harvest. That same summer, Evelyn was pregnant with her third child. Lorraine wrote letters to Evelyn. In one letter, Lorraine informed Evelyn that Wellen's drinking was becoming a problem, and that Charley and Wellen's younger brother, Bryan, was there to help out. Evelyn wrote a letter of comfort to Lorraine, as it was all she could do as her pregnancy advanced.

On March 9, 1933, Mantle saddled his horses. He helped his pregnant wife onto her horse with one of the boys. Then he mounted his horse, holding the other child. Leading a packhorse loaded with necessary items, the Mantle family rode out of Hells Canyon. Almost out of the steep rock canyon, Evelyn's horse stumbled and Evelyn came close to falling off. Mantle turned the horses and headed toward the Chew ranch, just a couple of miles away. Along the way Evelyn's water broke and she was scared to death she would have the baby right then and there. Thankfully, they arrived at the ranch, where Rial helped Mantle get Evelyn inside. There was no time to waste. Mrs. Chew threw clean linens on the bed just as the men brought Evelyn in the room. Thirty minutes later, Evelyn delivered a healthy baby girl. Mrs. Chew cleaned the baby and took her to her father, closing the door so that Evelyn could get some much-needed rest. Later that evening, Evelyn named her baby daughter Lorraine Evelyn, after herself and her dear friend and sister-in-law, Lorraine Mantle. The next day, Charley prepared the horses for the trip back to his ranch. However, Mrs. Chew insisted on keeping Evelyn and the baby for the next week.

When Evelyn and baby Lorraine arrived at the Mantle Ranch, Evelyn quickly resumed her normal routine of cooking, cleaning and caring for her livestock. She did manage to fit a little time to write to Lorraine and tell her all about the birth of the baby, her namesake. Because of the isolation of Hells Canyon, the Mantles only received their mail when they went to town for supplies, or when a neighbor might have picked it up and brought the mail to them on his next visit. Such was the case when the Mantles received a letter from Lorraine a month later. The letter told of the death of Wellen Mantle, Charley's brother and Lorraine's husband. It was tragic news that would change the lives of the Mantle family forever. Lorraine's letter, dated March 30, 1933, read in part:

My dear Brother Charley, Oh God Charley if I could just see you and tell you instead of trying to put it on paper. But I must try to tell you. For two months after we came home Wellen just seemed so contented and looked so well. Then after Xmas he started drinking and seemed to me he just had something just driving him. Always before I could seem to quiet him out of his terrible moods. Toward the last everything I did was wrong. Bryan never crossed him - just humored him like a child - and it seemed he felt every one [sic] was against him. The only thought was to get rid of me. He plotted every time he could get Bryan out of my hearing to knock me in the head. When Bryan was here he [Wellen] didn't touch me, but every time he felt we were alone, he would abuse me in a way no one can know but me. Then when those spells would pass how sorry he would be. I have known since Xmas that a terrible change had hold of him and I felt in time it must end in tragedy. Then a week before he died he had a sort of stroke after which he was never the same. He just raved about every one and said "I'll leave my mark in this country" and smile a twisted grin at Bryan. Then he'd say "I've fought these S... alone, alone, alone," and just glare at me with eyes I've never seen in any human's head before. Bryan went to the kitchen to boil some tea and something in Wellen seemed to snap - he lunged at me grabbing me by the throat with a fork in his hand. I screamed and George (my brother) grabbed him by the arm he was holding over me. He seemed to have the strength of a demon. He threw George off and against the wall like he were a child. Bryan shot him. He fell without a sound - never knew what hit him. Bryan knew that Wellen meant to Kill [sic] and that he couldn't be stopped once he had started. We buried him the next day. I put the clothes on him he liked the best - had everything at the grave as he would have had - just a few nice words and a song he liked. The coffin was nice and some pretty flowers. He looked so quiet after the terrible unrest and nervousness that had been hold of him for the past weeks. Oh God! Charley why did it all have to happen this way. He was so young but now he is gone and I am alone.[11]

Lorraine had included two newspaper clippings from the local newspaper in New Mexico. The first gave details of the shooting with the headline, "Fatal Shooting Climaxes Row Between Bothers." The second newspaper clipping covered the details of the subsequent murder trial with the headline, "Man Who Killed Brother Faints in Court When Case is Dropped."

The shock of his brother's death changed Charley Mantle. In mid-April, Mantle left Hells Canyon for Regina, New Mexico. Devastated at the loss of his brother, he also felt a responsibility to his widow. Charley's daughter, Queeda, later wrote, "He knew he could never forgive Bryan for shooting Wellen, but for Lorraine's sake, he was determined to be civil to Bryan. Then he hoped never to see him again."[12]

While Charley was in the town of Regina, an old friend offered to buy him a drink. During their conversation, the friend voiced his concerns about the manner of Wellen's death. He told Charley there had been no autopsy and that Wellen was hastily placed in box, not even a coffin, and quietly buried the next day, without a preacher or undertaker. He told Charley no one even knew about the burial until later. Then he said something to Charley that nearly stunned him. He said rumors in town were that Charley's younger brother, Bryan, and Lorraine were having an affair. Charley asked a few other acquaintances in town what they knew and they confirmed what he had been told. His daughter, Queeda Mantle Walker, later wrote:

> Charley had never trusted women. He thought all women were just out to use somebody, so it was easy for him to turn on Lorraine. In his tortured, grieving mind he came to believe that Lorraine had tempted and lured the young unworldly Bryan to fall in love with her. Then she had conspired with him to murder Wellen and make it look like self defense. He believed her motive was Wellen's monthly disability check of fifty-six dollars. He concluded that they had set Wellen up, killed him, then stuck him in a box and buried him like a dog, just as the man had thought.[13]

After Charley made a few more inquiries, he left New

Mexico for good. When he returned to the ranch, Evelyn was full of questions, the first being, where was Lorraine? Charley told Evelyn everything he had learned regarding the murder of his brother and the town gossip of an affair between Bryan and Lorraine. Evelyn didn't believe a word of it and said so. She offered Lorraine's tender letters and her later letters of Wellen's declining health. Their daughter, Queeda, related what happened next:

> Charley flew into a rage and she [Evelyn] feared he was going to strike her. He seethed with hatred and condemnation for all women. He said no woman should ever be trusted as they were just all conniving whores and added that under no circumstances ever was she to mention the name of Lorraine again. He said no baby of his would ever have that name.[14]

For the first time in her life, Evelyn was afraid of her husband. She left the room, rounded up the boys, and with the baby, left the cabin. Evelyn took the children to the granary and bolted the door. After a few hours, she left the shelter to check on her husband. Charley was slumped over the table, nearly passed out. An empty whiskey bottle lent evidence to his condition. Evelyn hastily gathered all the guns in the cabin, grabbed blankets and food and returned to the granary. She locked the door and braced it with wooden blocks.

The following morning Charley, in a hung-over stupor, realized his family was gone. After searching the outbuildings, he finally came upon the granary. Through the locked door, he told his wife how sorry he was and such an incident would never happen again. Eventually Evelyn opened the door. Queeda Mantle Walker later wrote, "But they both knew it would never be the same again between them. She had lost her complete trust in him, and he had lost his respect for her because she was a woman."[15]

Charley continued with his personal investigation regarding his brother's death. He became moody and for the first time, snapped at the children. During that summer of 1933, he instructed the boys not to call their baby sister Lorraine, which was confusing to everyone. As the baby began to crawl, visiting neighbors often commented that she was "growing like a weed." This started the family phrase, "Queen the Weed." The new name stuck and two years after their baby daughter was born, her parents finally registered her birth in Craig, Colorado, in 1934. The name on her birth certificate read Queeda Evelyn Mantle.

Now with three children to care for, and the responsibilities of running a ranch, Evelyn had no time for herself. As Queeda began to crawl, Evelyn made throw rugs from scraps of old clothes, which she carefully braided together until she had thick coverings over the dirt floor. She worked endlessly cleaning and cooking, with no running water, and still found time to care for the livestock and her precious chickens. However, by winter, Evelyn grew weak and began losing weight. A letter to her beloved cousin, Eva, gives an indication of Evelyn's desperation: "I'd give a lot if I could say 'wait until my next letter for my new address.' But since living so tucked up as I have I'm afraid I'd become lost in some one of the rooms and have to send out a distress signal."[16]

The following spring, Charley's sister Nancy and her two boys came to Hells Canyon for a visit. Unfortunately, Nancy's boys brought the measles with them. A few days after their arrival at the Mantle Ranch, both boys came down with the dreaded ailment. It was not long before Evelyn's children were also infected. To bring down the high fever the children were experiencing, Evelyn relied on an old technique her husband learned during his service in World War I. Sagebrush contains quinine, which relieves pain and brings down body temperature. Evelyn gathered a large batch of the plant and brewed the leaves in a large kettle over an open fire. She fed cup after cup of the tea to each of the children. Finally their fevers broke and the medical crisis was over.

The drought continued throughout that summer. The river was low and precious little water flowed to the crops. Evelyn watered her crops and her garden in the late afternoon and then closed the ditch for the night, hoping the water from the river would fill the ditch. This would be a routine Evelyn followed throughout the next summer, as the drought continued. To conserve the water, Evelyn would bathe the children in the river during the hot summer months.

While the Mantle family struggled through, living their isolated existence, unbeknownst to them the rest of the country was suffering from drought conditions as well. When Charley rode to Vernal to trade some livestock for winter necessities, he also bought a battery-operated radio. For the first time in her married life, Evelyn could now keep up with news and world events. Evelyn wanted her children to have a proper education. The boys were now of age to attend school, but the nearest school was over twenty miles north of the canyon at Brown's Park. The Mantles were told of a place for sale in the Park, and reluctantly, Charley rode out to take a look at it. However, when he arrived, he was told the property had been leased. Secretly, he was most likely relieved, for he never really wanted to leave Hells Canyon. However, the dilemma of the children's schooling still remained. It would be another year before Evelyn would be able to give her attention to the issue, as she learned she was pregnant again.

Later that fall, a Moffat County sheriff's deputy, a friend of Evelyn's, stopped by the ranch. Knowing how isolated Evelyn was, he was eager to tell her the latest news he had just learned. He told her the north side of Blue Mountain and the Yampa Canyon were going to be incorporated into the acreage of Dinosaur Monument, which was established in 1915. The area was to become the Dinosaur National Monument. Evelyn was also told the most exciting news: within a year's time, the government would have a road built through Hells Canyon and along the Yampa River. He further told her that although it would be a government road, their land would not be affected, nor their grazing rights. Evelyn was overjoyed with the news.

The following spring, Evelyn was able to purchase a stove from the estate of a woman who recently died at her ranch, not far from the Mantle ranch, and Charley had purchased a boat. Charley used the boat to transport the stove down the river to their ranch. When the stove was installed, Evelyn could not have been happier. It was a huge cook stove with a warming oven and a surface space for simmering pans.

Evelyn's joy was short-lived. That summer brought incredible heat and Evelyn, in her eighth month of pregnancy, quickly tired from her daily ranching chores as well as caring for the children and her domestic chores.

Toward the end of June, Evelyn left the children in Charley's care and rode on horseback, out of the canyon, to a designated area where her father met her with his automobile. From there, Fuller took his daughter to the Prowers ranch, at Bear Valley, for the night. The next morning they would drive into Vernal. However, Mrs. Prowers informed them Vernal was under a health alert, as an epidemic of chicken pox had spread throughout the town. Mrs. Prowers insisted that Evelyn stay with her. Four days later, at noon on July 1, 1935, twenty-seven-year-old Evelyn gave birth to a healthy baby boy. When Charley finally arrived, he named his son Lonnie Miner, after a one of Charley's uncles who had taken him in after the death of his parents.

During her two-week stay with Mrs. Prowers, Evelyn learned that the local school had been closed. If the Mantles were willing to build a schoolhouse on their property, the local superintendent of schools, with his authorization, would provide the needed items such as desks and books. Meeting with the school district superintendent, Evelyn was immediately appointed secretary of the school district. Elated at the prospect of a school for her children, at her ranch, Evelyn was eager to get back home with baby Lonnie. Charley was eager as well, for he had built his wife a new chicken house while she was away.

By the end of summer, Charley and many of the local ranchers had cut enough logs for the new schoolhouse. However, the men would have to wait until winter, as the logs would have to be brought into the canyon by sleds. In the meantime, Evelyn had found her first school teacher. Ruth Haslem was a school teacher from New Jersey who had recently moved near Jensen, Utah, following her marriage to Joe Haslem. Ruth accepted the teaching position and suggested the school term begin right after Labor

Day. The children would be taught in the dugout bunkhouse until the new school building was completed. Ruth would stay with the Mantles during the school term.

Once the snow fell, Charley and his neighbors brought the cut logs by sled to the ranch. Ruth's husband, Joe, came to help with the construction, as did Evelyn's father. By mid-November the building was nearly completed. Built at the southern edge of Castle Rock, the twenty-by-fourteen-feet structure included a heating stove and large window in the front and a second window installed in the west wall. By Thanksgiving, the new schoolhouse was finished. To reach the required number of days children had to attend school each term, as well as finish before summer ranching chores began, the children were sent to school six days a week.

As was typical with government projects, a year later the promised road into Hells Canyon had not even begun. Charley took it upon himself to build a road. It had taken a few months to clear a path, but he had gotten it done by November. It was rough and rocky in spots, but it was a road. It was an exciting event that the entire Mantle family witnessed when Charley drove the first wagon, loaded with desks and school supplies, through the canyon and to the front door of the Mantle cabin.

In the spring of 1936, Charley rode out of the canyon in comfort along his new road to Jensen, to pick up a delivery Evelyn had ordered from a catalog. When he returned, Evelyn was thrilled with the wagon load of fifty small fruit trees. She had dug out a large area of earth, near the wall of Castle Rock, where she had discovered the ancient petroglyphs on the rock wall so many years ago. This would be the spot where a fruit orchard would eventually grow. Charley and Evelyn, with the help of Potch and Pat, carefully unloaded the trees. Then Evelyn tenderly straightened the roots of each tree and planted them in the newly cultivated ground. Next, she used the precious irrigation water to soak the ground and then covered the ground with straw.

Charley and Evelyn had long talked of building a new home. In the spring of 1938, Charley and a group of his friends brought sleds loaded with building supplies over the frozen Yampa

River. Evelyn was overjoyed that her new house was about to become a reality. Her joy was dampened by dismay when in March Evelyn realized she was once again pregnant.

Evelyn Mantle, who had just celebrated her birthday, fell into despair. It seemed as if she had spent her entire life pregnant. As her spirits dipped into near depression, Charley spent more and more time away from the ranch, tending to the cattle and horses and working with the crops.

It was an unusually warm spring season and the snow melted quickly off Blue Mountain. The Yampa River was rising and Evelyn kept a close watch on it. She was a stern disciplinarian and forbid her children to go near the river during this time. Charley was away from the ranch, moving the cattle away from the river. One night, Evelyn was awakened by the sound of rushing water against the canyon walls. She ran outside to see that the water was flowing over the hardened ground and was almost to cabin. Frantic, Evelyn woke the children, covered little Lonnie with a quilt, and herded her children to cliffs behind the cabin. With her children out of harm's way, all she could do was hold them tight under the quilt and wait for daylight. It was a long night, as the thunder from the storm was deafening against the rock canyon. When the sun rose, Evelyn took the children to the safety of the school building. Then she opened the gates of the corrals so the milk cows could get away from the rushing waters. Her garden was destroyed. She noticed that the ditch was full of mud and broken tree limbs. Then she turned her attention to the cabin. The dirt floor was a muddy mess. It would take days to clean the cabin. As she began the work of restoring her home, she and the children slept in the school house at night. The summer was spent repairing the corrals and outbuildings and restoring the ditch.

That summer brought another obstacle Evelyn had to overcome. The school teacher would not be returning for the fall session. Evelyn, nearly six months pregnant, rode out of the canyon on horseback. She was determined to find a suitable teacher in Craig. The school district superintendent gave Evelyn the name of Florence Shank. She was the oldest daughter of Henry Shank, a well-known local rancher. Twenty-three-year-old Florence had just finished her first teaching assignment at the small ranching settlement of Lily Park, and came highly recommended. The young teacher accepted the position and would arrive at the Mantle ranch in the fall.

Back at the ranch, Evelyn learned that Charley had befriended a group of prospectors at Hardings Hole, not far from the ranch. Through some wheeling and dealing, Charley had arranged the trade of a side of beef and fresh vegetables for their help in extending his rough road out of Hells Canyon as far east as they could. Charley and Evelyn staked out the path for the road. It was a careful process, as they wanted the road built at a reasonable grade, so an automobile could traverse the high canyon ledge. The men blasted sections of the canyon with dynamite and then used picks and shovels to move the debris and clear a path. It was slow, hard work, yet they made good progress.

In the meantime, Charley was forced to ride horseback out of the canyon to bring Ms. Shank to the ranch for the fall school session. The Mantles were thrilled to have her, and Evelyn had set up a separate living quarters for her in the schoolhouse. The children and their new teacher got along very well, and Evelyn and Florence became fast friends.

Finally, in July, Moffat County had approved the construction of a road through Hells Canyon, in an effort to capitalize on the new tourist industry. The county brought in heavy equipment and bulldozers to complete the job that Evelyn and Charley had already begun. On Sundays, when there was no school, the Mantles took the children out to watch the bulldozers break rock and crush trees. Charley became friends with the crew who worked tirelessly throughout the fall. As Thanksgiving approached, he invited the them to his ranch for the holiday meal. Charley pitched in to help with the meal preparation, as Evelyn was in her eighth month of pregnancy. It was a fine gathering with plenty of food for everyone.

Just before dawn the following morning, Evelyn went into labor. Charley rushed to the schoolhouse to get Florence, and brought her to the cabin. Florence instructed Charley to put pots on the stove to boil water, and sterilized needed utensils that were available. Then she did her best to help Evelyn. After five hours of hard labor, Evelyn gave birth to a healthy baby boy. She had to cut the cord and tie it herself. Florence Shank later recalled, "Evelyn sure was one wonderful little woman, she told us everything to get ready and what to do when the time came and drilled Charley and me as to what each of us could do."[17]

For years, Evelyn had been corresponding with various professors at the University of Colorado regarding the many ancient Indian artifacts she had found on her property over the years. She received kind replies, but not much interest. Then, in the summer of 1939, a pickup truck bearing the University of Colorado logo drove right up to the porch of the Mantle cabin. Evelyn greeted the man, who introduced himself as Charles Scoggin, an archaeologist with the university. Scoggin explained that he had been selected to conduct an archaeological survey, now that federal funding had been allocated for the Dinosaur National Monument. Evelyn not only granted the man permission to survey the land, but offered to take him to the different caves and canyons where she had found the evidence of earlier life and show him the petroglyphs.

It was a summer filled with joy for Evelyn. She and Scoggin rode horseback deep into the canyons, where they explored caves and Scoggin sketched the petroglyphs. Evelyn also showed Scoggin her collection of baskets, a cedar bark bag, reed mats, stone utensils, and a horn from a desert bighorn sheep that had a hole carved through it to allow for scraping arrow shafts. Scoggin examined the ancient relics and estimated them to be from the Basket Maker Period, approximately thirteen hundred years ago. Scoggin was then allowed to make sketches of the ancient artifacts.

Charley and Evelyn also began the construction of their new home. Charley and several neighbors mined sand from the river bottom. A large wooden frame was erected for the process of mixing the cement. Then the cement was poured by hand to create the foundation. By the end of the summer, the framed house was in place, and together, Evelyn and Charley built the staircase.

As fall approached, Evelyn readied the children for the school term and Charley moved the livestock out of the canyon for the winter. Evelyn had another surprise before the winter season. Unexpectedly, a friend of Charley's arrived from Craig in a used Chevrolet pickup truck. He told Evelyn that Charley had asked to find a dependable vehicle for her, now that there was a dependable road in and out of the canyon.

The following summer, Scoggin and other archaeologists returned, asking for permission to excavate a few of the areas Evelyn had previously shown him. Evelyn granted the permission, and spent time with them when she could, as she and Charley were determined to finish building their new house. By summer's end, Evelyn had mastered the art of wood-work and built the frames for the windows and doors. She even helped in placing the roof, and nailed the shingles herself. Shortly after the new school term began, the Mantle family moved into their new home. It was far from finished, but with Evelyn's new wood-working skills, she would finish it herself. Evelyn spent the winter building closets, cabinets, shelves, and counter tops. She loved the work which became a hobby. She relished making new things and improvements to her home for the rest of her life.

In the fall of 1941 a new teacher arrived. Esther Campbell and her husband, Duward, arrived in Hells Canyon on September 16. Evelyn made the old cabin comfortable for Esther to live in during the school term. Once his wife was settled, Duward returned to his ranch at Douglas Mountain in Brown's Park. Esther enjoyed her pupils, and she and Evelyn became friends. Evelyn provided lunch for the children and then Esther would ring the school bell for recess. After the women chatted over a quiet lunch, Esther would again ring the bell and the school day resumed. Evelyn was disappointed when Esther chose not to teach the following year.

The war brought hardships to American families. Evelyn was forced to teach the children herself, as the local women were needed at home. During this time, her ranch work suffered, and her beloved orchard was often neglected. With gas rationing, Evelyn seldom left the canyon and made clothes for the children from old garments. Charley did his best providing fresh meat for the family from his hunting trips. Pat Mantle later recalled, "When I was a little boy, if my brothers and I told our daddy we were hungry, he would hand us a stick and say, 'There's a jackrabbit right over there.'"[18]

In the fall of 1944, Evelyn enrolled their two oldest children, Potch and Pat, in the Craig high school. They would stay with Walt Hammond, the postmaster for Craig. Pat enjoyed school and made many new friends. Potch hated school and spent most of his time with his new rodeo friends. When the school term ended, Potch returned to the ranch and declared he was finished with school. Evelyn was deeply disappointed as she had worked so hard to see that her children were well educated. Potch worked with his father at the ranch.

The following fall, Pat returned to the Hammond home in Craig to attend school. Not long after school started, Pat was at the home on the morning when Hammond committed suicide with a gunshot to the head. Pat heard the gunshot and rushed to the scene. He broke down the door of the bathroom and found Hammond on the floor in a pool of blood. He immediately called the police and kept the Hammond family members away from the bathroom until the police and ambulance arrived. It was a horrific experience for Pat that would stay with him for years.

That summer, both Potch and Pat worked with their father. Charley was a tough disciplinarian, and worked his boys hard. As the summer grew hotter, so did Potch's temper. He began arguing with his father and picked fights with Pat. One day the brothers got into an argument over their mother. Potch made a derogatory remark about his mother and threatened to kill her. Pat shoved his brother and boldly said to him, "If you ever set a hand on Mama or say anything like that to her, I'll kill you."[19] The two brothers took swings at each other until their father finally pulled them apart. Charley saw that his oldest son was out of control. After a long discussion between father and son, Potch told his father he wanted to leave the family ranch. Potch said, "I want to get out of this damned country and never come back. You can run this god-damned outfit any way you want to 'cause I'm leaving."[20]

With that, Charley gave his son what money he had with him and bid him good-bye. When Charley and Pat had finished moving the cattle, they rode in silence back to the ranch. As Pat tended to the horses, Charley went into the house for a quiet moment with his wife. He simply said, "Today we lost a boy." Charley told Evelyn that Potch had decided to leave and wouldn't be returning. Neither Charley nor Pat ever told Evelyn that she was the reason that led to her oldest son's desertion from the family. As Charley harbored the secret his disposition became dark and moody. Evelyn was dealing with her own sadness of losing her son. She wrote to her cousin Eva in New York, "If I can ever live through this it may all iron out. I have cried buckets of tears thinking of this."[21]

Evelyn's despair over losing a child was compounded the following fall when it was time to send her only daughter away from home to attend school in Craig. Evelyn was able to overcome her despair by immersing herself in making a new wardrobe of clothes for Queeda. Her cousin sent her patterns of the latest fashions and old clothing that Evelyn used to make new clothes for Queeda's school year in Craig.

Just before Queeda left for school, Charley, with Pat's help, had negotiated an extremely profitable sale of steers to a rancher near Craig. With the sale completed and the money in hand, Charley sent Pat by train to Denver to pick up a used Jeep he had been dealing on. A few days later, Pat drove to the Mantle ranch in a shiny, bright yellow Jeep. Evelyn was thrilled with the new vehicle. When the time came to take Queeda to Craig for the school year, Evelyn loaded Queeda and her new wardrobe into the Jeep and drove to Craig. There, Queeda would stay at the home of Henry Hobley, the Moffat County clerk.

On the return trip to the ranch, Evelyn encountered a rainstorm and the road was covered in mud. When she finally arrived at the ranch, she exclaimed to Charley that the Jeep was "a daisy in mud and on rough, impossible roads."

In the spring of 1947, an early snow melt off Blue Mountain caused the river to rise, bringing a torrent of water through Hells Canyon. The rushing waters destroyed the fences, the ditches, and the garden. Potch came home to help rebuild the ditches, dig a new well, and rebuild the fences. Evelyn was thrilled to see her son again. However, on Memorial Day, the day of Pat's high school graduation, Potch elected not to join the family on their trip to Craig.

That summer, tourists visiting the new Dinosaur National Monument arrived at the Mantle Ranch. Evelyn provided them with cool refreshments, and occasionally guided a group to the cliffs to view the ancient petroglyphs.

In June 1948, Evelyn's beloved garden and fruit orchard were invaded by grasshoppers. Evelyn used a homemade poison, but it was no use. Finally, she resorted to spraying a strong insecticide. It would not be known until the following spring if her precious fruit trees would live.

Queeda, Lonnie, and Tim helped their mother during the summer. Evelyn's fruit trees survived and most of them produced fruit, which Evelyn and Queeda canned. Pat was a great help to Charley and by the end of that summer, the ranch was again fully operational after all the repairs had been made. After Queeda completed high school, she attended the Wasatch Academy in Salt Lake City, Utah. When she graduated, with honors, in May 1950, she received a letter of acceptance to the University of Colorado in Boulder. Both Evelyn and Charley worried about their daughter being so far away from home, but after visiting the campus, they were reassured that Queeda would be just fine. It was a bittersweet time for Evelyn. As she saw her only daughter off to college, she also sent both Lonnie and Tim to Craig for the school year. Pat, who had been such a big help to his father, had accepted employment with the K Ranch, and was doing well on the rodeo circuit. Potch was nearby, working for his father's friend, Rial Chew, but he didn't visit often. Evelyn resigned herself to the fact that her children were leaving home to start their own lives.

Later that year, Evelyn began suffering from shortness of breath, which affected her ranch work. Finally, she took the Jeep and drove to Craig for a visit with the doctor. After a complete examination and a few tests, Evelyn, forty-three years old, was diagnosed with a heart condition. When Evelyn returned to the ranch, she did her best to cut down on her work load, but there was so much to be done. There was also sadness and tension in the Mantle household. Evelyn had received a letter from her cousin, Eva, with news that Julia, Evelyn's mother, had suffered an illness and was bedridden, and that her Evelyn's father, Evan, was drinking uncontrollably. Evelyn's parents had moved to Oak Creek, Colorado, shortly after the construction of the Mantle schoolhouse. After the move, there was no more communication between Evelyn and her parents. Queeda Mantle Walker later wrote, "Evelyn had still not told her children after all these years that their grandparents were alive and living in Oak Creek. Charley had insisted on her complete separation of them from his family, nobody but he and Evelyn would ever know why."[22]

Evelyn continued to care for her garden and can fruit from her orchard. Then, Charley was injured in a horrific horse accident. He was on his favorite horse, Star, checking the cattle approximately fifteen miles from the ranch, when Star suddenly began bucking. Charley hung on, but lost the battle and was thrown to the ground, landing on a pile of rocks. Star had run off and Charley was stranded. He felt the pain in his back and knew it was a serious injury. All he could do was slowly, and painfully, crawl to the main road and hope someone would drive by. He waited the entire day. Queeda Mantle Walker later described what happened next:

He [Charley] had always chastised Evelyn for worrying and made fun of her for checking on anyone who was missing longer then she felt they should have been. She waited worried until almost dark and still he wasn't home, so risked his wrath she took the Jeep and went searching for him. He was never so glad to see anybody in his life, but nonetheless chastised her

301

bitterly for not coming for him sooner.[23]

After Evelyn got Charley back to the ranch, he was bedridden for weeks with back pain. In the meantime, Pat had received his draft notice. America was embroiled in the war with North Korea, and Evelyn was worried what the future held for her sons, as Potch had recently enlisted with the United States Navy. With her boys facing combat in a faraway war, and her husband's back condition, most of the ranch work fell on Evelyn. Charley's back condition eventually improved, but a shoulder injury caused a setback that he never fully recovered from.

The war also took a toll on the economy. The Mantles learned that nearby ranchers, including the Chew family, were selling out. By the spring of 1953, more ranchers had sold their property. As it fell to Evelyn, she did everything she could to keep her ranch operating and profitable.

Evelyn and Charley were proud parents when Lonnie graduated from Colorado State University at Fort Collins, in 1957. Evelyn's joy turned to despair when Lonnie chose to enlist in the United States Armed Forces.

In February 1958, Lonnie left the ranch for basic training at Fort Hood in Texas. Shortly after Lonnie left, Evelyn was not feeling well. One day she told Charley that she felt weak and suddenly fell to the floor. Charley managed to get her into bed and did what he could for her. Their daughter Queeda later wrote: "She had all the symptoms of a heart attack. Charley couldn't leave her to go for help, and they figured there wasn't anything anyone could do anyway, so Evelyn was just 'resting it out.'"[24]

When a neighbor happened to come by the ranch, Charley asked him to send telegrams to the children. Pat, Tim, and Lonnie arrived as soon as they could and helped with the ranching chores. Queeda, who had recently married and lived in Texas, arrived with her new baby girl. Because of Evelyn's condition, Pat brought the doctor from Craig to the ranch. After Dr. Monahan examined Evelyn, he determined she had suffered a slight heart attack, but that there was no permanent damage. He gave Pat a bottle of iron pills and told the family that it would be best if they moved their mother into town where she could enjoy an easier life. At the very least, he said, her work load had to be decreased substantially.

With plenty of bed rest, Evelyn began to improve. However, Charley, who had no intention of living in any town, grew increasingly resentful over life's changes and his lack of control. Queeda later wrote, "Charley was sinking farther and farther into a dark, brooding existence. He seldom shaved, talked to himself constantly, and dreamed of 'leaving this god-damned ranch and finding a country where a man can still make a living.'"[25]

Meanwhile, the Mantle children were getting on with their lives. Lonnie was stationed in Frankfurt, Germany, and faithfully wrote letters home. He traveled the country when he had leave and was enjoying the area. Queeda and her husband Rex, had moved back to Colorado, and Pat joined them in starting a new business in the summer of 1959. Their new venture, Sombrero Stables, originally located in Estes Park, offered horseback rides for children. The following year, Tim graduated from Colorado State University. Both Evelyn and Charley made the trip to see their youngest son graduate from college. Later that summer of 1960, the Dinosaur National Monument area was expanded. The Mantles lost all but one of their grazing rights, as the government had acquired the land. The government also placed grazing restrictions on the Mantle Ranch. Queeda Mantle Walker later wrote:

It was like a last blow to Charley. The heart was out of him. Charley couldn't stand it any longer. He just had to get away and do some investigating of the world. It seemed to him that the ranch had gone to hell in spite of all his lifelong efforts. He left home and flew into the remote Amazon country of Brazil during the winter of 1960-1961.[26]

Queeda went on to describe how her mother reacted: "Evelyn was crushed that he would go off like that and she felt that he would surely die down there."

Charley Mantle seemed to be having the time of his life, according to the letters he wrote to Evelyn. She did what she could to keep the family ranch operational, and Pat came to lend a hand when he could.

On a rare shopping excursion, Evelyn stopped at the Singer sewing machine store and learned that there was an opening for a seamstress, making covered belts with buckles. She was told that the Singer Corporation provided all the material and the buckles, and that she would be paid by the piece. Evelyn could work from home, provided she could meet the pick-up and delivery date each week. Evelyn agreed and was given a sample to cover and assemble. She used one of their machines, quickly finished the item and was hired. Evelyn knew the job would not pay much, but she was thrilled that for the first time in her life, she was employed. Part of the paperwork needed for the employer was copy of her birth certificate, which she did not have. Her cousin Eva was able to obtain a copy from the courthouse in Cicero, New York, where Evelyn was born. For whatever reason, when Evelyn held the official government document with her maiden name on it, a sense of independence and pride came over her. Queeda later wrote, "Now Evelyn felt like she was more qualified to do business in her own name, and it looked like it had come to that. She was pretty sure she would not be making her living on the Mantle Ranch anymore."[27]

It seemed as if Evelyn's new-found independence was fortuitous as events unfolded. During that summer of 1962, Pat was busy setting up a second Sombrero Stables facility in Grand Lake, at the western edge of Rocky Mountain National Park. He was also heavily involved with his 7-11 Rodeo outfit, which provided stock for rodeos across the state. It was through one of his rodeo contacts that he learned that his father was back in the states and staying with Pat's older brother, Potch, in Montana. Not long after this news, Evelyn received a phone call from a representative with the Dinosaur National Monument. The man explained to Evelyn that he had received Charley's written permission to conduct a survey of the Mantle ranch for an appraisal and potential buyout.

The representative requested a date for the survey to take place in January 1963. Knowing that the winter months were not advantageous to an accurately reflective appraisal of the ranch's worth, Evelyn refused the request. Undaunted, the representative contacted Tim directly at the Mantle ranch. His answer was the same as his mother's, but he did agree to a date in June 1963. This gave Tim and his new wife, LaRue, time to make necessary improvements and generally "spruce up" the place. Evidently the plan worked, for the Dinosaur National Monument representative did not make an offer.

In the spring of 1964, Evelyn returned to the ranch from a winter stay with Queeda and her growing family. Queeda later recalled, "Evelyn was sure Tim and LaRue would want to spend time together riding and working the cattle, and she could keep the home ranch going. She remembered how much she had enjoyed working with Charley before their children were born. She eagerly drove her aging pickup back to the canyon home she loved."[28]

In 1965, Charley signed over the deed to the family ranch to his five children. Evelyn dutifully supplied the necessary paperwork for the transfer of ownership. Queeda later wrote, "She watched passively as the transfer of the ranch took place. Silently she suffered, as not Charley, not any of the children, asked her opinion or thanked her for the gift of the ranch she loved."[29]

Shortly after the deed was signed, and before it was recorded at the Moffat County courthouse, Charley evidently had another arrangement in mind. He submitted a letter of a land exchange to the Dinosaur National Monument authorities. Charley Mantle proposed to exchange the eighty acres of uninhabitable cliffs, bordering the northern edge of his ranch, for the eighty acres of land along the Yampa River that he had legally obtained from William "Billy" Hall, paying cash for his homestead claim, in 1923. The letter of exchange, legally drawn up by family friend and attorney, Stan Johnson, was filed in the Boulder County Court. However, no action was taken on Mantle's legally-filed exchange proposal by the DNM authorities. Queeda Mantle Walker wrote of this family episode, "He [Charley] was washing his hands of this ranch he had loved so much and worked so hard to make a living on for the last thirty-nine years."[30]

Lonnie and Tim took over the operations of the family ranch. That winter, Evelyn went to Boulder and stayed with Queeda and her family. Eager to get back to the ranch and her gardens and orchards, Evelyn returned the following spring. Working in her garden and tending to her orchard seemed to bring a calmness to her, despite the turmoil over the future of the ranch.

In 1968, Evelyn purchased a parcel of land in Boulder County, not far from Queeda's home. A friend of Rex Walker, Queeda's husband, built a fine house for Evelyn. Now Evelyn had a mortgage obligation and found work as a seamstress at the Fashion Bar department store in Boulder.

That summer Charley arrived at the ranch in Hells Canyon. He was getting older, had no means by which to make a living, and was broke. Tim and his wife were at the ranch and suggested that Charley move over to the old Blevin homestead at Red Rock. There was a water well and a great view of the rock cliffs.

Meanwhile, Pat opened a third Sombrero Stables facility in Steamboat Springs. He found the perfect location, complete with a rustic barn, at the foot of Mount Werner. Pat's new location was an instant hit with the local residents. By the time ski season was in full swing, the city of Steamboat Springs had a new marketing campaign complete with posters featuring Pat Mantle as the "Western Cowboy" of the ski resort town. Mantle soon became a legendary horse wrangler in the area and a respected resident of the town. Long-time friend and local newspaper reporter Tom Ross, later wrote of his friend, "Pat Mantle influenced a lot of young horseback riding guides in the region with his tough love balanced with his generosity and cowboy humor."[31]

In the fall of 1968, Charley left Hells Canyon with a female acquaintance he had recently met.[31] The two packed a vehicle with camping gear, Charley's bedroll and his pistol, and .22 rifle. His female companion packed her sleeping bag, and her .22 pistol and took her toy poodle dog along. The two traveling companions entered Mexico at Nogales, on December 27, 1968.

According to information the Mantle family later obtained, the two made their way to Los Mochis and attended a local New Year's Eve celebration. The following morning, Charley's companion chose to stay in the town, so Charley continued on his journey alone. Near the small town of El Fuerte, Charley set up camp, intending to stay for several days. Sometime during the night of January 4, 1969, Charley Mantle was murdered.

Early on the following morning, a Sunday, campers in the area found his body. The report of the murder was phoned in to the local police by a woman. Local officials from Los Mochis arrived at the crime scene. It was also about this same time that Charley's traveling companion, and the man she had been staying with, arrived at the police station in Los Mochis. The woman was carrying her poodle, which was bleeding profusely. She explained that someone had shot her dog. However, both she and her new friend were covered with blood. With a murder investigation just underway, the police placed both in jail. Their working theory was that the two people had committed the murder; a crime of passion. However, during interrogation, the woman claimed that her friend accidentally shot the dog, mistaking it for a coyote, and they had brought the dog to town seeking medical attention. Suspicious of the story, the police kept the two in custody.

Meanwhile, the Mexican authorities had identified the body and contacted his known next-of-kin, Rex and Queeda Walker. While Rex made arrangements to fly to Mexico, Queeda frantically tried to reach her brothers and her mother. Rex arrived in Los Mochis the following day. He was taken to where his father-in-law's body was held, and identified the body as that of Charley Mantle. Rex requested the body be embalmed as soon as possible, so that he could take it with him on his return trip. Rex was allowed to interview the woman in question. She maintained her innocence and repeated the story she had told the officials.

After four days in Mexico, Rex finally received Charley's body, his personal possessions, and his Jeep. He and the family provided the funds to fly the body to the states. Then Rex packed his father-in-law's possessions into the Jeep and drove to Nogales, where he crossed the border back into the United States.

Lonnie drove to Denver's Stapleton Airport to take possession of his father's casket. From Denver, he would take the body to Craig for the funeral service. Meanwhile, brothers Potch and Pat worked together to dynamite rock and then dig a grave on a hill at Red Rock on the Mantle Ranch.

On the day of the funeral, all of the Mantle children and their families were present, as well as Evelyn. Because of the large crowd, the service was held in the town community hall. Charley's daughter Queeda later wrote:

> There were well over 300 people there, and old friends got to visit quietly. Nobody seemed to notice that it was snowing and getting on toward night, and they had a hundred-mile trip to make to the grave site. The snow just kept coming, and the dirt roads were almost impassible. Since nothing was impossible to Charley Mantle in his lifetime, certainly nothing was going to stop his funeral procession. His friends and family got him to the grave site and sadly buried him. The tragedy and mystery of his death still haunts many people.[32]

Later that same year, Evelyn suffered another devastating loss. In November 1970, Evelyn's oldest child, Charles Evan Mantle—Potch—was killed in a car accident. He was forty-three years old. Once again it fell to Lonnie to claim the body of a family member. He drove to Hamilton, Montana, where he identified the body of his oldest brother. Lonnie made arrangements and paid the required fee for the funeral home to provide transportation of the body to Craig.

Evelyn her remaining children had all agreed that Potch would be buried on the hill at Red Rock, next to his father. Pat arrived from Steamboat Springs, and with a few friends, a grave was finally dug through the hard rock next Charley's grave. The funeral was held at Zoebels Mortuary in Craig. Queeda Mantle

Walker recalled:

> It is always a sweet and amazing thing how Western [sic] people get the word around about one of their own. People showed up from all around the country. They had known Potch when he was a youngster, or when he rodeoed, or when he ranched, or when they had worked with him at various places. Potch's body was transported in the pitch dark of the night by pickup to the grave site 100 miles west of Craig to the Mantle Ranch. He was buried beside his father.[33]

Queeda went on to comment on how yet another death was affecting her mother: "Evelyn buried her eldest son, who was only forty-two. It had been only ten months since she buried her husband of forty-three years. Her body carriage showed the grief she was holding inside, and her eyes showed all the agony of her soul."[34]

Indeed, Evelyn Mantle was struggling with emotions she had experienced over a lifetime of devotion, loyalty, hard work and dedication to her family. She remained saddened over the separation from her husband and grieved over his senseless death. Evelyn was also grieving over the death of her son and nearly overcome with thoughts of what could have been. Evelyn's daughter Queeda later reflected, "Evelyn was exceptionally sad and introverted after the funeral of her son, Potch. It ended a lifetime of difficulty between them, beginning when he was a child. All the love she could give him hadn't changed him much, although he had mellowed toward her some over the years."[35]

To escape the family sadness, Evelyn immersed herself in her work. The Christmas season was in full swing, and Evelyn's work for Fashion Bar doubled. She took work home with her, which she did not mind, as it kept her busy and away from family sadness. The added income also helped her to pay off her mortgage. By the summer of 1971, she only had two payments to make, and as Queeda later wrote, "By August it would be done. She was elated, because now she would have her own roof over her head."[36]

Evelyn's added earnings allowed her to purchase a dependable used vehicle. However, she grew tired of driving to work in the snow and ice and hated city traffic. Because of this, that winter she cut down on her workload. Evelyn also was not feeling well. She wrote the following to her cousin Eva, "I have numbness in arms and legs and passing out. Dr. put me on a new medicine that really did me in. I was a month getting back where I could do anything again. Dr. never did figure it out. They are too busy to really take care of anybody. But I really do have to slow down, and I hate it."[37]

For the next few years, Evelyn's health slowly declined. She was determined to remain independent, so she continued to work, but cut back even more. Not wanting to alarm her children, who had their own lives to lead, she did her best not to let on that she was not well.

In the summer of 1978, members of Hayden High School class of 1924 were having a reunion. Evelyn was determined to attend the reunion and visit, perhaps for the last time, old friends and classmates. Queeda agreed to take her and they would also make a trip to see Tim and his family at the Mantle family ranch. Evelyn thoroughly enjoyed her time at the high school reunion and even attended the local rodeo. At the Mantle ranch, she spent time with her grandchildren and Tim and LaRue. Evelyn walked through the garden, spending time alone with her thoughts. It would be the last time she would see the ranch and Hells Canyon that she had come to love.

On January 2, 1979, nearly two weeks before her seventy-second birthday, Evelyn Fuller Mantle died following complications from a surgery to remove her spleen. Her funeral and burial took place in Boulder, Colorado.

The former city girl from New York who had worked most of her life as a rancher in an isolated rock canyon, suffering unmeasurable hardships, was finally at peace.

# Notes

1.  Walker, *The Mantle Ranch*, pg. 1.
2.  *Steamboat Today*, July 23, 2013.
3.  Walker, *The Mantle Ranch*, pg. 5.
4.  ibid.
5.  ibid., pg. 15.
6.  ibid., pg. 36.
7.  ibid., pg. 2.
8.  Walker, *The Mantle Ranch*, pg. v.
9.  ibid., pg. 74. ibid., pg. 81.
10. ibid, pgs. 98, 99.
11. ibid, pg. 103.
12. ibid.
13. ibid.
14. ibid.
15. ibid, pg. 110.
16. ibid, pg. 155.
17. ibid.
18. Walker, *The Mantle Ranch*, pg. 211.
19. ibid.
20. ibid.
21. ibid.
22. ibid, pg. 247.
23. ibid, pg. 248.
24. ibid, pg. 279.
25. ibid.
26. ibid.
27. ibid., pg. 78.
28. Walker, *Last Ranch in Hells Canyon*, pg. 9.
29. Walker, *Last Ranch in Hells Canyon*, pg. 9.
30. *Steamboat Today*, July 23, 2013.
31. Walker, *Last Ranch in Hells Canyon*, pg. 122. Perhaps because the subsequent murder of her father was never solved, the author does not provide the identity of the female companion.

32. Walker, *Last Ranch in Hells Canyon*, pg. 124.
33. ibid.
34. bid.
35. Walker, *Last Ranch in Hells Canyon*, pg. 134.
36. ibid.
37. ibid.

*DPL*

# REMINISCENCES OF LIFE IN THE COLORADO MOUNTAINS

*Julia T. Biskup Kawcak*

# Julia T. Biskup Kawcak

**M**ountain ranching in the nineteenth century was often a lonely, lonesome, and isolated existence. It took extreme inner strength, determination, and sheer will power to overcome many of the obstacles of the rugged life.

Julia T. Biskup Kawcak was one such mountain rancher who possessed these qualities and much more. At the age of fifteen, Julia married Panko Paul Kawcak in Craig, Colorado. Julia ran their ranch while Paul, as he was known, worked in the nearby coal mines. Over the years, Julia would give birth to sixteen children. In 1984, Julie Jones Eddy interviewed Julia Kawcak in Craig, Colorado.[1]

A few years later, in 1987 at the age of eighty-eight, Julia T. Biskup Kawcak died. Following her death, family members discovered a manuscript Julia had been writing. It was a memoir of sorts. Family members worked together to assemble the one-hundred-page manuscript that was eventually published.[2]

It is through these writings, her interviews (all unedited), as well as reminiscences from family members, that we get a true sense of Julia's life on a mountain ranch:

> I was born on June 29, 1999, in Rockvale, Colorado, a coal mining town about nine miles south of Canon City, Colorado. My father was a coal miner and worked inside of the mine. My father Steve Biskup came to the U.S.A. in March of 1894 and mother Mary Biskup and two small children Joe and Mary came over from Austria in the fall of 1896 and dad worked in a coal mine in Texas. But they soon moved to Rockvale, Colorado and lived there about thirteen years and five more

children were born, Anna, Katherine, Julia (me) Steve, and John. Mother had more, but she miscarried.[3]

And I think they just didn't eat right, or something, but she did bring Joe and Mary over on the ship, and she was sick. It took nine days or something to come over, and she was sick, so the captain took care of the kids for her. He'd come in in the morning and help them get dressed, because she was in bed. He'd help them dress, and he'd take them to the kitchen, and feed them, and then he'd take them up on the deck, you know, in the daytime, and make them sit there, or something, and they were scared, because there was a lot of people on there. They'd sit right where he'd put them.

In 1907 my father and a friend heard of Craig, Colorado, and all of the good farming land that would soon be released for homesteads so father and his friend came to Craig in July 1907 and father bought a 160-acre farm that was already a deeded farm. He bought the land from Judge R.A. Breeze who lived about a mile west on a farm. Our farm was 160 acres of sage brush so tall you couldn't see cattle or horses out on it.[4]

Craig was a long way from everywhere. Rawlins was about 125 miles north and Glenwood Springs about 130 miles south with the small towns of Meeker and Rifle between so if anyone needed building materials like doors, windows, and hardware they had to make trip to Rawlins and Glenwood Springs to obtain them. Craig was very isolated and freight was being brought in from Rawlins, Steamboat, and Glenwood by four and six horse freight wagons so you couldn't even buy a bed, it had to be brought in by wagon.

When dad sent for us, mother sold our four room house and a one room office of my oldest brother who was a civil engineer or surveyor for four hundred dollars, two milk cows at $35 apiece to friends who had children. We kept two milk cows and we delivered milk to eight families at five cents a quart and my sisters and I delivered the milk, some in the evening and other in the morning. So when mother sold the house, office, and cows, she crated her Singer sewing machine, put cardboard between the bedstead, wired them together, rolled up the mattress, and tied it, and shipped them to Craig because you couldn't buy them there.

Mother wrapped our big key-winding shelf clock in a blanket and carried it in her lap so the glass door wouldn't break. We boarded the train on April 9, 1908, in Florence, Colorado where the stage of Hack as it was called took us to the train. We came through the Royal Gorge through Salida, Leadville, Wallcott, down through the Glenwood Canyon and into Rifle, the end of the train trip for us. In our party were mother, two little brothers, two sisters, I and my brother Joe and his bride of eight months and a friend who wanted to take up a homestead too.

And then the next morning after we got off of the train, we slept on the seats in the depot down there all night, and next morning the stage coach come and picked us up, and brought us up to Craig. We arrived in Craig about six or seven p.m. and stayed over night at the Webb Hotel which was on the corner of Yampa and Victory. It was a big two story wood building and it was up on stilts or posts because there was a wide ditch under the hotel. Father and Tony Bakos, his friend, met us the next morning after breakfast with the wagon team and took us out to the farm that is the present Mrs. Marie Biskup ranch. Neighbors gave us a wagon load of sweet smelling hay that we spread on the floor in the room and covered it with a canvas. Mother and dad had their bed set up in the kitchen which served as a dining room too.

My father had the well dug when we got there. See, that's the first thing they done. And then in a year or two, why, we got a windmill. We had a nice garden, you know, and it would pump the water and run it down like ditches, you know. We always had a nice garden, lots of stuff.[5]

Our house was a hewed log house with a dirt roof so when the first fall rains came the roof leaked everywhere. We put canvas canopies over the beds and put buckets, pans, and cans all over the house. It was a two room house and each room was 14 x 14 feet. The floor in the house was 10 inch rough boards and all the windows had to be replaced. The ceiling was cheese cloth tacked to the pole rafters that held the roof up to keep the dirt from falling into everything. And if there was a mouse up in that dirt, you could see it running around on that cheesecloth!

Dad bought a four hole or four burner coal and wood stove and we got along with it for one year. Then one day when dad arrived home from bringing in a load of freight to the J.W. Hugers Co. General Store he brought a coal range with a warming oven above and a nice big oven to bake the bread in. It was a show piece with shining chrome so mother was very happy to have a dependable cook and bake stove. It even had a hot water reservoir on the right hand side so we had hot water at all times. It was a treat to us kids to keep it filled with water. Clothes were all washed in a tub on a washboard and boiled in a big boiler on the stove.[6]

We cleared and plowed about five acres and we made a fence of sage brush all around it to keep the horses and two cows out of the oat crop dad had planted. The brush was piled in a square and when our oats was about six inches high we were hit by the Mormon crickets which came from the west. We could hear a lot of banging on tin pan tubs and anything that would make noise and soon neighbor Van Tassel came running to tell us that the Mormon crickets were coming and him and his family run them out of his garden. There were so many they ate everything that came in their way. They were so thick that they couldn't go around anything. They'd come to the buildings they climb right over if they came to your leg they would climb up your leg so if you made a lot of noise you could scare them and they move faster and would not stop to eat. You was always stomping when you was around them. I was about eight or nine. It was around 6 p.m. and the crickets all climbed into the brush barrier and stopped for the night and that night we went out after dark and lit all of that brush so we got rid of millions of crickets but we had to tie the cows and the horses until the men could build a barbed wire fence. Barbed wire was hard to get so that is why we built the brush barrier. There weren't very many crickets left at our place the next morning. Only those were left roosted in the sage brush that wasn't cut down yet. We didn't see any more crickets for several years. You know, grasshoppers did that to some farmers back on the eastern slope.

Soon more people came into Craig about 1910 and settled all of the Breeze Basin Country and all of Austrian nationality so we were good friends and worked to help each other. It was in 1909 when the crickets hit us that the other men folks came in to file on their homesteads.

In 1910 my sister Mary and husband [Mike Kawcak] and four children came in and settled up in the Elk Head Community... so we had the Austrian and Slovak communities settled there. Even if land changed hands it is still owned by immediate families of the first owners.

My sister Kate and I had to be dad's helpers so we didn't get much schooling because every spring we had to quit a month or a month and a half ahead of time for school to close to help put in the crops. We helped put up rye hay to feed the cows and horses. School was the old Breeze Basin or South Side School about a fourth of a mile West of the Roscoe Morton Ranch. We had almost three miles to walk to school. We had to go around a fence and get to it. And we had to bring water to school. You didn't have any water at the school.

Dad was an awful hard worker. Dad always went to Oak Creek in the fall after all the fall work was done to work in the coal mines there to keep us in food and clothes for the winter and pay taxes and try to save money for the summer.

Us children milked the cows and mother would make butter which we would exchange at a little local butcher shop. Just exchanged butter and garden vegetables for beef each week for our Sunday dinner. Dad was a good hunter so kept us in sage chicken and rabbits so we never lacked meat. We didn't have ice boxes or refrigerators so mother would cut and then salt it [the meat] layer by layer in a big bucket and dad would drop it down into the well just above the water and it kept cold as the well was at least 45 feet deep.

In 1914 my sister Kate married John Hoza. John was a brother to our first sister Anna's husband. So that left me alone to help dad with the farm work but I was a husky, strong girl so we plowed up more brush so that by the time I left home we had about 70 acres cleared, plowed and in crop.

Among the many European immigrant families in the Breeze Basin region were the Kawchack and Kawcak Austrian families. Panko "Paul" Kawcak was Julia Biskup's future husband. In her taped interview, Julia spoke of Paul's family:

He came from the old country then, in 1903, and my sister and his brother were getting married that fall, so he came, and he was 15 then. And when he came there, why he played with us, but he couldn't talk, you know. He couldn't talk American, from Austria, and so we talked to him in our language, and we had a lot of fun. He never did have anything like that in the old country, because when they had a wedding there, they went to the saloons to dance and all. Nobody had a place to dance at home. So they'd go down to the saloon, and the kids had to stay home. See, so they'd have their good times down there, dance all night so this was a treat to him.

He [Paul] was still working at the coal mine when his brother, told him to come, [to Craig] so he'll get a homestead right next to him. So we had joining homesteads. But he only got 80 acres to start with, because the rest wasn't turned loose.

I was married August 1, 1915 to Paul Kawcak a brother to my oldest sister Mary Kawcak's husband [Mike Kawcak] so again two sisters married two brothers. Paul had filed on a homestead up on Elkhead joining his brother's land.

We still didn't have a church at the time, see. I was married at the old court house. We all come from the ranch, from my father's, over there on Breeze Basin, on a wagon, with a team of mules. And we come across the river to get into town, and my father come on his wagon, and different neighbors come from up above, because all of them were Catholics, see. Old Father Myers, he came down, and so we were married.[7]

My brother played for my wedding. We danced all day and all night in the old house. There was even a chivaree. Van Tassels, and Breezes, and Tuckers, they lived further down the river, you know. They all came, and they were pounding on all kind of things, well, nobody was outside, and it really did kind of give us a scare when it first started.[8]

But they all came, each brought some little thing. The women brought me a doily or something like that, a bowl, or something. I never got much gifts, that's for sure. Nobody had the money. Judge Finley and Judge Breeze, well, they both were judges, and they came, all of them came up there that night. They rode up to Van Tassels on their wagons, you know,

321

and then they come walking up in the dark, so when they got there, we had cake and chicken, and everything on the table. Mother had everything piled up around there. So they all took something to eat, you know, and had cake. I didn't have a wedding cake, just had a cake. Mother baked it.

So two days after our marriage we moved up to his brothers and sisters and lived with them while we dug our water well. Paul, my husband, would dig the dirt and we had a windlass with a quarter inch rope with a five gallon nail barrel on the rope. Paul would fill the bucket with dirt and I would pull it up and dump it out until we got down about 14 feet and ran into sand rock and gravel and the deeper we dug the harder the rock was. We had to drill holes and I'd go down and help we had two ladders hanging on ropes so I'd go down and help drill the holes. Then we'd put in dynamite and fuse them. I'd hurry up the ladder and get out while Paul lit the fuse and hurried up the first ladder. As soon as he got on the second one I'd pull the lower one up. We would run away because rock and sand blew clear out of the well. Then back down he would go fill buckets and I pulled them up and dumped them and we repeated this day after day until our well was forty feet deep and water showed up but it was very little water, hardly enough for the house. We finished off the well by putting a box over it with a pully and rope to pull the water up in the oak buckets we bought and put the rope though the pully and tied a bucket to each end. When you were pulling up one bucket of water the other one was going down into the well.

We built a reservoir, just with the horses and a scraper, you know, he built a reservoir just above where we were going to build our house. So we had water in that the next year, and you know, from that, we got a lot of water in our well. We could get about 1100 or 1200 gallons of water at a time out of there. After we got electricity, see, we got a pump in, and pumped water. Well, anyway, we got our well finished.

After the well was all finished we started to haul logs. We were up in the mountains hauling logs, he was, [Paul] and his brother. [They] hauled logs to the sawmill. Bower had a sawmill up there on Black Mountain, and they sawed the lumber. It was just rough lumber, and while they were doing that, I was grubbing sagebrush. I grubbed out about two acres of brush where we were going to build the house so there wouldn't be anything to catch fire real close. Well, I had all that dug out and everything when they brought the lumber, then they were building. First he dug a little cellar under the house. And they rocked it, made a rock foundation, just out of rocks. And then built the house on top of that. And it was four 14 x 14 rooms, and we had a pretty high attic. And our house was up on a kind of a little hill, you had about 50 feet or more, maybe to go down to the well and get the water and pack it uphill. We just had a bedspring and a mattress. The mattress was just made out of some material, heavy material, and filled with hay.

After that was all finished we started to haul fence post to build a fence around the land that was our homestead. We got a permit for 600 posts from the forest ranger then we started to get up at 4:00 a.m. because Paul had to get up before dawn and go out and look for our team of horses and chase them home. Sometimes he could catch one or both a mile or more from the house. Paul would chop down the quaking aspen trees and I would trim the branches off them and drag 2 or 3 long poles and put them together and slip a log chain around them and pull them up to the wagon undo the chain and go get more. I would pull them in with the team. After we had about 27 or 30 poles we would make three posts out of each so we brought home up to 90 poles each day. I helped get all the posts set and I would stamp the dirt in around each post after that we hired a neighbor Mr. Vassek to help Paul string the wires and stretch it then staple it to the posts. By July we had our fence up and well dug then I found out I was pregnant with my first son. But that didn't stop us. Next thing was to haul in pine logs to build a barn, granary, chicken coop, and a pig pen.

They hauled logs off of Buck Mountain there in Breeze Basin, way back there. And for fences, and they built the chicken coop, the hog pen, and the granary and everything. We done all the daubing, us women. The men still had other work to do, and we were daubing. That's putting the mud in between the logs. You stir the mud up [and] put a lot of straw in it. The straw keeps it in there, doesn't crumble so easily. So we'd daub it all, you know, and they'd put the roofs on and everything.

That first winter after we had our barn and granary built Paul helped his brother do some fall plowing then got a job at the Mt. Harris Coal Mine, the Colorado Utah Coal Company. I stayed with my sister and brother-in-law until snow fell then my brother-in-law took me down to my parents' home at Breeze Basin where we stayed until our first son Steve was born, March 31, 1917. We stayed with my parents until snow went off and the ground was dry so people could start farming.

There would be sixteen children born to Julia and Paul Kawcak. Julia talked about her child-rearing days in an interview with Julie Jones Eddy.

And after that, they [the children] were all born up at the ranch. I never did go to a doctor, or examine, or nothing else. The neighbor lady would come, and take care of everything. She'd come for a couple of days, to bathe the baby and wash the diapers, you know, and all that. I didn't have any Loveys, or anything to put on the baby! Sixteen. Sixteen children. Nine boys and seven girls. And I love them all!

Julie Jones Eddy asked Julia, "Did you ever have any trouble with any of the pregnancies?" Julia replied:
Nothing, nothing. No, that's what I say. And all these women

go to doctors for examinations, and go to the hospital, have the doctor there, and still, something will go wrong. I just thank God everything went right. I've had some women tell me they think part of that is that the hard work, the physical hard work that you did outside, made you stronger, so that having children was easier too.

In 1917 after Steve was born we lived with my sister and brother-in-law during the long winter and [we] had around 40 head of cattle and several horses. Mike and Paul went out looking for hay straw or just anything to feed the cattle and bought a ton or two of hay miles from home but it wasn't enough. So, they had to turn them out into the sage brush hills to feed but they started dying off. One night we were all asleep and all of a sudden my husband and I heard cattle bawling and we heard horses galloping down the road past the house. One horse had a bell on so we heard it. Paul and I both jumped out of bed and ran to the door to see what was happening. We opened the door and looked out and there was a wet snow coming down. Several head of cows were huddled up along the house, cold and hungry, but all quiet with no horses running anywhere.

Paul and I and our son were still living with Paul's brother and my sister's family. They had a large two story house. After the men had the crops planted Paul and I started working on an old adobe cabin that Mike and Mary lived in until they built their own big house. We put in new windows and fixed the floor and we moved in about July first. It had a dirt roof on it with three big logs spaced apart then split posts laid across the three log beams with the middle one higher than the side ones so that made a good spread on the split rails laid side by side. Then dirt was hauled in on the wagon and put on the roof at least ten inches deep. We moved in right away and one morning while preparing breakfast I heard something crack and I looked up and seen that the center beam or log was breaking and my husband was still asleep so I woke him and he jumped up and put on his overalls. I grabbed the baby from his cradle and ran out and Paul ran out and got a post about eight feet long and an ax. He hurried back in and he made a brace to hold up that center beam so as it was propped in place we went back in the cabin. We ate our breakfast knowing the roof wouldn't fall in on us. The post was right in the middle of the cabin but we managed.

About the last of July Paul and brother Mike got a permit to cut down big pine logs and haul them to the Bower sawmill to cut into lumber so the only cost was cutting or sawing into rough lumber that when it was cut they took two wagons, just the wheels, and hauled the lumber down to our homestead where we had a barn, granary, coop, and pig pen and we built a two room house, 28 x 14, and built it with the rough boards over building paper that was nailed to the two by fours for insulation. Then clapboard was put over the crack of each two board joinings. It was quite comfortable with a nice big attic, but not finished and no walls finished with wall board or anything. In about two years after we had a couple of good crops we put ship lap on the walls and put kalsomine on so it looked like a mansion to us in our first home. In this house six children were born with my sister as the midwife. I never had a doctor for any of them.

Over time and as more children were born the house was enlarged, and Paul also added a second story. Julia explained the living conditions of such a large family:

Well, after the kids were big enough to go from downstairs to upstairs, they slept some in one end of the attic, and some in the other. The girls had a blanket in the middle, there, so the boys wouldn't be seeing them. The boys were at one end, and the girls were in the other.
We proved up on everything, see. So after we got our

homesteads proved up on, you had to live there three years, and have 20 acres plowed and fenced. Well, we had all that, and we proved up on it. Well, from then on, we were paying taxes. Then later on, well, we were to get 160. Then, a couple or three years later, they turned loose that land, so we took that up. We got 360 acres. There was one 40 left there, 40 acres, that was just between everybody, and the government gave it to us.

After these children were born we moved a half mile to the two story house that Mike and Mary Kawcak were living in. We bought their place and they moved down on Elkhead Creek to the Starr Ranch on the Creek, it was a hay farm. Our first milk cow we bought from Mr. R.A. Breeze over in Breeze Basin after whom the basin was named.[9]

Paul bought a red muley cow that was giving quite a lot of milk and my father bought a cow at the same place and gave it to me as a wedding gift but was so wild she broke out of the barn and ran away back to their old home so Paul and Mike went after her and brought her home on a rope then tied her to the manger and fed her hay and water in the barn for a few weeks until we got her gentled a little. After she had her first calf I broke her to milk and she got used to only me and if anyone came around the corral she would jump the corral and turn out into the pasture. That one cow had a heifer every year until she had six and with that cow and her six heifers we raised a herd of cattle. Then one day she was out in the alfalfa feed that had frosted and she bloated and came to the house. Paul and I were not versed on what to do in case of bloat but he called his brother and he said to get a good butcher knife and stick it into her side that is bloated the worst and we did it but it was too late she fell over and was dead. We saved many a cow by sticking them to relieve the gas pressure and we would tie a big knot in a heavy rope and stick it in their mouths to make them keep their mouths open and tie it up behind their ears.

Chewing on this rope would help the bloat gasses to escape.

Life was no bed of roses on a homestead ranch!

# Notes

1. Julia's reminiscences are from an interview given in 1984, her own memoirs, and a newspaper article written by family descendants. Because these are often contradictions regarding names and dates, or typos in the interview transcript, and the audio of the interview is often hard to understand, I have relied on Julia's own writings.
2. The taped interview conducted on September 29th, 1984, as well as the full transcript, are located in the archives of Colorado College, Colorado Springs.
3. Steve Biskup paid Judge Breeze $1500 for the land. Julia Kawcak taped interview.
4. Passages from Julia's memoir, *A Very Fruitful Life: The Story of My Life*, are taken as written and are unedited.
5. Taped interview with Julia Kawcak located in the archives of Colorado College, Colorado Springs.
6. The general store was actually the J. W. Hugus Company. Historic corrections to Julia's *A Very Fruitful Life* have been made by Dan Davidson, Director of the Museum of Northwest Colorado in Craig, Colorado.
7. Because there was no Catholic church in Craig at the time, Father J.J. Myers came from the Catholic church in Steamboat Springs to perform the wedding of Julia Biskup and Panko "Paul" Kawcak.
8. A chivaree (or shivaree) was an eastern European custom of a post-wedding noise party where the newlyweds were serenaded by family and friends in a noisy, raucous manner.
9. According to an article written by members of the Kawcak family and published in the Craig Press on August 1, 2014, the older boys eventually moved out to the bunkhouse. Today, the ranch house contains the original four rooms of Julia and Paul's homestead home. The Kawcak ranch is still in operation on the original homestead land and operated by Julia and Paul's son, Ivan and his wife Regina.

# INDEX

## A

# BIBLIOGRAPHY

## Books

Anderson, Meg and Lake, John. *Castle Entertaining: From Ranch Hands to Royalty*. Cherokee Ranch & Castle Foundation, 2018.

Appleby, Susan Consola. *Fading Past, The Story of Douglas County*, Colorado. Filter Press, LLC, 2001.

Athearn, Frederic J. *An Isolated Empire: A History of Northwestern Colorado*. Bureau of Land Management 1982.

Beaton, Gail M. *Colorado Women: A History*. University Press of Colorado, 2012.

Burroughs, John Rolfe. *Where The Old West Stayed Young*. William Morrow and Company, 1962. DeJournette, Dick and Daun. *One Hundred Years of Brown's Park and Diamond Mountain*. DeJournette Enterprises, 1996.

Drumm, Stella M. *Down the Santa Fe Trail and Into New Mexico: The Diary of Susan Shelby Magoffin*. Yale University Press, 1962.

Ellison, Douglas W. David Lant, *The Vanished Outlaw*. Midstates Printing, Inc., 1988.

Gulick, Bill. *ManHunt: The Pursuit of Harry Tracy*. Caxton Press, 1999.

Hensley, Marcia Meredith. *Staking Her Claim*. High Plains Press, 2008.

Hughel, Avvon Chew. *The Chew Bunch in Brown's Park*. San Francisco: Scrimshaw Press, 1970. Kaelin, Celinda Reynolds. *Pikes Peak Backcountry: The Historic Saga of the Peak's West Slope*. Caxton Press, 1999.

Kawcak, Julia. *A Very Fruitful Life: The Story of My Life*. Self-published by the Kawcak family, 2008.

Kouris, Diana Allen. *The Romantic and Notorious History of Brown's Park*. Wolverine Gallery Publishers, 1988.

Lavender, Davis. *Bent's Fort*. University of Nebraska Press, 1954.

Lecompte, Janet, Editor. *Emily, The Diary of a Hard-Worked Woman*. University of Nebraska Press, 1987.

McClure, Grace. *The Bassett Women*. Swallow Press, 1985.

McNatt, Lindsay. *Kate Slaughterback: Legendary Rattlesnake Kate*. Filter Press LLC, 2013.

Mantle, Queeda. *The Mantle Ranch*. WestWinds Press, Portland, Oregon, 2005.

Mantle, Queeda. *Last Ranch in Hells Canyon*. Lifetime Chronicle Press, Montrose, Colorado, 2009. Marr, Josephine Lowell. *Douglas County: A Historical Journey*, B & B Printers, Gunnison, Colorado, 1983.

Merrell, Pat and Jim. *The Merrells*. Self-published, 1979.

Propst, *Those Strenuous Dames of the Colorado Prairie*. Pruett Publishing, 1982.

Sammons, Judy Buffington. *Riding, Roping, and Roses*. Western Reflections Publishing Company, Montrose, Colorado, 2006.

Whiteley, Lee. *The Cherokee Trail: Bent's Old Fort to Fort Bridger*. Johnson Books, 1999.

Wommack, Linda. *From the Grave: A Roadside Guide to Colorado's Pioneer Cemeteries*. Caxton Press, 1998.

Wommack, Linda. *Ann Bassett, Colorado's Cattle Queen*. Caxton Press, 2018.

## Manuscript Collections

Bassett, Ann. Unpublished memoirs. Denver Public Library.

Bassett, Josephine. Taped interviews by Murl Messersmith, July 6, 1961. Dinosaur National Monument, Jensen, Utah. J.S.

Hoy Manuscript. Colorado History Center.

Willis, Ann Bassett. "Queen Ann of Brown's Park," *Colorado Magazine*, Volume XXIX, April 1952; Volume XXIX, January 1952; Volume XXIX, October 1952; Volume XXX, January 1953. Denver Public Library.

Willis, Frank. Unpublished manuscript entitled *Confidentially Told*. Colorado History Center.

## Magazines, Periodicals and Journal Publications

Colorado's Cattle Industry, Las Animas, CO: Boggsville Committee, 1957. "Homestead Proof-Testimony of Claimant on October 27, 1885"

A guide provided by the Florissant Fossil Beds National Monument.

Hurd, C.W. "Boggsville: Cradle of the Colorado Cattle Industry, Boggsville Community, Las Animas, Colorado, 1957.

Lively, David. "The Harbisons: An Ordinary Family Who Led an Extraordinary Life."

Rocky Mountain National Park archives.

Wommack, Linda. "Josie Bassett, Pioneer Hellcat." *Wild West Historical Journal*. Summer, 2016.

## Archives and Additional Sources

Dinosaur National Monument/Florissant Fossil Beds National Monument, Utah Department of Community and Culture

Utah State Historical Society Research Center and Collections.

## Interviews and Correspondence

Beaton, Gail

Bishop, Freda Walker

Davidson, Dan

DeJournette, Daun

Jessen, Kenneth

Kaelin, Celinda Reynolds

Kawcak, Regina

Greeley Museum

Kauffman House Museum, Grand Lake, Colorado

Museum of Northwest Colorado, Craig, Colorado

Ouray County Ranch History Museum and Friends of Ouray County

Ridgway Museum

Sterling Museum
Trail of Pioneer Museum, Steamboat Springs, Colorado
Uintah County Library and Museum, Michelle Fuller, Vernal,
Utah
Yampatika Group, Hutchinson Ranch, Steamboat Springs,
Colorado

## Newspapers

The various local newspaper archives accessed for this work are
noted in the exact quotes used throughout the text. In addition:

"Bartley Marie Scott," the *Denver Post*, May 29, 1983.
"Castle West of Wildcat," *Empire Magazine*, November 1, 1953.
The *Delta County Independent*, interview with Annie Huffington on
        her 90th birthday. By Mike Wood, December 26, 1995.
The *Denver Post*, "William Bent's Life Saved by a Cheyenne
        Doctor," January 25, 1920.
"The Lady of the Castle," *Douglas County News-Press*, May 8, 1996.
        This is an interview with Tweet Kimball, written by
        Susan Casey.
The *Loveland Reporter Herald*, March 24, 2012. "Adeline Hornbek,"
        by Kenneth Jessen.
The *Vernal Express*, "Ann Bassett," February 2, 1901.
The *Steamboat Today*, "The Mantle Ranch," by Queeda Mantle
        Walker, July 23, 2013.

# ABOUT THE AUTHOR

A Colorado native, Linda Wommack is a Colorado historian and historical consultant. She has written eleven books on Colorado history, including *Murder in the Mile High City; Colorado's Landmark Hotels; From the Grave: Colorado's Pioneer Cemeteries; Our Ladies of the Tenderloin: Colorado's Legends in Lace; Colorado History for Kids; Colorado's Historic Mansions and Castles; Ann Bassett, Colorado's Cattle Queen;* and *Haunted History of Cripple Creek and Teller County*. She has also contributed to two anthologies concerning Western Americana.

Linda has been a contributing editor for *True West* Magazine since 1995. She has also been a staff writer for Wild West magazine, contributing a monthly article since 2004. She has written for *The Tombstone Epitaph*, the nation's oldest continuously published newspaper, since 1993. Linda also writes for several publications throughout her state.

Linda's research has been used in several documentary accounts for the national Wild West History Association, historical treatises of the Sand Creek Massacre, as well as critical historic aspects for the Lawman & Outlaw Museum in Cripple Creek, Colorado, which opened in 2007.

Linda feeds her passion for history with activities in many local, state, and national preservation projects, participating in historical venues, including speaking engagements and hosting tours, and is involved in historical reenactments across the state.

She is a member of both the state and national Cemetery Preservation Associations, the Gilpin County Historical Society, the national Wild West History Association and an honorary lifetime member of the Pikes Peak Heritage Society. Linda currently is on the Heritage Legacy Committee for Cherokee Castle. As a member of Women Writing the West, Linda has organized quarterly meetings for the Colorado members of WWW for the past twelve years, served on the 2014 WWW Convention Steering Committee. Linda currently serves on the board of WWW and is the DOWNING Journalism Award Chair.

The author in the front room of Josie Bassett's cabin on Cub Creek. *Wommack*